To La-Eista,

Congratulatrs on the Wedding! I hope you enjoy the book!

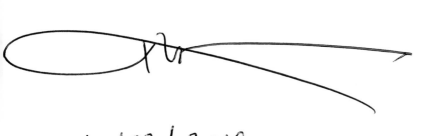

12/02/2019.

Islam as Critique

Islam of the Global West

Series editors: Kambiz GhaneaBassiri and Frank Peter

Islam of the Global West is a pioneering series that examines Islamic beliefs, practices, discourses, communities, and institutions that have emerged from "the Global West." The geographical and intellectual framing of the Global West reflects both the role played by the interactions between people from diverse religions and cultures in the development of Western ideals and institutions in the modern era and the globalization of these very ideals and institutions.

In creating an intellectual space where works of scholarship on European and North American Muslims enter into conversation with one another, the series promotes the publication of theoretically informed and empirically grounded research in these areas. By bringing the rapidly growing research on Muslims in European and North American societies, ranging from the United States and France to Portugal and Albania, into conversation with the conceptual framing of the Global West, this ambitious series aims to reimagine the modern world and develop new analytical categories and historical narratives that highlight the complex relationships and rivalries that have shaped the multicultural, poly-religious character of Europe and North America, as evidenced, by way of example, in such economically and culturally dynamic urban centers as Los Angeles, New York, Paris, Madrid, Toronto, Sarajevo, London, Berlin, and Amsterdam where there is a significant Muslim presence.

Amplifying Islam in the European Soundscape: Religious Pluralism and Secularism in the Netherlands, Pooyan Tamimi Arab
Islam and Nationhood in Bosnia-Herzegovina: Surviving Empires, Xavier Bougarel
Sacred Spaces and Transnational Networks in American Sufism, Merin Shobhana Xavier

Islam as Critique

Sayyid Ahmad Khan and the Challenge of Modernity

Khurram Hussain

BLOOMSBURY ACADEMIC
LONDON • NEW YORK • OXFORD • NEW DELHI • SYDNEY

BLOOMSBURY ACADEMIC
Bloomsbury Publishing Plc
50 Bedford Square, London, WC1B 3DP, UK
1385 Broadway, New York, NY 10018, USA

BLOOMSBURY, BLOOMSBURY ACADEMIC and the Diana logo are trademarks of
Bloomsbury Publishing Plc

First published in Great Britain 2020

Series design by Dani Leigh
Cover image © Brian Stablyk / gettyimages.co.uk

A catalogue record for this book is available from the British Library.

Library of Congress Cataloging-in-Publication Data
Names: Hussain, Khurram, author.
Title: Islam as critique: Sayyid Ahmad Khan and the challenge
of modernity / Khurram Hussain.
Description: New York, NY: Bloomsbury Academic, [2019] |
Series: Islam of the global west | Includes bibliographical references and index.
Identifiers: LCCN 2019018776 | ISBN 9781350006331 (hardback) |
ISBN 9781350006355 (epdf) | ISBN 9781350006348 (epub)
Subjects: LCSH: Islamic countries–Relations–Western countries. |
Western countries–Relations–Islamic countries. | Islamic modernism. |
East and West. | Aòhmad Khan, Sayyid, Sir, 1817-1898–Criticism and interpretation.
Classification: LCC DS35.74.W47 H87 2019 | DDC 303.48/2176701821–dc23
LC record available at https://lccn.loc.gov/2019018776

ISBN: HB: 978-1-3500-0633-1
ePDF: 978-1-3500-0635-5
eBook: 978-1-3500-0634-8

Series: Islam of the Global West

Typeset by Deanta Global Publishing Services, Chennai, India
Printed and bound in Great Britain

To find out more about our authors and books visit www.bloomsbury.com
and sign up for our newsletters.

To my father

Contents

Prologue   viii

   Introduction   1

1   The Language of Reform   19

2   Modernism and Humanism   47

3   The Meaning and End of Time   61

4   The *Viva Activa*   103

5   Knowledge and Wisdom   137

   Epilogue: Can the Muslim Speak?   157

Notes   169

Bibliography   194

Index   204

Prologue

Only a year into his presidency, Mahmoud Ahmadinejad of Iran sent a curious letter to George W. Bush. Curious not so much in its content but in the very fact of its existence. No direct communication had taken place between executives of Iran and the United States in almost thirty years. And whatever indirect talk there had been was more of kin to Japanese *kaiju* movie titles than international diplomacy: The Great Satan versus The Axis of Evil, Death to America versus Tehran Terror Theocrats, and so on. It was an odd sort of thing then, this personal letter, from one head of state to another when the states they presided over had persisted, for so long, in carefully preserving a perpetual state of reciprocal enmity. Tensions with Iran had only intensified in the preceding years with the American war on terror grinding on in neighboring Afghanistan and Iraq. And now, in 2006, the international community was becoming increasingly apprehensive about Iran's nuclear energy program and debating possible sanctions at the UN Security Council. The letter was an exceedingly polite litany of complaints to Bush about US foreign policy, Western imperialism, and international double standards that ended with Ahmadinejad highlighting their common Abrahamic monotheism as a possible source of détente between their two societies and a peaceful new world order. But it landed amid all the rancor as a feisty snowflake on oozing lava, preserving its form for the barest of moments before being obliterated. Bush quickly rejected any future official response from his office. The press reported state department officials (anonymously) deeming it "a window into Iranian mentality . . . [an] inclination to dwell on myriad grievances of the past rather than . . . [deal] with its intransigence over the nuclear issue."[1] Condoleezza Rice was the only cabinet member to even minimally address the letter, calling it a calculated distraction from "issues we are dealing with in a concrete way."[2] The American media took turns being flabbergasted and amused by it. *The Wall Street Journal*'s editorial page likened its "philosophical depth to the Unabomber's soliloquies."[3] Some even declared it a Trojan horse, a "peaceful overture" which when analyzed using ancient Islamic precedence, "is in fact a declaration of war."[4] Late night talk show hosts briefly played up its length (eighteen pages), its obscure language, and its religious references for laughs. Like all curiosities, this letter too faded quickly from public memory. It didn't lead to any détente between the West and Iran, nor did it make the situation any worse. It provided occasion to ridicule Ahmadinejad for his naivete or his lunacy, an unnecessary addition to the brimming annals of the bizarre from the Orient. Other than that, this curious letter accomplished nothing.

Still, even as a faded curiosity, this letter deserves attention. It may have fizzled out abruptly and ignominiously in the West, but it received far more salutary and sustained attention in the Muslim world. Pakistan's paper of record (*Dawn*) lauded Ahmadinejad for his pragmatism in trying to break the old taboos of directly addressing the Great Satan, a move to which the only opposition and derision appeared to be coming from Iranian hardliners and the US administration.[5] Lebanon's *Daily Star* seriously jumped the gun in declaring that "for the first time in years, there is cause for hope."[6] Writing for *Hurriyet Daily* in Turkey, Professor Alon Ben-Meir of New York University suggested that

> although his letter did not address the nuclear issue, it was clearly meant as an opening, and only by directly engaging the Iranians can Washington establish its own agenda for discussion. If it chooses not to, the administration, to the utter dismay of its friends and allies, will forfeit the chance afforded by a great opening to de-escalate tensions in the Middle East.[7]

An editorial for Egypt's *Daily News* called it "one of those moments of clarity that show the huge gap between how the United States and the West see the world and how Muslims in the Middle East perceive it."[8] No one was laughing and nary a soul was confused.

This makes sense. Nothing in Ahmadinejad's letter was particularly obtuse. I will not regurgitate the entirety of the letter's contents here; meriting the seriousness of its substance, the letter deserves a more considerable précis than space permits. The salient points raised were the various different ways in which Western powers have continuously asserted their power over Muslim majority societies (Latin America also earned a brief mention) in exploitative, oppressive, and restrictive ways that render any claim to a moral high ground not just bogus but also constitutively corrupt. His tone is questioning and polite throughout, but critical, with an edge. He demands common standards of evaluation and judgment. He seeks underlying frameworks of shared vintage for understanding and dealing with the problems of the world. This last concern leads him to an emphasis on the traditions of the prophets and Jesus Christ and their shared monotheism as a possible basis for a conversation with the Christian Bush. Other than the unfortunate (and unfortunately obligatory) brief mention of Israel and the Holocaust, Ahmadinejad stays on message throughout. If in fact he was "play[ing] to the bleachers," as the Council on Foreign Relations' Iran expert Vali Nasr put it, at least he knew to speak to them in a language they understood, in words that communicated meaning of historical significance and not in pleasantries or jests.[9]

One need not have any position on Ahmadinejad's politics to understand both the appeal of his letter to Muslims around the world and its summary rejection and ridicule by Western audiences. It has little or nothing to do with his politics. Depending on point of view, Ahmadinejad's offenses or accomplishments are one and the same. From a self-consciously Muslim point of view, and informed by the history of Muslims in West Asia (and not the West), he is questioning the commonsense paradigm that equates Western modernity and its institutions and values with universal progress. And he is seeking a conversation from an assumed position of discursive equality with his Western counterpart:

> The people of the world are not happy with the status quo and pay little heed to the promises and comments made by a number of influential world leaders. Many people around the world feel insecure and oppose the spreading of insecurity and war and do not approve of and accept dubious policies. The people are protesting the increasing gap between the haves and the have-nots and the rich and poor countries. The people are disgusted with increasing corruption. The people of many countries are angry about the attacks on their cultural foundations and the disintegration of families. They are equally dismayed with the fading of care and compassion. The people of the world have no faith in international organizations, because their rights are not advocated by these organizations. Liberalism and Western style democracy have not been able to help realize the ideals of humanity. Today these two concepts have failed. Those with insight can already hear the sounds of the shattering and fall of the ideology and thoughts of the Liberal democratic systems.[10]

To reverse the critical gaze is to peddle in madness. It is no wonder that the *Wall Street Journal* compares the letter to the Unabomber's manifesto, and so many in the West dismiss such rhetoric as a distraction from the *real* issues at hand. Ahmadinejad does not just question the West's intentions and its motivations. He questions the universal efficacy of its values. Whatever one thinks of Ahmadinejad's brand of Islam, or even his casual anti-Semitism, the summary rejection of his words with derision, ridicule, and worse, silence has tremendous symbolism. After all, if casual anti-Semitism was grounds for generally rejecting anything anyone has ever said, the West's own canon of important figures and thinkers from before the middle of the twentieth century would suffer a catastrophic decline in numbers. So, what does this rejection of Ahmadinejad symbolize? *Abjection.* The state of being cast out. Muslims can be in or out but not indwelling, immanent. Muslims can be friends or foes but not critics.

Then there is also this to consider. The sources of "Muslim rage" cannot be reduced to the economic, political, and ideological deficiencies of the status quo, important as these deficiencies may certainly be. The appeal of Ahmadinejad's letter to Muslims everywhere was far more visceral than any of these proximate causes would imply. It was an instinctive rejection of the silences that currently inhabit their speech. Or as the Editorial in Egypt's *Daily News* put it:

> The letter that Iran's hardline president sent to U.S. President George W. Bush this week opens a window onto the underlying rage and powerlessness many Muslims feel toward America, going some way toward showing why the United States still struggles to win hearts and minds in this troubled region. That is not irrelevant but a vital issue if the United States wants to blunt Islamic extremism. Bush has put money and high-profile aides into that public diplomacy effort. Yet many Americans find it incomprehensible that the Muslim world views their country as a bully. In short, the West and the Muslim world are talking past each other in classic fashion. Perhaps it is a clash of civilizations, as some believe. Or, perhaps there are still small openings for understanding.[11]

If recent history is any guide, whatever openings there are, they are very small indeed.

Introduction

What would it mean to imagine Islam as an immanent critique of the West? An obvious objection to such a proposition is to argue that "Islam" and "the West" are distinct lifeworlds with peculiar histories and discrete normative vocabularies. Islam represents a seventh-century prophetic dispensation that subsequently generated a world-system of ideas, values, norms, and institutions and its own autonomous set of meaning-making language(s). The West, on the other hand, is one name for the emergence in early modern Europe of radically new ways of looking at, describing, and evaluating the world and for the evolution of this new sensibility into a force of tremendous global transformation. As ideological artifacts of distinct historical processes, Islam and the West cannot be critically immanent in each other's frame. This manner of objection is a version of Rudyard Kipling's rhyming exhortation that goes like this: "Oh, East is East and West is West, and never the twain shall meet, Till Earth and Sky stand presently at God's great Judgment Seat."[1] A second, different objection to the above proposition is to claim that Islam and the West are not unitary or well-defined categories at all but rather represent such a bewildering diversity of histories and societies that to imagine "an Islam" as an immanent critique of "a West" is to fundamentally misconstrue the aggregate nature of these entities. These are both valid objections. But they are not insurmountable. Let me explain.

First, those who cite Kipling's verse in offhand conversation as a measure of his learned evaluation that the East and the West are incorrigibly distinct clearly have not read the rest of the poem, and perhaps not even the next measure: "But there is neither East nor West, Border, nor Breed, nor Birth, When two strong men stand face to face, though they come from the ends of the earth!" Kipling's poem, in fact, tells the story of how an initially agonistic encounter between an Englishman and a tribal chieftain in the borderlands of British colonial India eventually leads to constructive engagement across their differences and the mutual affirmation of each other's humanity. I will not belabor the point. The reader is free to look it up. Kipling came of age in a world that was for the first time in history becoming a world in full. Partly as a consequence of European imperial expansion, the far-flung corners of this world were being knitted together into a whole, crisscrossed and interpolated by transformative encounters between peoples and ideas. The processes that undergirded these encounters have only escalated since. Now, this world has become a networked hydra of interconnected nodes where the flow of goods and information, the (voluntary or involuntary) movement of peoples, and the reach of ideas and institutions have assumed a truly global scale. And we need ways of talking about this world that fully acknowledge both the plurality of these peoples, goods, and ideas as they jostle and compete with each other in a globalized public square and the interdependent and networked unity of the context of these encounters. "Islam" and "the West" can be said to represent nominally discrete zones of experience within this newly emergent world with distinct ways of talking about, describing, and evaluating this common world, of arguing for this or that interpretation of its pasts and presents, and of articulating its possible futures. It is against the humanistic ether of this shared world that Muslim strategies for making sense of it can be said to become critically immanent in their engagement with other accounts and different strategies, including Western ones.

Second, while there is clearly no single Muslim way of speaking about this world (and certainly no single Western way either), centering Muslim experiences in our deliberations can reveal aspects of this world that would otherwise be unavailable to us. Consider, for example, that there is no such thing as a single, unified, or simple "woman's experience" of this world. Women represent as diverse and multifarious a set of experiences, descriptions, and evaluations of this world as Muslims, perhaps even more so. Yet feminism as critique is a viable way to isolate and identify those sets of debates, arguments, and conversations that center women's experience and to highlight the new avenues of intellectual and normative exploration that such centering generates. The same is true of intellectual and political mobilizations around the experience of being black, queer, or colonized, for example, and the furious social movements such mobilizations have generated in the past and continue to generate today. Not only are these categories of identity each in and of themselves aggregates of a varied set of experiences, but they often also intersect with each other in the complex whole of a subject's identity. One can be queer and black, a (formerly) colonized person and a woman, or any combination of these and other historically marginalized subject positions now operationalized in the service of critique. Still, such composite intersectionality is no reason to throw up one's hands but rather an opportunity to attend appropriately to each vector in the intersectional unity of said identity to properly resist oppression.[2] To imagine Islam as critique is to identify "Muslim" as one distinct (and aggregate) vector in the intersectional network of critique generated by peripherally positioned subjects in the modern world. The Western consensus on the meanings of foundational ideas such as freedom and equality, or what constitutes a properly "political" space and action, or the nature and limits of human agency have all been challenged and often are radically transformed through critical intervention from hitherto unfamiliar perspectives. To imagine Islam as an immanent critique of the West is to recognize it similarly as an outsider tradition challenging the West's regnant norms and values against the backdrop of a common world emergent as an interconnected unity in the modern age. In fact, if "modernity" is to be rescued as a useful concept in our descriptions of this world, it must be reimagined as precisely the parallel emergence of intense and ongoing contests among various actors about the meaning and nature of this new world and of its pasts, presents, and futures.

The West as a way of talking about the modern world is peculiar only insofar as it serves as a kind of clearinghouse for "legitimate" and consequential debates about the world as such. Not provincial concerns of this or that region or religion, nor of this or that identity or disposition, but matters of universal and general significance. The West is one name then for what the poet Audre Lorde calls "the mythical norm," an abstract representation of what counts as "normal" and also the ideal normative standard against which all other claims to normalcy are to be judged.[3] As a norm-generating concept "the West" is, therefore, the universalization of a provincial moral lexicon imagined as a repository for master narrative accounts of the world. And of those in it. At any given point in time, the moral consensus of the West (which is, of course, ever-changing) therefore serves in the West as a measure of the civilization (or lack thereof) of its many "others." Muslims have been judged against this measure for decades if not centuries even as the reasons for their lack of civilization keep changing. Once upon a time, for example, they were judged uncivilized for being too permissive toward homosexuality. Now they are often judged uncivilized for the opposite reason. To imagine Islam as critique of Western ways of looking at the world is nonsensical from a Western perspective. This is because in Western accounts of Islam, it is either assimilated into being a familiar but insufficiently developed version of the West (Islam needs a Reformation, Religion of Peace, "modernist" Islam, real Muslims share our values, etc.) or it is banished to the outside as a wholly unfamiliar and/or dangerous ideology (political religion, Religion of Violence, "fundamentalist" Islam, real Muslims do not share our values, etc.). The West as a way of talking about Islam does not recognize a complex other but instead is largely self-referential. In the mirror of the West, Muslims appear as friends or enemies but not critics. They can either confirm and regurgitate the West's norms, values, and priorities, even the West's history of Reformation(s) and Enlightenment(s), or confirm their infernal character in their rejection of the West. The middle space of critique, of contest, and of conversation about a shared humanity in the open *agora* of a common world has been hollowed out and made unavailable.

Inasmuch as "Islam" is not allowed publicity as a distinct and viable vector in their intersectional identity, this hollowing out of the middle space of critique represents a *depoliticization* of Muslims in the global public sphere. And I believe this is the primary normative problem with the contemporary status quo on Islam in the West. By depoliticization I mean the incapacity of Muslims to participate critically and meaningfully, as Muslims, either in matters that directly affect their lived experience of the modern world or in the affairs of this world as such. While Islamophobia is clearly a moral wrong, depoliticization more accurately describes the problem associated with the lived experience of Muslims in the West and elsewhere. Such depoliticization takes many forms: from Western meddling (or worse) in the affairs of Muslim majority countries to legal regimes at the national and international levels designed to limit Muslim public expression and participation (in the West and elsewhere), to neo-colonialist exploitation of resources in Muslim lands, to the near complete absence of Muslim voices in global institutions and deliberations, to the marginalization of the Muslim experience of modernity as irrelevant to the world's future, and myriad other ways too numerous to list here. But the one important way this depoliticization works is the manner in which Islam is often talked about in the West and how in Western accounts Muslims are processed discursively into their proper place in the modern world. Such talk reduces the complexity of Muslim identities to an either/or of submission to the West as the definitive account of the good life and of humanity, or an outright rejection of the West and all its attendant values and concerns. This is what it means to argue that Muslims can be either friends or enemies but never critics. As depoliticized insiders in the West and dehumanized outsiders out there in the rest of the world, Muslims, therefore, represent a failure of the status quo to properly integrate them into this new world order, rendering this order unstable and unsustainable. Islam only emerges as a problem in the regime of such depoliticization, and as epiphenomenal to these failures. Against all those who posit the politicization of Islam as a problem, I would, therefore, like to argue, perhaps counterintuitively, that what Islam needs is not depoliticization but re-politicization.

* * *

But what would such repoliticization look like in practice? I believe that as a scholarly matter, we must first begin by re-reading the archive of the Muslim experience of modernity not within the sealed-off silos of Islamic and Middle Eastern Studies but rather in critical comparison with other accounts and descriptions of the modern age. The critical reflection of Muslim thinkers on such matters is often too hastily cordoned off into the "eithers" and the "ors" of "modernist" or "fundamentalist" Islam and "liberal" or "jihadist" Muslims. This obscuring of the complexity of Muslim thought and reflection into the either/or of familiarity or unfamiliarity with the West is what I call a "Commensurability Thesis" on the status of Islam in the West. According to a set of evaluative standards generated by Western consensus, "authentic" Islam is acknowledged and explained either as commensurable with modernity or as an arrangement of sociocultural and ethical parameters that are essentially incommensurable with it. While it is certainly true that more sophisticated methodological approaches emerging from postcolonial studies and comparative philosophy have been making slow inroads into Islamic Studies scholarship in recent years, they have to date exerted minimal influence in reshaping the regnant architecture of the field. Such approaches have also largely failed to instigate any sustained interest in excavating the critical potential of modern Islamic thought and to unfetter Muslim thinkers from the normative shackles of the commensurability thesis. This book is an attempt to begin remedying this situation. Instead of participating in scholarly discourses that tend to evaluate and explain Islam primarily with reference to tropes of Western vintage, I seek to change the terms of the debate. Using the life and work of the nineteenth-century Indian Muslim polymath Sayyid Ahmad Khan (1817–98) as an orienting axis, I reimagine Islam as an alternative interpretive strategy for investigating the modern condition. And along the way, I identify Muslims both as a viable resource for critical intervention in important ethical debates and as legitimate participants in normative discourses to underpin a just global order.

Islam as Critique takes on this task through a comparative methodology that is both novel and accessible. Sayyid Ahmad Khan lived in a time of great tribulation for Muslim India. Following an unsuccessful rebellion against British rule in 1857 by disparate groups and factions in various parts of the Indian subcontinent, Muslims found themselves in the crosshairs of their colonial masters, singled out as the chief instigators of what was in fact an amorphous and general uprising by the people of India. Under these circumstances, Khan's reinterpretation of Muslim theology and his re-conceptualization of Islam were provoked by the necessity of beginning and maintaining a viable critical conversation between the Muslims of India and the British in the grim shadow of deep mistrust and a flammable political situation. Though the specifics of the post-9/11 environment are indeed very different, they share with Khan's India the important general problematic of a critical and constructive engagement in the inhospitable aftermath of a paradigm-shifting catastrophe. I believe this makes Khan an ideal contemporary even 120 odd years after his death.

But since Khan was identified very early on as a "modernist" and a "liberal", scholarly treatment of his work rarely delves into the critical elements of his reconstructed Islam as an orienting paradigm for judgments concerning modernity.[4] By examining Khan's work as a critical expression of modernity rooted in a Muslim experience of it, this book is a long overdue corrective to this trend. Khan's political acquiescence to British rule constituted neither an ideological conversion to Enlightenment values nor an abandonment of traditional Islam. It did lead him to scrutinize this tradition in light of Western dominance in worldly affairs and to offer a systematic normative appraisal of both his fellow Muslims and the British.

It is in this sense that Khan represents a vital discursive marker in the broader historical and intellectual context of Muslim India as it evolved from the early modern Mughal period into the late-colonial twentieth century. I argue that between the traditional theological reconstructions of Shah Wali Allah (1703–62) and the Romanticist modernisms of Muhammad Iqbal (1877–1938), Sayyid Ahmad Khan represents a pivotal discursive node essential to understanding the problematics of modern Islam and its relationship to the West. Khan explicitly brings a critical Muslim apparatus to bear, for example, on such questions as the nature of modernity (*jadidiyyat*), the meaning of history (*tarikh*), the status of the human self (*insaniyyat*), the ideal of human sociality (*'asabiyyat*), and what counts as knowledge (*'ilm*). But his perspectives are already internally informed by a critical reconstruction of Islam in his encounter with Western epistemology and rationality. Khan practiced an engaged comparative mode of scholarship that allowed him to retrofit the classical moral lexicon of Islam for effective use in a new age. Traditional constellations of ideas and norms are re-arranged and new ones identified. Khan, therefore, offers us an alternative cartography of modernity that is paradigmatically Muslim.

But an alternative cartography comes with both promise and peril. The promise is the discovery of new terrain hitherto undiscovered. The peril is illegibility. Sayyid Ahmad Khan's value lies in his Islamic distinction. Yet such distinction can also lead many to callously dismiss his work as provincially Islamic with little to offer to a wider conversation. To re-ghettoize it, in short, in the commensurability trap. I overcome this problem by employing a comparative approach. I argue that if the purpose of comparison is an engaged critical re-evaluation of values and norms, then a comparative study in fact necessitates "both a conception of meaningful distinction and a common object of inquiry."[5] The common object of inquiry here, of course, is modernity in the abstract. But for the purposes of comparison, this book focuses on a certain set of concepts that ground a common experience of modernity both for Muslim intellectuals like Khan and for their Western counterparts. Yet these same concepts also generate conflict between the two sides as to their significance. I identify ideas like freedom, sovereignty, progress, the human self, the meaning and end of history, "Islam" and the "West," and of course modernity itself as constituting a shared arena in which contest about their meaning can ensue. Additionally, I juxtapose Khan's treatment of these ideas with that of three thinkers from within the Western tradition who engage critically with this tradition as insiders: Reinhold Niebuhr (1892–1971), Hannah Arendt (1906–75), and Alasdair MacIntyre (1929–).

Reading Khan's work along with these Western critics allows us to imagine Islam as part of a conversation in the West about the modern world, rather than as a conceptual apparatus wholly foreign to the West. Using this guiding paradigm, I compare and contrast Khan's notion of *taklif*, or burden/obligation, with Reinhold Niebuhr's conception of Christian *sin*, and argue that both ideas are essentially different versions of a realist critique of Western liberal optimism concerning progress and freedom.[6] I also juxtapose Khan's take on the Islamic imperative for *jihad*, or struggle, with Hannah Arendt's understanding of *action* as that paradigmatically human way of being in the world now threatened by modern understandings of agency rooted in negative rights. Finally, I explore Khan's understanding of *'ilm*, or knowledge, in relation to Alasdair MacIntyre's emphasis on *tradition* as the only viable mechanism for a coherent practice of judgment and his critique of liberal Enlightenment philosophy as a deficient resource for the generation and preservation of viable human communities.

Each of these juxtapositions is a shared narrative engagement with common objects of inquiry that de-provincializes Khan's work while still maintaining its critical Islamic edge.

On a more general level, this book locates Sayyid Ahmad Khan within a broader strain in modern Islamic thought that is neither a rejection of the West nor a wholesale acceptance of liberal or conservative principles. This is what has often come to be called *Critical Islam* in the writings of contemporary Muslims like Ziauddin Sardar, Malek Chabel, and Tariq Ramadan (among many others), and was more recently featured in Irfan Ahmad's excellent new book *Religion as Critique: Islamic Critical Thinking from Mecca to the Marketplace*.[7] The emerging field of Critical Muslim Studies, for example, aspires to study Islam not only as a "spiritual tradition, or a civilization, but also as a possibility of a decolonial epistemic perspective that suggests contributions and responses to the problems facing humankind today."[8] The journal attendant to this emerging field, *ReOrient*, imagines itself as "a sustained collective thought experiment that seeks to explore the consequences of producing knowledge that is no longer organized around the axis of West and non-West."[9] Another journal, *Critical Muslim*, has since 2012 featured the work of a variety of Muslim (and non-Muslim) authors "showcasing groundbreaking thinking on Islam and what it means to be a Muslim in a rapidly changing, interconnected world." Over the years this journal has done an excellent job of "providing a Muslim perspective on the great debates of contemporary times, and promoting dialogue, cooperation and collaboration between 'Islam' and other cultures, including 'the West.'"[10] At least since 9/11, and increasingly more urgently since the Arab Spring of 2011 turned into a sour winter for many of its participants, Muslims around the world have been rethinking their place in the larger global order and trying to make sense of their pasts and presents, and their possible futures. But I argue that this tradition of critical Muslim thinking about the modern world is in fact much older. From at least the mid-nineteenth century onward, Muslim thinkers have sought to address the novelties of the modern age by deploying both dynamic resources made available by their own traditions and newer forms of knowledge emanating mostly from the West. Interspersed throughout the text and with Khan's life and work as an organizing axis, this book introduces a diverse mix of Muslims such as Jamal al-Din al-Afghani (1838–97), Muhammad Iqbal (1877–1938), Ali Shariati (1933–77), Fatima Mernissi (1940–), and Abdul Karim Soroush (1945), among many others, as together constituting a partial but coherent project of critical reflection within modern Islamic thought. This project offers accounts and evaluations of modernity that are often in conflict with dominant Western interpretations but are also always an engaged response to these interpretations. It is in this sense that Critical Islam represents an immanent critique of Western accounts of the nature and meaning of modernity.

* * *

Of course, Sayyid Ahmad Khan's value to this project is not self-evident. He lived more than a century ago, in India not in the West, and seems far removed from the problems of the present. Why look to him and not someone more contemporary like the Oxford Islamic Studies scholar Tariq Ramadan, for example, a Muslim who is literally enmeshed in the modern Western world? I believe there are good reasons for attending to Khan instead. First, inasmuch as the *object* of someone like Tariq Ramadan's project is détente between Islam and European society, Khan's was one of the earliest such projects to have an enduring impact on Islamic thought and practice in the modern age. It provides us insight into the issues and concerns attendant to such a project as yet unburdened by a century and a half of accumulated prejudices on either end of the divide between Islam and the West. Khan grew up in a traditional Muslim household and was educated in the traditional manner. His world was irreversibly shattered by the "Great Rebellion" of 1857 when the British finally wiped away all remaining remnants of Muslim sovereignty from the face of India and established unequivocal hegemony over its people. His writings clearly illustrate that this was not merely a political rupture for the Muslims of India but also a psychological rupture that tore apart their sense of self. In this sense, Khan's project was a personal one. In trying to stitch together all the disparate parts of himself that had been splintered by the events of 1857, Khan came face to face with the need for a reformed language of Islam that would incorporate the novelty of the circumstances in which Muslims found themselves. The political and economic domination of the West had a corollary in its scientific and technological superiority. If Muslims failed to account for their obscurantism in such matters, they would surely be relegated to the dustbin of history. Khan postulated that moral questions could not be detached from epistemological ones. The fact of inferiority was always already a sign that something had gone wrong with the language that Muslims had hitherto used to give meaning to their lives as Muslims. Still, he continued to believe in the superiority of Islam as an abstract ideal that stood in judgment of both Muslims and the West. His was therefore an early, clear articulation of Islam as an *immanent* critique of both Muslims of his day and the West. I believe that more than a hundred years on, it still remains one of the clearest articulations of its kind.

Second, while Khan did not live in Europe, he did live in a sociopolitical milieu that was being shaped and re-configured by European intervention. The British were the masters of India, and their subjectivity was normative by definition. Khan witnessed firsthand the absolute carnage of the final destruction of the *ancien regime*, the old Muslim order of India. And he was there when the British turned their suspicious attention to his co-religionists in the aftermath of the revolt. In 1869, Richard Southwell Bourke, the 6th Earl of Mayo, and Governor-General and Viceroy of India, mooted the now-famous question: "Are Indian Musalmans bound by their religion to rebel against the Queen?" The answers came fast and furious. Sir William Muir wrote a multivolume biography of the Prophet, called *The Life of Mahomet*, which not only skewered the reputation of the Prophet by describing him as a warmonger but also dismissed all Muslim accounts of the Prophet's life as based on flimsy evidence and unscientific sources.[11] And Muir's was by far the most considered account. As in the wake of 9/11, Islamophobia was rampant in Britain's imperial administration after 1857. The general European public was not much better. Muslims faced a steady barrage of attacks on Islam as a backward, barbaric, and uncivilized religion from Christian missionaries, from European newspapers in and outside India, from Hindus and other non-Muslims in India eager to distance themselves from their erstwhile rulers, and from overly circumspect colonial administrators who did not want to be blindsided again by a Muslim rebellion. That the rebellion was hardly only perpetrated by the Muslims seemed beside the point at the time. This question of loyalty to the crown appears anachronistic now since most Muslims no longer live under the direct colonial rule of European powers. And fealty to the Queen may seem to us a rather strange way of framing the question of Muslim commensurability with Western modernity. But that is exactly what it meant in those days. There is a discursive thread that runs directly from these accounts of Islam as a contagion within British India and the critiques of those who see Islam as an existential threat to the regnant Western order.

In many ways, Sayyid Ahmad Khan's entire career is one long response to this question of loyalty. To his credit, Khan refused to take the bait. He recognized the danger in fanning the flames of anti-British feeling among the Muslims of India. In any case, he was as disturbed by the backwardness of Indian Muslims as he was by British bigotry. So he responded instead in the only manner he thought constructive, progressive, and useful. He set up magazines and journals such as the *Aligarh Scientific Gazette*, *The Muslim Social Reformer*, and many others. He focused on educating his co-religionists by creating the Muhammadan Anglo-Oriental (MAO) College, the first institution in India that explicitly integrated religious education with the study of European sciences and philosophy. And he wrote and traveled widely across India, Europe, and the Muslim world. In this sense, his was *the* paradigmatic attempt at finding common ground between Muslims and Europeans, since his reconstructed theology of Islam had such a détente as a *core* concern. He did not think of it as incidental to Islam. Islam was precisely that mode of religious experience that allowed disparate forms of knowledge, and different systems of social and political organization, to be integrated into a harmonious whole. Islam's was the method of *tatbi'a*, harmonization, of the many into the one. Human flourishing is only possible through such integration. The question of loyalty could not be answered because it was the wrong question to begin with. It was based on false assumptions about the nature of the human animal, and its purposes in this world. Khan understood this implicitly and, in much of his writing, expressed it beautifully.

* * *

In the aftermath of 1857, Sayyid Ahmad Khan decided to refute the conspiracy theories about Muslim disloyalty then rampant in the colonial administration by taking it upon himself to write an alternative history of the rebellion. The result was a brilliant little text called *Asbab-i-bhagavat-i-Hind* (*The Causes of the Indian Revolt*) that has not received much scholarly attention over the years.[12] Whatever little focus there has been on this text has pointed to Khan's dawning realization that his community was in a state of intellectual and economic disrepair, and so in need of much reform. This is certainly true. While the book is written in an apologetic mode that defends the Muslims of India from the then commonsense notion that it "was Muslim intrigue and Muslim leadership that converted a sepoy mutiny into a political conspiracy, aimed at the extinction of British Raj," the process of writing this book also put him face to face with the dilapidated condition and extreme economic decay of Muslim society in India.[13] "I could not even bear to contemplate the miserable state of my people," he declared, "for some time I wrestled with my grief, and believe me, it made an old man of me. My hair turned white."[14] The veneer of formal Mughal sovereignty having been wiped off the face of India, the reality of Muslim subjecthood and the backwardness of the Muslim populace was suddenly put in stark relief for Sayyid Ahmad Khan. It is for this reason that his later work as an educationalist and a reformer has its roots in the time he spent researching this book. Still, a less discussed aspect of the book is ironically what the book was ostensibly about: Why did the Indians revolt? As I have already indicated, the going theory was a Muslim conspiracy fed in equal parts by the resentment of the former ruling classes and the religious fanaticism of the Muslim masses. Khan disagreed. His answer was profoundly simple:

> The primary causes of rebellion are, I fancy, everywhere the same. It invariably results from the existence of a policy obnoxious to the dispositions, aims, habits and views of those by whom the rebellion is brought about. . . . I believe that [the Indian Rebellion] owes its origin to one great cause to which all others are secondary Branches so to speak of the parent Stem. . . . Most men, I believe, agree in thinking that it is highly conducive to the welfare of Government, indeed is essential to its stability, that the people should have a *voice* in its Councils. It is from the voice of the people only that Government can learn whether its projects are likely to be well received. The voice of the people can alone check errors in the bud, and warn us of dangers before they burst upon and destroy us. . . . From the beginning of things, to disregard [this voice] has been to disregard the nature of man, and the neglect of [this voice] has ever been the cause of universal discontent. . . . The evils which resulted from the non-admission of natives into the Legislative Council of India [meant that the Government] could never know the inadvisability of the laws and regulations it passed. It could never hear as it ought to have heard the voice of the people on the subject. The people had no means of protesting against what they might feel to be a foolish measure, or of giving public expression to their own wishes. . . . At length the Hindustanees fell into the habit of thinking that all the laws were passed with the view to degrade and ruin them, and to deprive them and their fellows of their religion. . . . Our Government never knew what troubles each succeeding sun might bring to its subjects, or what sorrow might fall upon them with the night. Yet day by day troubles and anxieties were increasing upon them. Secret causes of complaint were rankling in their breasts. Little by little, a cloud was gathering strength, which finally burst over us in all its violence. . . . When the Governors and the governed occupy relatively such a position as this, what hope is there for loyalty or good will?[15]

Khan goes on to add that "a needle may dam the gushing rivulet; an elephant must turn aside from the swollen torrent; the *voice*, however, can never be heard and this security never acquired, unless the people are allowed a share in the consultations of government."[16] It is tempting for us to think of Khan's appeals as a demand for democracy. But this is not the case. Khan's primary concern was always with the capacity of Muslims (and other Indians) to communicate with those under whose rule they lived. The events of 1857 were merely the end point of a gradual disintegration of such a capacity to speak. This incapacity to speak also entailed an incapacity to listen. Mutual incomprehension bred discontent. It bred contempt. Khan saw his project as the recovery of a Muslim voice. Internal to this project was also the recovery of the ability and capacity to listen. Khan viewed many of his co-religionists as hopelessly insular and provincial, set in their ways and unwilling to change with the times. Together, to speak and to listen constituted the twin demands for the recovery of Muslim agency through a renewal of Islam itself. Khan saw the decay of Muslim power as epiphenomenal to these twin disabilities, one feeding back into the other until this doomsday loop had finally rendered them completely deaf and mute. For Khan, this state of affairs was the very antithesis of Islam.

Back in those days, questions of loyalty were the main obstacle to the articulation of an authentic Muslim voice in the public sphere. In contemporary times, the Commensurability Thesis serves to do much the same. To imagine Islam as critique is to imagine it the way Sayyid Ahmad Khan imagined it: as a continuing, critical conversation with the world. History is the subjective experience of such engagement. The survival of Islam and détente with the West is part of the same process of revival. And the basis of this détente is the recovery of an authentic Muslim *voice*. When recovered, this Muslim voice will speak of values that are as universal as those of the European Enlightenment. It will speak of *tauhid*: to make whole, that which is broken. To Sayyid Ahmad Khan, this was the only way forward for both Muslims and the West.

*   *   *

A chapter summary is customary for introductions, so let me briefly lay the book out for you. In Chapter 1, I provide an overview of Sayyid Ahmad Khan's underlying concern with the theological and epistemological relevance of the concept of *tauhid* in Islam. *Tauhid* has been misconceived by both Muslim traditionalists and Western observers as referring narrowly to the idea of the unicity of God. It is understood primarily as an emphatic affirmation of monotheism in Islam. While this is certainly true, Khan has a more expansive understanding of this term and its relevance to the human condition as such. *Tauhid* is the ontological basis for the practice of *tatbi'a*, harmonization, through which the many disparate elements of human existence and knowledge are to be constantly integrated into a coherent whole. Reality is at its core unified and whole, just as the creator of reality is one. Yet, the subjective experience of reality exposes the human animal to the temptation of polytheism. The fact of difference becomes the basis for moral, political, and social differentiation. For Khan, Islam provides the epistemological apparatus for holding these disparate elements of reality together by focusing on interdependence and on the movement of history. He therefore provides us with a searing critique of many of his own co-religionists' unwillingness to appreciate the moral and sociological imperatives that a belief in *tauhid* entails. This internal critique will set the stage for how Khan's work can be applied critically to Western notions of modernity as well.

In Chapter 2, I introduce Khan as a practitioner of peculiarly Muslim forms of modernism and humanism grounded in his experience of the aftermath of 1857. As cascading events overtook Indian Muslims' ability to make proper sense of their new reality, Khan offered both critique and introspection as the twin mechanisms of Islamic renewal. But the disorienting consequences of an escalating modernity are hardly only relevant to the Muslim experience of it. In fact, such disorientation is evident across the modern world, including in the West. This chapter therefore makes the case of reading Khan with others in the West who are similarly engaged in a critique of modern Western ways of describing and evaluating this world and for the dehumanizing effects of an intensifying modernity. This "reading with" is not a straightforward comparison but rather what Edward Said called a "contrapuntal" approach to the archive of modernity, the putting together in close discursive proximity parts of the archive that are usually kept apart in distinct silos of inquiry; Said, for example, suggested reading Jane Austen with Frantz Fanon![17] Acceding to Said's advice, I identify Reinhold Niebuhr, Hannah Arendt, and Alasdair MacIntyre as viable interlocutors for Khan and make the case for a contrapuntal exploration of Khan's critical assessments of the modern age in conjunction with their work.

To this end, in Chapter 3, I put Khan's reinterpretation of the theological notion of *taklif*, or burden/obligation, in conversation with Reinhold Niebuhr's concept of *sin*. Modern conceptions of freedom and progress are too often imagined and articulated in opposition to restraint and finitude. They are also characterized by a future-perfect sensibility: a persistent optimism about the perfectibility of the human condition. But the modern age has also produced fundamentalisms of various sorts that hold a past-perfect worldview: a relentless pessimism about the human capacity to create a perfect order leading to an obsession with past perfected states of society, existence, or being. This chapter centers on Sayyid Ahmad Khan's and Reinhold Niebuhr's common identification of freedom not with lack of restraint but with a ceaseless negotiation of the relationship between morality and history in the regime of human finitude. In fact, freedom is epiphenomenal to the more fundamental condition of finitude built into the human condition: *taklif* for Khan and Christian conception of sin for Niebuhr.

Using a wide-ranging discussion of scientific positivism, Shi'i millenarianism, and utopianisms of all varieties, this chapter offers Khan's and Niebuhr's realist alternatives to the utopian optimisms and pessimisms generated by (and against) Western modernity.

In Chapter 4, I juxtapose Khan's take on the Islamic imperative for *jihad*, or struggle, with Hannah Arendt's understanding of *action* as the paradigmatically human way of being in this world. Modern public discourse is often characterized by an identification of meaning with utility, instrumental rationality, and provincial reason. A pervasive ethic of consumption, survival, and reproduction suggests a disturbing regression of human masses into animal-like states of being. This chapter offers a productive juxtaposition of Khan's conception of *jihad* with Hannah Arendt's theory of action as a basis for alternative anthropologies of the human condition. When evaluated by the normative standards of Arendt's neo-Aristotelianism and of Khan's reformulated Islam, many aspects of Western modernity appear deeply dehumanizing. And modern nationalism, whether wedded to a liberal-democratic or authoritarian/totalitarian ideology, is equally implicated in divesting the public sphere of humanizing political action and speech. I use both Khan and Arendt to frame a discussion of freedom as an active principle rather than a negative right. I argue that they also eschew a politics of equality for one predicated on the importance of distinction, deliberation, appearance, and truth.

In Chapter 5, I discuss Khan's understanding of Islam in relation to Alasdair MacIntyre's emphasis on *tradition* as the only viable mechanism for a coherent practice of judgment. The problem of tradition in the modern age is a symptom of the normative unmooring of knowledge production from wisdom. This unmooring, either glorified as progress or vilified as a descent into moral chaos, has rendered the very notion of tradition an odd counterpoint to modernity. This chapter uses the work of MacIntyre in conversation with Khan to identify possible alternative framings of the relationship between tradition and modernity. It offers a novel re-definition of "wisdom" as an artifact of knowledge. As knowledge accumulates, it sediments into layers of meaning that provide evaluative foundations for further accumulation. This is what MacIntyre calls "tradition." Knowledge both grows on the foundations of wisdom and constantly produces new wisdom as an artifact of such growth. A robust emphasis on tradition not only is therefore essential to properly describe human societies but also is a necessary basis for a coherent practice of judgment. This is what makes traditions like Islam not just objects of scholarly study and description but also repositories of critical wisdom that can inform serious inquiry into the modern world.

In the epilogue, I circle back to the present and the post-9/11 "problem" of Islam in the modern world. I tell the story of a well-known American Salafi Yasir Qadhi, Dean of Academic Affairs at the al-Maghrib Institute and professor of Religious Studies at Rhodes College, Memphis, Tennessee. Qadhi has advanced postgraduate degrees from the Islamic University of Medina and a doctorate in Islamic Studies from Yale University. Qadhi comes from a deeply religious family that also inculcated in him the peculiarly deep immigrant's love for America. But this love has been sorely tested in the years since 9/11. He has had, for example, the unfortunate distinction of being interrogated numerous times at airports traveling to and from conferences organized by Homeland Security and the State Department where he was an invited guest. Qadhi believes in the urgent necessity of conversations about controversial issues like the status of *jihad* in Islam, or the relationship between political citizenship and obligation to the *umma*, or the proper role of *shari'a* in modern Muslim life, or a critical Islamic take on the institution of secularism. In contemporary America, the urgency is even more profound because, in the absence of frank conversation in the community, the young have a tendency to turn to the basements of communal life where radicalism resides. But by all accounts his greatest challenge has been teaching Islam to Muslims in America with its distinct critical apparatus intact: "My hands are tied," he says, "and my tongue is silent." As a critical Muslim, Qadhi views the world through organizational paradigms like *jihad, taklif,* and *fiqh.* Still, teaching and transmitting this distinctive worldview is difficult: "What stop[s] us [from offering courses on jihad]? Picture two bearded guys talking about the *fiqh* of *jihad.* We would be dead. We would be absolutely finished."[18] The conclusion to the book uses the struggles of Qadhi and other contemporary Muslims as an occasion to reflect on the value of recovering the practice of Islam as critique as a viable way of being in the world.

*   *   *

I should note at this point that this book is not an exhaustive study of the life and thought of Sayyid Ahmad Khan, or of his three interlocutors. I lack the training adequate to such a task, and in any case, I do not intend this project to offer a complete biographical sketch of this or that person. Khan's corpus runs thousands of pages long and his complete works are contained in a sixteen-volume behemoth of a collection. This is on top of his social, political, and educational activities that spanned decades and continents. Niebuhr, Arendt, and MacIntyre are similarly panoramic in their intellectual output and led widely interesting lives.[19] But more so than their lives in full, I am narrowly interested in certain aspects of their reaction to the rapid transformations happening in the world they inhabited and their critical appraisals of this world's emerging normative architecture. To read Khan alongside Niebuhr, Arendt, and MacIntyre is to *read into* him a broad critique of a world dominated by European power, a critique that was always present but has seldom been highlighted. It is to read him *out of context* and to evaluate him against the generalized ether of the world he lived in and not just the specific place he called home or the particular religion to which he belonged. Such *reading into* and *out of context* runs against much of the consensus in the modern Western academy when it comes to the study of non-Western peoples and cultures. This consensus was forged against decades of scholarship that paid little heed to the peculiarities of time and place, and that often inappropriately used insights gleaned from the study of Western societies as the standard framework for investigating the world as such. The "cultural turn" against such scholarship has been instrumental in making visible hitherto obscure systems of social organization and in rendering legible the meaning-making activities of people around the world. This has all been for the good. But the appropriate next step must be to elevate the voices of these people into general conversations about the world. The deconstructions attendant to the project of unearthing meanings and excavating truths about oneself and others must at some point give way to the constructive project of building a better world together. The Sayyid Ahmad Khan of this book is therefore not the man in full but rather the version of him best suited to this project of world-building, together with folks like Niebuhr, Arendt, and MacIntyre.

With this as the orienting paradigm for the book, what would it mean then to imagine Islam as an immanent critique of the West? This is a simple question for which there are no simple answers. Some may argue that the question itself is a distraction or a chimera. The problems run so much deeper than the ability or inability to critique that to waste time and mind on such abstract questions is itself a scholarly pathology reflective of the decline of Islam. Others may claim that this entire project is a not-so-subtle form of Muslim apologia. That under the cover of criticism, I am trying to sneak Islam into conversations where it does not belong. I disagree. Critical Islam is neither chimera nor apologia. It is an aspirational formulation in response to the question, and the possibility, of Muslim agency in the modern world. Abstract or not, surely such a project deserves our attention.

The Language of Reform

The year is 610 CE. The place is the cave of Hira in the mountain now called Jabal an-Nur on the desolate sandy plains of the Hijaz. The angel Jibril commands Muhammad to "RECITE (*iqra*)! In the name of thy Lord who created. He created man from that which clings. RECITE! And thy Lord is most Bountiful, He who has taught by the pen, taught man what he knew not." Muhammad is to be God's apostle, his prophet to the people of Arabia and to the rest of the world. Of the hundreds of idols in the "Cube" (Ka'ba) in Mecca, none are worth worship.

Only God (*Allah*) is godly. All else is sham and masquerade.

The Meccans have made a mockery of the divine. Arab society is corrupt and ignorant. Its ways are violent. Its people are prideful and quick to anger. As if mirroring the hundreds of gods they worship, they are bitterly divided, fragmented, and degenerate. Muhammad must preach submission (*islam*), purification (*tazkiya*), and peace (*salam*). Muhammad is to bring them out of the darkness and be a light to the world. On that first night of destiny (*laylat al-qadr*), Jibril confounds and confuses him. Still this much is clear to Muhammad soon enough. There is no god (*la ilaha*) but God (*il Allah*), and Muhammad is to be His messenger (*Muhammad al-rusul Allah*).

But some years later, a most curious incident takes place. The Meccans are tough. They are not easy to preach to. They do not listen. Worse, they mock Muhammad and persecute his followers. And there are precious few followers to begin with. Muhammad is dejected and losing faith. The Meccans have no interest in Allah as the one true God. He may be a high god, but he is distant and absent. He does not know them and does not care. The Meccans need his three "daughters," the goddesses (Al-) Lat, Manat, and (Al-) Uzza, the beautiful cranes (*gharaniq*) who they worship and revere above all else, and who intercede on their behalf with distant impersonal powers. They have no interest in Muhammad either, the orphan who pretends to be a prophet. That is until the incident. This time the place is the Ka'ba. The time is six years on. Muhammad stands alone in a crowd. The Meccans have their backs turned to him. They mock him and deny him their faces, their respect, their religion. Muhammad stands estranged from his community. Is there no hope for reconciliation, for peace, for God? Suddenly Muhammad begins to chant, as if in a trance: "Have you then ever considered [what you are worshipping in] Al-lat and Al-Uzza, as well as Manat, the third, the other?" The Meccans turn to face him, interested, intrigued, suspicious. Will he mock their goddesses, will he belittle their religion again as he has done so many times? But this is a different sort of revelation: "They are the exalted *gharaniq*," he continues, "whose intercession is approved." There is excitement and jubilation. "Muhammad speaks with favor of our goddesses." They too are tired of quarrelling with their tribesman. "If Allah shall have our three goddesses, we shall have Him as well." Muhammad shall have his peace, the community shall have its relief. It is decided. The Arabs will have fewer gods than before. Many fewer. But not One. Allah will have his daughters, and Mecca shall honor Muhammad as His prophet.

Why then is Muhammad still feeling uneasy? Something is not quite right. Was it really God who spoke through him of the *gharaniq*, the cranes, His daughters? Soon, Jibril confirms his worst fears. "O Muhammad, what have you done? You have recited out loud something to the people that had not been given to you by God, and you said something that was not said to you." Muhammad has made a terrible mistake. Like so many prophets before him, a satan (*shaytan*) has fooled him, tempted him into uttering a blasphemy that suited his own trivial concern of reconciliation with his tribe. The verses uttered in the Ka'ba were satanic. They are abrogated. And on the same question about the *gharaniq*, a stunning reversal: "What are you males, and He female? That were indeed an unjust division. They are naught but names yourselves have named, and your fathers. . . . God has sent down no authority touching Him . . . and to God belongs the First and the Last."

Thereafter, Meccans return to being Meccans. In fact they are worse. They are insulted beyond bearing and want Muhammad's blood. Soon he will have to leave with his followers for the oasis city of Yathrib to escape the destruction of his fledgling Muslim community. In the meantime, as if in direct response to the satanic verses, a new revelation. Here, a verse (*ayah*) from the *surah* of Sincerity (*al-Ikhlas*):

"Say He is God, One
God forever
Not begetting, unbegotten,
and having as equal, none!"

The incident of the cranes has revealed to the community its most fundamental tenet. On this there is no compromise, no equivocation, no ambivalence: God is one. And He is alone. There is none with Him, none associated with Him, none of his Nature. He is unified, integrated, whole. He requires nothing other than Himself. He is made one (*tauhid*) by Himself, in Himself, forever. From this point on, the cardinal Muslim sin is associationism (*shirk*)—literally, "idolizing" beings or values other than God as if they are God or are like God or are associated with God.

In time Muhammad will learn the social and political value of this oneness: a unitary God demands an integrated worshiper, a unified subject to His call for submission. For now though, Muhammad is again alone in the crowd. It will be many years before he can pray in the house of God and not be mocked. As the old Jewish saying goes, a prophet is always without honor in his own country. But this is only half the story. Prophets put up with so much because they know another, more basic truth:

Being right with God has transcendent utility. *All else is sham and masquerade.*

* * *

Is it a historically sound hypothesis and a discursively legitimate claim to identify the events of 1857 as marking India's definitive entry into modernity? Some scholars look much earlier focusing instead on the battle at Plassey in 1757 where the armies of the British East India Company defeated Nawab Sirajudullah of Bengal and gained a permanent foothold in what was then Muslim India. These scholars equate the modern with the mere appearance of Europeans on the scene. They are incorrect. The modern is never mere appearance. Something has to die, to pass, before the modern emerges from the innards of that which it kills. Before 1857, the British were self-consciously interested primarily in the preservation of their economic interests in India. Some even went native, producing an entire class of Euro-Indian "Mughals" whose fascinating late eighteenth-century lives augured an intriguing future that unfortunately never materialized.[1] After 1857, the mission increasingly also took on the quintessentially modern turn of civilizing the natives. It is in this sense that 1857 represented the passing of an age and the beginning of a new one. Nothing passed at Plassey; nothing changed. In fact, as far as battles go, it wasn't even much of a battle. Not very many people died. There was not much blood. It was good old-fashioned palace intrigue and co-optation, divided factions played against each other that won the day for the Company. Even putting aside the aesthetic value of blood and guts to origin stories, Plassey at best only marked the entry of the British into the medieval political order of sovereign Mughal rule in India. This political order was in itself a continuation of the nearly thousand years of almost uninterrupted Muslim sovereignty over largely non-Muslim populations in the Indo-Gangetic plains of the north. This order remained sacred and sacrosanct. Plassey did not change that.

This Mughal order was sovereign on par with the empires of the ancient world, like Rome or Persia. The north Indian population did not understand sovereignty outside the Mughal framework. To say empire was to mean the Mughal Empire, to say emperor meant the Mughal *Shahenshah* (King of Kings) in Delhi. The city of Delhi itself was the *axis mundi* of this sovereign order, built, rebuilt, and added to for millennia, the seat of power in India from time immemorial. It bears mentioning that Delhi was in 1857 a Muslim city in every sense; its political language was Islam, its culture and refinement born of a peculiar synthesis of Persian high culture with native ways. Native here meant not just the "Hindu" (a term notoriously difficult to pin down) culture of the masses but also the many layers of cultural and political sediment left by earlier instances of Muslim rule and its concomitant Muslim populations. Islam had been in India for a thousand years. Delhi was the integrated edifice of this Muslim political power, and the apotheosis of the refinement of the order it represented. It is this order that the British entered in 1757 as subjects and then vassals of the Mughal emperor, and which they obliterated a hundred years later.

The events of 1857 actually render the term obliteration a euphemism. Catastrophe, collapse, and carnage. Unequivocal barbarity was visited on the people of India after the defeat of the mutinous Company sepoys (soldiers) and the pacification of the rebellion(s) that had haphazardly engulfed much of northern India. The Bengali corps marched onto Delhi and (much to his chagrin) proclaimed the Mughal emperor Bahadur Shah Zafar their sovereign and leader. The old order groaned and turned, awakened from its stupor to make one last violent stand. Some historians have suggested that in the first few weeks after the mutiny, it could have gone either way. This is wishful thinking. The old order had been decaying for more than a century. It lacked unity, uniformity, integration. The Great Rebellion was great only in extent not in ideological clarity. Bahadur Shah Zafar was an uncomfortable and opaque personification of a fading ethico-political system, and its attendant economic and social infrastructure, and he was not much of a spokesman for anything.

The terror that followed the defeat of the rebellious forces was not arbitrary, but it would have appeared so to many of its victims. There was no class, no caste, no community that was safe. The British were as if drunk with passion, crazed with an animosity that was racial, religious, and feudal all rolled into one. Delhi was practically razed to the ground by continuous, relentless cannon fire, its largely Muslim population killed or expelled, its institutions and its way of life totally destroyed. Those feudal and political elites who had rebelled were summarily executed in the thousands, nay hundreds of thousands, and usually in spectacular fashion to terrorize the population. The message was clear. There was a new sheriff in town.

Sayyid Ahmad Khan was one of the first Muslims in India to see this writing on the wall after 1857 and to decide to do something about it. This chapter is chiefly concerned with Khan's efforts to remember the ideological fragments of the language of Indian Islam after it had been rendered inexplicable by the catastrophe of defeat. More specifically, I will look at certain key features of his theological re-interpretations of Islam that were designed to integrate the classical purity of the Islamic religion with the emerging scientism and rationality of the new order and to imagine the Muslim subject as the personification of precisely this integration. Internal to this reimagination was an emphasis as old as Islam itself: *tauhid*, "to make one." Khan understood the crisis of Indian Islam as an indication of the loss of *tauhid*. Muslims had lost the capacity to authentically practice their own religion. In the process, they had also divested themselves of agency in their own history. The British obliteration of Delhi was merely a sign of this divestment, a symptom of a disease far advanced. Even in the near aftermath of these catastrophic events, Khan already recognized that how Muslims respond to these signs and symptoms would determine their place in the new world order and their station in the new age dawning amid the blood and carnage of 1857. This situation demanded a new *'ilm al-kalam* (theology) to guide Muslims through the novelty of the times. But this theology would still be rooted in foundational ideas, and in a concept as old as Islam itself: "Say He is God, One, God forever, not begetting, unbegotten, and having as equal, none!" A unitary God demands an integrated worshiper, a unified subject to His call for submission. Before they could proceed with confidence into a salutary future, Muslims of India would have to pick up the many pieces of their fragmented existence and put them all together as a coherent whole fit both for Islam and for the modern age.

* * *

To properly assess Sayyid Ahmad Khan's theological and intellectual interventions during the discord and rancor of the times he inhabited, it is first necessary to lay out, in brief, the character of the antecedent world to which he belonged and those sedimented influences of his family background that never fully left him. Khan was born in 1817 to a noble Muslim family that still drew a *wazifa* (stipend) from the court of the Mughal emperor and was well respected in aristocratic circles of imperial Delhi. The family belonged to the *ashraf* classes of north India who claimed descent from non-Indic stock. In Khan's case, "Sayyid" was an indication that he was descended from the Prophet himself. The historical authenticity of such claims is not relevant. The elitism of the *ashraf* classes against "native" Muslims (*ajlaf*) rivaled the caste system of Hindu society. Khan never entirely eschewed the values attendant to being a *sharif* (sing. of *ashraf*), even when in later years he did begin to see the Muslim body politic in more holistic and egalitarian terms.

Khan's family had a strong Sufi background. One of his uncles was a noted adherent of the controversial Sufi doctrine of *wahdat al-wujud* (Unity of Being) first articulated by the thirteenth-century mystic Muhyiddin Ibn 'Arabi (1165–1240). Unity of Being was a quasi-pantheistic doctrine that declared the absolute immanence of God. It proclaimed "the mystical truth (*haqiqat*) that no real separation exists between God and the Self" or between God and His creation.[2] While Ibn 'Arabi is usually credited with the first theological explication of this doctrine, even as early as the tenth century the ecstatic Sufi master Mansur al-Hallaj (d. 922) had famously declared *ana al-Haqq* ("I am the Truth/the Real"). This outraged the traditionalist authorities and al-Hallaj was executed. *Wahdat al-wujud* found a fertile religious environment in India where it shared much conceptual affinity with the pantheistic aspects of Hindu Vedantism. Some mystical Sufi poets like Kabir (1398–1448) went one step further and suggested that even the distinction between Muslim and non-Muslim was a mere illusion, and that any kind of devotional practice would do if the ultimate end is a mystical union (*wisal*) with God, or annihilation into God (*fana*).[3]

The thoroughgoing syncretism of the doctrine of *wahdat al-wujud* produced a reaction not only among the traditionalist *ulama* but also within the Sufi mainstream itself. Khan's mother belonged to the *Naqshbandiyya Mujaddidiyya* (a Sufi *tariqa*/order) of Shaykh Ghulam Ali who was himself an adherent of the *silsila* (lineage) of seventeenth-century master Shaykh Ahmad Sirhindi.[4] The great theological contribution of Sirhindi was the doctrine of *wahdat al-shuhud* (Unity of Perception). Sirhindi suggested that Sufis who claim the underlying unity of all existence with and in God have mistaken their perception of reality with reality in and of itself. Human beings by definition have narrow, circumscribed perceptions, and their subjective experience of reality is limited by their finitude. Only God has a truly objective vantage point and can perceive reality, in whole and as such. God is absolutely transcendent, and this transcendence is absolutely essential to maintaining a distinction between the *is* and the *ought*. Muslims are special precisely because they alone have access to the undiluted word of God and the Sunna (tradition) of his Prophet. It is this peculiarity that gives Muslims their station in this world as those who proclaim not just the existence of God to others, but also live in this world with an eye to the next. Sirhindi believed that the creeping syncretism in much of the Sufi practices of his time endangered the distinction of Muslims from non-Muslim. To combat this trend, he advocated *tawakkul*, a strong reliance on God and the traditions of the Prophet for moral and other concerns, and a deep antipathy toward superstition: "God alone should be approached in everything, and He will do what He pleases to do."[5]

Khan navigated these tensions within the Sufi life of the Indian subcontinent throughout his career. In this he was walking on already well-trodden ground. The biggest single influence on his pre-1857 writings is clearly the work of Shah Wali Allah, the greatest Muslim thinker/reformer of eighteenth-century India, and a towering figure in early modern Muslim theology. Wali Allah is a most interesting and complicated figure because he combines in a single coherent theology both what we moderns might call conservative and progressive ends. At times he appears a quintessential, orthodox, traditionalist in his insistence on the purity of Islam. He is clearly unnerved by *bid'a* (innovation) in Muslim thought and practice that renders it "almost a synonym for the Hindu folkways and mores which were retained by the converts, and because of them were diffused into Indic Muslim society."[6] His Islamic revivalism thus included a sociological imperative to "[eschew] Hindu cultural patterns and [an adherence] to those cultural values of the Arabs which were accepted and exemplified by the Prophet Muhammad and his Sunna."[7] So he exhorts his co-religionists "not to abandon the customs and mores of early Arabs, because they were the immediate followers of the Prophet Muhammad, . . . [and to] not adopt the mores of the Hindus, or those of the people of *'ajam*—countries beyond Arabia."[8] There is much criticism in Wali Allah's writings of everything from the prohibition of a second marriage for women (which he identified both with Hindu norms and as an example of pre-Islamic *jahiliyyah*), to the extent and expenditure of numerous ceremonies surrounding marriage (including the use of dowry), to the extended period of mourning after a death which far exceeded the precepts set by prophetic example. Wali Allah also believed that *bid'a* extended to many mystical practices of Indian Sufis and to the excessive visitation to the tombs of

Sufi saints. The preoccupation of some Muslims "in the domain of annihilation and eternity, and the mystical practices" appeared to Wali Allah "as causing a deep malaise among the Indic Muslims," while visitation to tombs and excessive honoring of dead saints smacked of *shirk* and Hindu idolatry.[9]

Still, Wali Allah's greatest contribution to Islam was a theological concern of a very different variety. This was the doctrine of *tatbi'a* whereby he attempted to "[smooth] out the differences among theologians, philosophers and traditionalists . . . to harmonize the two schools of [Sufi thought] *wahdat al-wujud* and *wahdat al-shuhud* . . . in *fiqh* the differences between the four *madhahib* [schools of law] . . . and to clarify the difference between the Sunnite and the Shi'ite traditions by researching the origins of the dispute."[10] Wali Allah had a strong historical focus, looking at Islamic history and the developments of Muslim society as in and of itself an internal feature of the essential meaning of Islam. This is especially evident in his treatment of the history of *taqlid* (emulation) and *ijtihad* (independent, interpretive reasoning) and harmonizing these two supposedly opposite conceptions of knowledge and tradition. For example, while he maintains that following the *shari'a* of God is an absolute imperative, he employs two other principle concepts as legitimate sources of a continuing *ijtihad*: first, *al-masalih,* or salutary purposes, whereby law must be harmonized with the demands of human flourishing and welfare: and second, *al-fitrah,* or nature, whereby law must be harmonized with our developing knowledge of God's creation and especially of human nature. These concepts allow him to imagine the *Shari'a* as having "inherent flexibility" and to demonstrate an understanding of the meaning of the Qur'an, the Sunna, and of Islam that is essentially diachronic.[11] Islam moves with time and is sensitive to the context of its practice. In addition, *tatbi'a* suggests that it is simultaneously ever-changing and yet unitary. Harmonization not only accepts the diversity of the world as real and determinative of Islam but also imagines Islam as that particular method by which such diversity is held together in a single over-arching framework that gives it meaning, purpose, and stability.

The sociopolitical context of Shah Wali Allah's reformist theology was the continued existence of formal Muslim sovereignty in India, even as Muslim power as such was in precipitous decline. The Mughal state persisted throughout the eighteenth century but it no longer exerted the kind of political and cultural influence it once had. India was divided into contesting and fractious Muslim polities being threatened by the Hindu Marathas of Central India, the Sikh Rajputs in Punjab, and by the rising British influence in Bengal. The focus on the harmonization of disparate forms of Muslim practice was in this sense a theological correlate to the political fragmentation of Indian Muslim life and all its attendant anxieties of being over-run by Hindu influences. The British as yet were a distant presence in the western delta of Bengal and were mostly ignored as a relevant threat to Muslim religious life in India. Shah Wali Allah believed that the political fortunes of Muslims in India were closely tied to their practice of a pure Islam. The loss of the former was epiphenomenal to the loss of the latter.

* * *

Khan's pre-1857 writings show a strong adherence to the concerns first articulated by Wali Allah, which were already his own concerns due to the competing influences of his Sufi upbringing. His focus in these early days was on reiterating Wali Allah's insistence on finding a mechanism for uniting all the disparate elements of Islamic theology under one coherent rubric and preventing Islamic life from being any more corrupted by the polytheistic influences of Hindu culture. Khan's first known work of theological reflection was the 1841 treatise *Jila al-qulub bi dhikr al-Mahbub* (Polishing of the Hearts by Remembering the Beloved). This was a *maulud risalah* (a biography of the Prophet) sans any unreliable material or superstitious content. Khan was interested in "relating the (actual) events in the life of the Prophet without apocryphal stories" and "to restrict rank popular belief and fantasy."[12] It was a self-conscious response to criticism by Christian missionaries and other Europeans who claimed that Islam was a backward and obscurantist religion riddled with magical thinking. It was also an attempt to "purify" Islam by ridding it of superstitious innovations that had crept into both belief and practice due to pantheistic Indic influences. One aspect of these influences was the gradual decline in the veneration of the Prophet and his Sunna. Khan wanted to bring the Prophet back into the mainstream of Muslim moral life through a renewed focus on *tariqa Muhammadiyya* (the way of the Prophet).[13] But Khan reimagined this *tariqa* in a rather unorthodox manner. He avoided the overly legalistic and ritualistic concerns of the *ulama* and focused instead on the devotionalism of Sufi practice as the proper paradigm for understanding a Muslim's relationship to the Prophet. Still, he held on to the fundamental priority of *Shari'a* at all times, and for all Muslims, in contradistinction to many Sufis. As Yohanan Friedman has pointed out, a fundamental ethical question for Islam has always been "in what way does the Muslim community maintain its contact with the Divine after Prophecy has come to an end?"[14] The Muslim legal tradition, or *fiqh*, developed in response to this concern. The Quran and the reliable traditions of the Prophet, or *ahadith*, provided the normative framework for the formulation of *Shari'a*. This *Shari'a* stood in stead, so to say, of God and his Prophet as a guide for and a judge of the Muslim community. From a very early time, Sufis in Islam had come up with a different solution to this same problem. Through mystical practices and extreme devotion, Sufis believed that they could have direct, unmediated access to the Divine. The *ma'rifa*, or experiential knowledge/gnosis, gained from such access could then be passed down from *shaykh* to *murid* in chains of transmission (*silsila*) that constituted distinct Sufi orders, or *tariqa*. In this sense, the *tariqa* of the elect was considered superior to *Shari'a* of the masses. The traditionalist *'ulama*, on the other hand, found the Sufi emphasis on esoteric practices (and their public attestation that they could supersede the *Shari'a*—"I am the Truth/ the Real") as clear signs of *shirk*.

Even at this early stage of his intellectual development, Khan took pains to avoid the extremes and seek instead some mechanism for imagining these competing viewpoints as signs of an underlying unity. The *'ulama* had always imagined the Sufi practice of *tasawwur-i-shaykh* as idolatry by another name. This practice was the use of a mental image of one's *pir*, or guide on the Sufi path, as a meditative tool for the *murid*, the student, to reach higher stages of consciousness. The *'ulama* felt that the undiluted word of God, and the reliable traditions of the prophet, were the only true sources of moral knowledge and this reliance on esoteric techniques was a sign of *shirk*. In the formulation of *Shari'a*, the *alim,* or religious scholar, relies on these incorruptible sources, not the words or images of another human being. But Khan instead wondered what it would mean to imagine the Prophet as a *pir*? As a living, ever-present embodiment of God's law on this earth? The Prophet may have passed on many hundreds of years ago, but he is still available as an object of devotional focus. And in fact, without such devotion, his words and deeds have the potential of becoming staid and moribund, mere words that neither sate the soul nor provide emotional imperatives for moral action. For Khan, "Islam means to love Muhammad personally, and to follow *out of this love*, his *sunnah* as closely as possible" (emphasis added).[15] *Tasawwur-i-shaykh* is therefore only one stage in the broader concern with maintaining a devotional link to the Prophet in the time of his absence from this world. As the great Indian poet and *Naqshbandi-Mujaddadi* Sufi saint Khwajāh Mir Dard (1720–85) put it, "The *shaikh* is in his group like the prophet of his people."[16] Khan was a great admirer of Mir Dard and fashioned his treatment of the *pir-murid* relationship closely after Dard's idea of *tahdhīb al-akhlāq*—the "polishing of the moral faculties" leading to one of the four different forms of *kashf* (disclosure) which Dard enumerates.[17] *Tasawwur* allows the *murid* to rid his mind of extraneous concerns and seek the annihilation of his own ego in the person of the *shaykh* (*fana al-shaykh*). According to Khan, this is merely the first stage in the development of God-consciousness, since the *murid* must realize it as provisional. *Fana al-shaykh* is accompanied by the realization of a still nagging incompleteness, which leads the *murid*, through the *shaykh*, to seeking *fana al-rusul*, annihilation in the Prophet. Ultimately, of course, the Sufi imperative is *wisal* (divine union) or *fana Allah* (annihilation in God). But Khan has little to say about the nature and parameters of such an experience, or even whether this is an advisable sort of end to seek at all. For the Muslim, the ideal human, the Prophet, is the ultimate guide. And it is through devotion to Muhammad (and of course, the words of the Qur'an) that humans can and do have access to God. God is *immanent*, yes, but immanent in these particular ways only. He is transcendent, yes, but not transcendent enough as to be wholly unavailable through anything but his words, and the words of His Prophet. All of existence is a sign (*aya*) of His immanence, with the Prophet and the Qur'an being the most unequivocal signs of them all.

In another early text, *Namiqah dar bayan-i mas'alah-i tasawur-i shaikh*, or "A letter explaining the issue of *tasawwur-i shaykh*" (1853), Khan suggests that "in the *rational* soul of sheikh and seeker, there will come about a mutual attribution and the grace of companionship, and guidance will take root in the rational soul (*nafs-i natiqah*) of the seeker, and, cleansed from vices, he will reach higher stages."[18] Moral knowledge in the human realm has a complicated relationship with moral knowledge as such. God's *shari'a*, which the rational soul seeks, is ultimately beyond human comprehension, it being perfect and timeless. In this sense, the *Shari'a* of the *'ulama* and the *tariqa* of the Sufis are imperfect and provisional attempts at explicating God's *shari'a*, which stands in judgment of both. The Prophet embodied this *Shari'a* as perfectly as any human being could. In this sense, his embodiment of God's law, made *concrete* in his example, is iconic; it points to, within time, that which is essentially eternal, timeless, the Truth. Or as Khan put it, "whatever gracious gift there is, it is in the Sunna of the Prophet, by God in nothing else, in nothing else, in nothing else."[19]

Khan splits the difference between the extreme devotionalism of Sufi practice and the legalistic, rational theology of the *'ulama*. It is in *Kalamat al-haqq*, or "The True Discourse" (1849) that we find the clearest, and most powerful, explication of his early theological ideas. Ostensibly a somewhat technical discussion of the proper *pir-murid* relationship, *Kalamat al-haqq* soars in its theological implications. The Prophet is revealed as an ideal human and in being the ideal human, the ideal *pir*. But the fact of his humanity is front and center. Khan has very little patience with the attribution of magical, and supernatural, powers to the Prophet which were so prevalent in much Sufi practice. Devotion to the Prophet has to do with meditation on his moral excellences and his capacity as a leader of the nascent Muslim community. How did this illiterate man manage to unify and civilize a ragtag group of Bedouins living at the very margins of the world? In a similar vein, in dismissing the traditional, orthodox opinion of the uniqueness (*'ijaz*) of the Quran as located in its miraculous rhetoric and style, or its *fasāhat o balāghat* (eloquent clarity), Sayyid Ahmad Khan argued that this book is unequaled rather because of its quality of *hidāyat* (eminent guidance).[20] The Qur'an's teachings are "all the more astonishing when viewed against the moral and religious depravity of Arab society in Muhammad's time."[21] And yet it is also a teaching that remains eternally relevant for all times and all places for all people.[22] God is immanent in this *natural* miracle attendant to the existence of the Qur'an. In fact, all of existence is a kind of miracle in this sense; a grand, incontrovertible sign of God's perfection. But as with all things created, it is ultimately only a sign. It points, imperfectly, and in so doing provides the motive force of human history. God's *shari'a* exposed to time is human *tariqa*, in all its different varieties. God's *tauhid* exposed to time is human *tatbi'a*, the imperative to harmonize the diversity of human experience of God and of the world He has created into a single, meaningful, purposeful, and yet ever-evolving narrative about the world and man's place in it.

In Sayyid Ahmad Khan's reading, Islam represents a kind of grand humanism. It takes the fact of the humanity of the human animal very seriously. God's will is immanent, but only in and through the human vessels through which it can and has been communicated. By focusing on another human being, the *shaykh*, the *murid* learns to forego the prejudices of his own will in search of the grand, impersonal design lying at the core of existence. This relationship between the *pir* and the *murid* is not merely esoteric but also epistemological since it constitutes the practice by which *ma'rifa* or gnosis is itself transmitted through the ages via the sanctified mechanism of *tradition*. Gradually rising to higher levels of impersonal consciousness, he may, in the end, begin to see, dimly, the faint outlines of divine purpose and act accordingly. But divine knowledge remains opaque. Human beings have the wisdom of the ages and of all their experiences in the world, and of the Prophets and of the holy books, to guide them. But ultimately, divine knowledge, can and will only be revealed at the end of time, on the Day of Judgment (*yaum-i qiyamat*), when all spheres of human experience and knowledge will finally coalesce in a climactic moment of moral certainty:

the end of Time itself. To seek moral certainty in history, as the Sufis do through their devotional practices, or as the *'ulama* do through their over-reliance on the words of the Qur'an and Hadith to formulate their versions of *Shari'a*, is to seek something that is unavailable in Time. Yet, this is no reason to lose heart. The moral adventure of human history is precisely the condition of human existence sanctified by God. To think otherwise would be to deny one's humanity, and worse to misunderstand God's divinity. This denial, this misunderstanding, is the quintessential form of *bid'a*, or corrupting innovation, which inevitably leads to the corruption and decline of Muslim society. The struggle to affirm one's humanity in the regime of divine purpose is a most fundamental concern, the denial of which is akin to apostasy. For Khan, the primary purpose in this early phase of his theological development was to ensure that the fault lines between different kinds of Muslim practice be minimized through the articulation of a mediatory discourse that explained the nature of their differences and accounted for their essential similarity. It is for this reason, that "perhaps the most remarkable feature of these [early] writings is the fusion of the Sufi and the alim tradition, of tariqqa and shari'a—a trend that had started much earlier [in Khan's writings] but which found a remarkable expression in *Kalamat al-Haqq*."[23]

* * *

By all accounts, the revolt of 1857 and the subsequent loss of formal Muslim sovereignty in India had a profound effect on Sayyid Ahmad Khan. It provided the locus and guiding framework for all his future literary and social work. Stationed as *na'ib munsif* (assistant judge) in the municipality of Bijnor at the time, Khan experienced firsthand the devastation wrought initially by the local population and eventually on them by the British forces. Subsequently, as British cannons reduced Delhi to smoldering ruins, some members of his family living in the city were killed as well. The witch hunts that followed left the Muslim elites of India cowering and immobilized. Whereas his early work dealt almost exclusively with issues internal to the Muslim community of India, and its relationship to the Hindu majority, he now had to turn his attention to the more general problem of Muslim life in a rapidly changing world dominated by Western power and technology. Muslims in India had no real language to describe this world or their place in it. Their Islam was provincial, and in the aftermath of the revolt, in danger of extinction.

In book X of *Confessions*, St. Augustine of Hippo famously pronounced *quaestio mihi factus sum*, "a question, I have become for myself." For Augustine, this was the most pathetic form of self-realization; to know that one does not know oneself is terrifying anguish. He lived in an age when the winds of change were sweeping the world around him. The emergence of Christianity had created a new and hybrid language of religious and political order that was as yet not fully constituted but which nevertheless had begun to exert ideological and social pressures that would ultimately transform the ancient Mediterranean world. Augustine was both a victim of this transformation and one of its perpetrators. He dealt with his anguish by creating a new language with which to understand and explain his anguish, to give his anguish meaning, and hence to render it affective rather than merely receptive.[24]

Much like Augustine, Sayyid Ahmad Khan also sought to transform the pain of inexplicability into an ideological re-configuration of the meaning of his own existence and of the existence of his community. It is interesting that for Augustine, the above question is raised in the presence of God, "in whose eyes I have become a question for myself." God renders man *grande profundum*, a great mystery to himself because man is unable to understand fully the nature and purpose of God's creative activity. It is in this same sense that God's plans had suddenly become totally incomprehensible to the Muslim elites of north India following 1857: What was the meaning of this catastrophe, of this devastation? What is one to make of this desertion by God of His own people? This is what Wilfred Cantwell Smith meant when he writes "the fundamental malaise of modern Islam is that something has gone wrong with Islamic history. . . . The fundamental spiritual crisis of Islam in the 20th century stems from an awareness that something is awry between the religion that God has appointed and the historical development of the world He controls."[25]

Smith spoke generally, and about the twentieth century. But the basic problematic is clear enough in mid-nineteenth-century India. After the veneer of formal Mughal sovereignty is wiped off the face of Muslim India, what remains is a face unrecognizable to itself in the mirror. It is disturbing and hauntingly unfamiliar. What the continued Mughal presence in Delhi had masked was the gradual decline of India's Muslim population in every sphere of life that mattered in the emergent order: modern scientific education, commercial and economic activity, technological skills, administrative training, etc. The list is long. Sayyid Ahmad Khan argued that for a Muslim, this condition of "subjecthood" and "backwardness" is a theological problem: if the Muslims of India were indeed God's people, then why had their God forsaken them? Political decline and other "this worldly" issues were not devoid of spiritual valence; that kind of dualism, which is the easy last refuge of much of Christian theology, does not hold for

Islam. Khan therefore sought to (re)construct a new language of Islam that could make an unfamiliar world familiar again, a new theology that could both account for the present and provide direction for the future.

Consider, for example, that in the years preceding the Great Rebellion, the main themes of Urdu and Persian poetry, the most sublime literary forms of Delhi's then-thriving Muslim culture, were romance, the life of pleasure and passion, and the Sufi motif of separation from the divine beloved (and its attendant sorrows). Post-1857, a new motif emerges: *shikwa* (the complaint). This was the literary expression of Muslim dissatisfaction not merely with their material and political condition but also with the various explanations for this state of affairs. Altaf Hussain Hali (1837–1914), a disciple of Sayyid Ahmad Khan (and one of his early biographers), wrote *Shikwa-i-Hind* in the 1870s, this being the Muslim complaint to the land of India for making paupers out of kings: "You've turned lions into lowly beings, O Hind, Those who were hunters came here to become the hunted ones."[26] Despite its sometimes strident tone, Hali's *shikwa* is also an elegiac ode to an India he fears has now passed, "which gave us wealth, government and dominion" and whose many kindnesses he takes much time to enumerate. But times have now changed: "Farewell O Hindustan, O Autumnless garden, we your homeless guests have stayed too long."[27]

More important than his laments, Hali provides poetic expression to Sayyid Ahmad Khan's quasi-theological explanation for Muslim decline: "So long as O Hindustan we were not called Hindi, We had some graces which were not found in others. You've made our condition frightening, We were fire O Hind, you've turned us into ashes."[28] This explanation has two interlocking contentions: one that Muslims are "foreign" to India and the other that Muslims have been irredeemably "changed" by India. The Muslim *ashraf* classes (to which Khan and Hali both belonged) had always maintained that their ancestors had come to India from those lands of West Asia that were the ancient core of the Islamic polity: the Arabian peninsula, Egypt, present-day Iraq, Syria, Jordan, and Palestine.[29] Even Iran was acceptable as a land of origin, perhaps only because it was the source of Indian high culture and Persian had always been the language of the Mughal court. But other than this rather minor caveat, the vast majority of Muslim elites were, impossibly, under the impression that they were Arabian immigrants! Considering their numbers, and knowing the historical record, this is on its face absurd. But unlike his elite co-religionists, the valence of Sayyid Ahmad Khan's emphasis on Muslim foreign-ness was not geographical or ethnic but religious.

For Khan, as it was for Wali Allah before him, foreign-ness was code for distinction, for those "graces that were not found in others." It was that set of peculiar features that made Islam and its followers unique. Muslim political power had never been based exclusively on force of arms, or superior numbers, or technology. Nor had their economic, cultural, and social innovations been the result of contingent historical circumstances. Muslims had a better system, a more coherent and effective structure of beliefs that translated into a superior social organization. The language of Islam was both normatively and instrumentally a more advanced language for understanding reality and hence for managing the world. In India's case, the uniquely Islamic character of the Muslim polity, its foreign-ness, had gradually eroded and been "naturalized" by polytheistic influences from the native Hindu populations. This is what Hali meant by Muslims becoming "Hindi"; they were no longer foreigners, no longer so different socially or religiously from the "native" masses. It is in this sense that the language of Islam was not extant anymore; no one appeared to be speaking it properly and no one seemed to know how. In fact, Khan feared that Islam itself was passing, disappearing, not merely in India but everywhere he looked. What was taking its place was a monstrous parody of Islam. Little wonder then that these so-called Muslims were in decline. Their counterfeit practices, their bastardized beliefs, their supernatural and ritualistic excesses, were a pale imitation of Islam's sublime simplicity. The proof of their corruption was, so to say, in the pudding of their circumstances. Feigning a self-reflexively "Hindi" fatalism, Hali blames fate, *qismet*, for the ignominy of Muslims: "We were convinced that adversity would befall us in time, And we O Hind will be devoured by you."[30] Corruption was inevitable; throughout the ages, India had done this to the best of them.

*   *   *

The technical term for this corruption is, as noted earlier, *bid'a*. For us moderns, innovation has only positive connotations. It is the engine of progress, the *raison d'être* of modern life. This is partly because we tend to think of innovation as primarily a technical matter; a smaller iPhone, a faster computer, a more fuel-efficient hybrid car. We have a hard time imagining innovation as pertaining to value systems or to social norms. But it is precisely in this sense that innovation can be death for a traditional moral order. Sayyid Ahmad Khan was hardly the first Muslim in India to express concern about the innovating influences of the local environment. Unlike their counterparts in North Africa and West Asia, Muslims in India had taken over a society that remained mostly pagan and polytheistic even after a thousand years of Muslim rule.[31] Native culture was not only unfamiliar to the early pioneers of Muslim rule but it was also deeply abhorrent. These early Muslim rulers were (in)famous for their idol-smashing and temple-destroying ways.[32] The traditionalist *'ulama* had also always been gravely concerned about Muslims "mixing" with locals and taking on native customs. These concerns only became more urgent (and certainly more strident) with the decline of Mughal power. As Muslim political control became less relevant to the everyday lives of Muslims, the exhortations of priests, scholars, and preachers became more so. It is in this context that north India had witnessed a series of reform movements and revivals since at least the beginning of the eighteenth century. These movements sought to return Indian Islam to a supposedly pristine "Arabian" purity by ridding it of its Indic accruals.[33] The thinking behind such reform is not hard to grasp; a self-consciously perfect system of beliefs, norms, and practices needs no innovation.

Within the reformist worldview, *bid'a* is perhaps too complex a concept to be ideally rendered by "innovation," and considerably more insidious than this term suggests. Pollution, infection, disease; a cancerous growth that destroys the Muslim body from within; the golden kernel of truth covered over by layers of mud, accumulating through the years like millions of tiny barnacles on the underbelly of an unsuspecting ship. Danger lurks in every social interaction with a non-Muslim, behind every encounter with an idol/god being paraded through the streets come festival time, underneath all compromises of belief and practice that accrue over generations until there is little left of the truth. *Bid'a* is also the temptation of assimilation to the ways of the world around you. It is the same temptation that Muhammad faced in Mecca all those years ago. Muslims in India had faced this temptation, and they had failed. The fabric of pure Islamic practice based on the *shari'a* of God, the primacy of the Quran and the Sunna of the Prophet had gradually unraveled. The dissipating uniqueness of the Muslim populace had its theological corollary in *tauhid* giving way to *shirk*, in the One becoming the many. The Muslims had become divided into petty fiefdoms and kingdoms, fighting each other like infidels. The moral life of the individual was as much in crisis as the larger political order. The gods had multiplied. There was little interest in piety and submission to the will of God. In the desert of human existence, knowing the *shari'a*—literally "the way to the watering hole"— is essential for survival. The Muslims of India had lost their way.

Sayyid Ahmad Khan identified strongly with the tradition of reform and its attendant distaste for *bid'a*. But whereas the mainstream revivalist focus had been on the corrupt ritual practices of native Muslim populations (like tomb visitations and saint worship), Khan began to imagine the problem of *bid'a* in more abstract ways. There was something fundamentally wrong with Muslim understandings of Islam. This was not the incidental *bid'a* of tomb visitation, or magic, but the essential *bid'a* of the nature of Muslim practice. The problem was not vocabulary, but the grammar of Islam. After 1857, Sayyid Ahmad Khan focused on more clearly articulating this problem and finding solutions for it. This was a grand project and as such engendered much resistance. Within a few years, Khan managed to alienate vast swaths of Muslim public opinion and the orthodox authorities of Sunni Islam. He was verbally burned in effigy by that great hero of late nineteenth-century Islamic anti-imperialism Jamal al-Din al-Afghani (1838–97) for being a British stooge and an apostate. He even had *fatwas* issued against him in Mecca and Medina, the venerable centers of Islam.[34]

On the other hand, he was also hailed as a savior by educated Muslim elites and by many in the beleaguered *ashraf* classes of north India. His social activism, educational work, and publishing projects drew praise from the British, who saw him as a "liberal" bulwark against the dangerous conservatism of his co-religionists. An entire generation of young Muslims, among them Altaf Hussain Hali, regarded him as their spiritual and intellectual mentor, their leader, their captain. Sayyid Ahmad Khan had become a lightning rod for both the fears and the aspirations of his fellow Muslims. This hysterically bivalent reaction had its origins in the theological "innovations" that Sayyid Ahmad Khan introduced as self-conscious adjustments to his earlier positions. One such adjustment was his then-controversial contention that the blind following (*taqlid*) of the existing juridical traditions (*madhahib*) needed to be supplemented by the use of reasoned interpretation (*ijtihad*) to deal with novel problems and changed circumstances. This was particularly grating for the religious authorities of his day because Khan, an amateur theologian and an "ordinary" Muslim, himself wanted to contribute to the development of a new *'ilm al- kalam*, a reformed apologetic theology fit for modern times. No surprise then that the "experts" were not happy with him at all.

*   *   *

Sayyid Ahmad Khan wrote his *Asbab-i-bhagavat-i-Hind* (*The Causes of the Indian Revolt*) in 1858. The book was written as a response to the virulent theories being bandied about by some in the Company elites that Muslims had instigated the revolt and that they were bound by their faith to be disloyal to British authority. In a curious reversal of the oriental and occidental "types," Khan responded to these passionate, knee-jerk attacks with a reasoned sociological analysis that pointed to a lack of communication between the government and the governed as the primary cause of the violence. He argued for greater native representation in the East India Company administration. The tone of the book was apologetic but researching it put Khan face to face with the rampant obscurantism at all levels of the Muslim community. He was apologizing for a dinosaur! More importantly, it was a dinosaur that did not know it was a dinosaur. Self-deception may be wonderful medicine for the weak but it is also that which sustains their weakness. Khan realized that none of the earlier reformers had appreciated the profound extent of the problem, nor had they properly diagnosed the nature of the infection.

In a nutshell, the problem was that Muslims had, literally, become detached from Islam. The main feature of this detachment was the loss of *tauhid* and the creation of a moth-eaten construct to take its place. The earlier reformers had rightly noted that Muslims were adopting the ways of the pagans and polytheists around them, visiting tombs and venerating saints, practicing *shirk* in all but name. But these reformers had missed the forest for the trees; *tauhid* was a forest, not a tree. It was a panoramic concept, an icon for insight into the very nature of reality. They had turned *tauhid* into merely a standard of judgment for ritual practice and for the moral development of individuals. In this they were not wrong, but their efforts betrayed a fundamental narrowness of perspective that was indicative of another, more obscure moral failing; the *shirk* of division. The integrated life of Islam had been broken into so many different pieces, and parts internal to its meaning and practice banished into exile. Muslims no longer had access to Islam, because Islam had become an abstract concept, a set of unified beliefs and practices that no longer existed as a whole in the Muslim world, or the world in general. Devoid of such wholeness, aspects of Islam were floating around in different places, and in different societies absent the one-ness which endowed them with their purpose and meaning. This was the fundamental problem of modern Muslim existence, the true nature of the pollution. Purifying Islam (*tazkiya*) did not just mean removing contagion. It required putting the pieces of Islam back together again.

In 1869, Sayyid Ahmad Khan went on a trip to Europe that lasted about eighteen months. He spent time in London, Paris, Berlin, and many other European capitals. On the way back he visited extensively the Muslim lands as well, including making a pilgrimage to Mecca and Medina. On his return to India, and obviously still in a state of high excitement following the trip, Khan made a most astounding statement in a letter to a friend:

> My faith in the fundamental principles of Islam was strengthened more by my
> exposure to the conditions of Europe and by gaining the knowledge of European
> scholars' views rather than by going on a pilgrimage to Mecca, *nā'awz bi-Allah*
> (God forgive me). . . . After my arrival in London, I became a true and faithful
> Muslim by *tasdīyq-i qalabīy'* (that my heart verifies it).[35]

Elsewhere, Khan stated that "on borrowed money on interest, I consider it
better to go to London than to Mecca . . . for the innovations that are current
in the revered city of Mecca and that are against revealed law of the Messenger
of God are not made permissible by the fact that they are practiced by the
people of Mecca."[36] This juxtaposition of Islam and Europe is curious especially
considering the long history of unequivocal animosity between European
society and its Muslim neighbors. It is just as well that Khan did not say this in
public. For the flamboyant iconoclasm of this statement conceals a rather more
simple sentiment. Sayyid Ahmad Khan was not talking about Muslim history or
even Muslims as such. He was talking about *Islam*, and what he had discovered
in Europe were "pieces" of Islam in exile, banished from Muslim lands but alive
and well in the centers of Christianity!

   This idea of using the term Islam to refer to a body of practices and beliefs,
a religio-ethical system independent of its believers was of recent and reformist
vintage in India and elsewhere. But it was a most useful construct. And Sayyid
Ahmad Khan took to it like a fish to water. *Tauhid* was the fundamental nature of
this Islam; submission to the one true God was epiphenomenal to a realization
of *tauhid*. But Indian Muslims were enmeshed in a practice defined by its
dualisms and divisions. Quite aside from the deeply problematic practices of the
common man, even those who professed to be the defenders of orthodoxy had
themselves literally painted "Islam" into a corner by identifying it with one side
of a quasi-Cartesian divide. These so-called leaders of the Muslim community
had appropriated Islam and made of it a fighting creed, a warring faction in a
battle with aspects of its own totality. They had dismembered the unity of God
into the multiplicity of the *gharaniq*.

   The divisions would be familiar to any student of European history.
Superficially, there was nothing novel about the manner in which the sides were
defined and the battle lines drawn in Indian Islam. The dualisms followed the
standard paradigm with the world partitioned irreconcilably between forces of
religion and science, faith and reason, revelation and empiricism, the sacred
and the secular, the spiritual and the material. In this Manichean construct,
Islam was crammed into the "good" side of the divide by its champions and
adherents. It was in fact the very embodiment of the good and as such the

bulwark against the forces of corrupting change. It stood with tradition against modernity. It was the last refuge of virtue in a world ravaged by the barbarity of novelty.

For a time early in his life, Sayyid Ahmad Khan was a run-of-the-mill traditionalist himself in his attitude toward the sciences, just as he was, by his own admission, a kind of Wahhabi fundamentalist in matters of virtue and vice. Until late in the 1850s, he continued to defend the Ptolemaic representation of the universe against Copernicus since Greek astronomy was internalized by Islamic thinkers early on and was now part of the established orthodoxy. But it was precisely the example of the Greek sciences that gave Khan an important insight into the true character of Islamic history. In the golden age of their political ascendancy, Muslims had also been ascendant, naturally, in the production of knowledge. Greek philosophy and sciences were integrated seamlessly into Islam because they provided modes of understanding the world that were superior to those otherwise available. Khan realized that it was misleading to imagine such integration as supplementing Islam or even adding to it. How does one supplement perfection? Instead, the discovery of the Greek sciences was an aspect of the progress of Islamic history; it was internal to Islam not an addition to it. Islam is an integrated view of reality, a single coherent truth that unifies the disparities and dualities of existence. It is timeless truth but it is not static. One aspect of the subjective experience of Islam is the growth of all forms of human knowledge. Islamic history unfolds in the continuing development of our moral faculties as well as in the evolving maturity of our knowledge concerning God's creation. The material and the spiritual are not separate or antagonistic spheres of human activity nor even different tracks of parallel but distinct human progress. *Tauhid*; they are made one in Islam.

* * *

Of course, the unity of these spheres had long been shattered under the influence of the environment in which Muslims found themselves, and due to the temptation of assimilation to the ways of the world. These *bida'at* (pl. of *bid'a*) had become so standardized that Muslims were living in a topsy-turvy, "looking glass" world; to advocate for the original purity and unity of Islam appeared as *bid'a* to most Muslims, whereas divisions and dualisms appeared the very essence of *tauhid*. Sayyid Ahmad Khan realized that these divisions were not merely ideological. They had a geographical component. While the value system of Muslims was superior, informed as it was by whatever pieces of Islam were still in their possession, the Europeans had appropriated the Islamic emphasis on

knowledge and material advancement and made it their own. Muslims were the
guardians of the "word of God" (Qur'an); their facility with the moral sciences
afforded a superior knowledge of ethics and value systems. But Islam's geography
was more complicated than the peaks and valleys of normative prohibitions
and permissions. The Europeans had far outstripped Muslims, and just about
anybody else, in the development of the technological and philosophical
sciences. They had developed modes of knowing and manipulating the "work of
God" (*qudrat*/nature) that elicited little interest from most Muslims; possession
of revelation had unfortunately made reason an unnecessary distraction to most
Muslims.

There are, however, limits to such indifference; one cannot indefinitely keep
one's head in the sand without the risk of losing it. Sayyid Ahmad Khan realized
the urgency of the danger in 1857 when Muslims paid for their backwardness
and obscurantism with their blood and with the total decimation of their culture
and power. This was to be expected considering the circumstances. The loss of
reason had rendered their material existence precarious. More importantly, it
had also made their Islam a monstrous parody of itself. Hidden underneath
heavy layers of self-referential jargon and parochial traditions, this Islam never
saw the light of day. It was timid and defensive. Khan looked at this "religion"
and its practitioners with contempt:

> Present times are different from the past. No person has the power anymore
> to prevent the rays of these sciences from shining forth. In fact if the people of
> religion, instead of proving the truth of their religion in the light of the sciences,
> obstruct their spread, they thereby avow publicly that religion is not capable of
> bearing the light of the sciences.[37]

There is nowhere to run, and nowhere to hide. There is no escape. Muslims must
leave their caves and come back into the light.

At issue was not the survival of their race or even the reconstitution of Muslim
political power. These concerns were epiphenomenal to the re-emergence of pure
Islam (*thet Islam*) in human history. Khan is philosophical about the reception
of his views in the Muslim community, especially among the so-called religious
elites of India. He notes that while his inquiring mind made him arrive at "the
truth which I believe to be 'pure Islam,' conventional (*rasmi*) Muslims may hold
it to be 'pure unbelief' (*thet Kufr*)."[38] Conventional Muslims had abandoned
inquiry and reversed the very meaning of Islam. With this reversal, Islam as a
lived and practiced entity had disappeared from the world.

Consider, for example, a text titled "Refutation of the Materialists" published
in 1880 by Jamal al-Din al-Afghani as a very thinly veiled attack on Sayyid

Ahmad Khan and his followers.[39] Afghani was the great peripatetic philosopher of Islamic resistance to European imperialism and as such was irritated with Khan's close relationship with the colonial authorities in India. But this work avoids any explicit mention of politics. Instead, Afghani strikes in precisely the manner Khan had come to expect. He condemns "naturalism" in religion as *shirk* and calls the "sect" of the *neicheris* (a pejorative bastardization of "naturalist") the direst threat to Islam in the Indian subcontinent. The text is a long and often meandering meditation on the nature and function of religion. The relevant critique is quite simple. The ethical and social function of religion can only be properly served if God's transcendence is unequivocal. Incorporating the human experience of the world, the laws of nature, and scientific descriptions of reality into the Islamic value system "naturalizes" God. It renders His transcendence provisional rather than absolute. As a fellow "modernist," Afghani is certainly not against science and reason. He is merely wary of the natural world serving as a standard for judgment concerning religious truth. These are different species of truth and Afghani wants to keep them separated.

Khan is viscerally allergic to such separation. The natural world is no more and no less real in the religious sense than the word of God or the Sunna of the Prophet. Ultimately, the Truth of God is unitary. This is not equating nature with God; it is merely acknowledging that like the word of God, the work of God must provide access to real knowledge about God and His plans for the human world. But Khan goes further, adding fuel to the fire, so to say, and all but admitting to the charge of being a *neicheri* while redefining what it means to be one:

> A true principle [is that] with which man must bring all his powers of will, body, soul and spirit into harmony as long as he is in control of his physical and mental powers. . . . If we want, therefore, from among different religions to establish critically the true religion, we should see whether it is in harmony with this true principle or not. . . . As far as man can know by his rational powers (*quwat-i 'aqli*), [this true principle] is nothing but nature (*qudrat*) or the law of nature (*qanun-i qudrat*). . . . Thus this [nature] alone is true and those principles alone which are in harmony with it are true principles, not those which depend entirely on the belief of a passing being capable of error and sin—the belief of man.[40]

Harmony is the subjective human experience of unity. God's creation is naturally in harmony with God's history. It is only human beings, endowed with free will (their curse and their blessing), that require a reflexive experience of history to appreciate its meaning and participate righteously in its unfolding. And they often get it wrong. The laws of nature are the material artifacts of God's creative activity. They are by definition signs of His perfection. God Himself admits as much when He claims "thou [Muhammad] canst see no fault in the Beneficent One's creation; then look again; Canst thou see any rifts? Then look again and yet again, thy sight will return unto thee weakened and made dim."[41] It is for this reason that the perfection of moral faculties cannot be divorced from the development of knowledge concerning God's creation. These are not distinct faculties, as if one could excel in one without caring for the other. God's perfection is a unitary perfection: it requires man to "bring all his powers of will, body, soul and spirit into *harmony*." The "true principle" admits no discord and separation. Like its author, it too is one.

This is the true philosophical meaning of the distinction between *dar al-Islam* (abode of Islam/peace) and *dar al-harb* (the abode of war). Islam is the experience of harmony, *tatbiq*, within the human being, among human beings, and between human beings and the natural order. Such harmony is only possible through knowledge of the conditions of natural and social existence. It is in this sense that the disintegration of the Muslim order in India did not represent the defeat of Islam. Mughal India was already a house of disharmony and discord. Its imminent destruction could have been foretold by any minor prophet. As it is, it probably was. But no one listened.

*   *   *

In 1909, the great Indian poet Allama Muhammad Iqbal published the epitome of all "complaints." His pithily named *Shikwa* is perhaps the most glorious piece of Urdu poetry of the twentieth century. Written as a response to a *bulbul* (nightingale) singing ruefully in the *gulistan* (garden) of life, *Shikwa* is a scathing verse of protest directed at God Himself: "Hear, O Lord, from the faithful ones this sad lament / From those used to hymn a praise, a word of discontent."[42] The poem is a hard-hitting tour de force. It's an elegiac history of the Muslim people, their many accomplishments and their courage in spreading the word of God far and wide: "On every human heart the image of Your Oneness we drew / Beneath the dagger's point, we proclaimed your message true."[43] And yet God has abandoned the very people who fought and bled for the glory of His name: "Strangers revel in the garden, besides a stream they are sitting / Wine goblets in their hands, hearing the cuckoo singing / Far from the garden, far from its notes of revelry / Your lovers sit by themselves awaiting the moment to praise You."[44] Iqbal shames God, questions His faithfulness, and dares God to provide an answer. Four years later, God responds.

Jawab-e-Shikwa (Response to the Complaint) is God's point by point rebuttal to *Shikwa*, as imagined by a now supposedly chastened Iqbal. God is not shamed.

In fact, God finds the complaint both humorous and somewhat juvenile: "Could celestial heights have become the aim of man's striving? Could this pinch of dust have learned the art of flying?"[45] On a more serious note, God denies that these lamenting nightingales are the same Muslims that He raised up in Arabia for the glory of His name: "You are bent on self-destruction; for honor and self-respect they were known / All you do is talk and talk; they were men of action, deeds and power." But God is not without favor for the scions of His erstwhile followers, and He provides Iqbal with the framework for renewal: "With reason as your shield and the sword of love in your hand / Servant of God! The leadership of the world is at your command / The cry—Allah-o-Akbar—destroys all except God; it is a fire / If you are true Muslims, your destiny is to grasp what you aspire." The response concludes in an emotional crescendo with a climactic challenge for the ages: "If you break not faith with Muhammed, We shall always be there with you / What is this miserable world, to write the world's History, pen and tablet We offer you."[46]

In *Shikwa* and its *Jawab*, the intellectual and theological reconfiguration envisioned by Sayyid Ahmad Khan reaches its most sublime form, its clearest exposition. Iqbal is both stylistically and substantively a very different kind of thinker than Khan. But sentimentally they are cut from the same cloth; they are both theorists of Muslim despair, its causes, and its consequences. And their concerns are both descriptive and prescriptive. Iqbal turns the Augustinian question around, asking God to explain Himself and in so doing explain man to himself. The explanation God provides is an elucidation of the true nature of Islamic history and of the Muslims' place in it. The Muslim is precisely that subject in which the totality of Islamic agency is unified, in which the movement of Islamic history itself is embodied. It is instructive that Jibril's command to Muhammad ("RECITE!") is reversed in God's offer to man of "pen and tablet." But agency is a function of integrity. Pen and tablet are for those who stand before God not as questions for themselves but as answers for those around them. *A unitary God demands an integrated worshiper, a unified subject to his call for submission.* To be faithful to Muhammad is to hold together in your person the love of God and a rational engagement with His creation, reason and revelation, the shield and the sword, and to appreciate the magnificent character of *the first and the last*. This is Iqbal's *mard-i-momin*, the man of perfect faith. Only he has the right to ask God for an explanation, although he has no need for one.

Sayyid Ahmad Khan's emphasis on scientific progress and education is consistent with his rather orthodox belief that Islam in its pure, unadulterated form, must epitomize the ideals of human civilization in *all* respects. In the modern era, the shortcomings of Muslims in politics, education, and, ultimately, civilization are an indication that Islam's true essence, which is necessarily "progressive" in its orientation, is better reflected in the progress of Western civilization. What his visit to Europe allowed him to do was "to 'discover' Islam as a political ideology whose value system was superior to contemporary ideologies of the West,"[47] but whose contemporary adherents were continuing to "[resist] the spirit of free inquiry [which] confined Muslims within the narrow limits of a stultifying past, even when they knew that it hampered the growth of their culture and personality in India."[48] Hence a viable test for the truth of orthodox traditionalism, what Khan pejoratively called "Islamic Obscurantism," must be an engagement with the political, social, and economic conditions of Muslims rather than with merely a truncated notion of "religious" revival un-representative of Islam as a complete ideology of life and society. Instead, Khan "strove first of all after a social, economical and cultural uplift of his co-religionists with the motto: the more worldly progress [Muslims] make, the more glory Islam gains."[49] Islam, by definition, is always a united front. The orthodox conception of Islam was inadequate at articulating a comprehensive vision of Islam that must, by definition, be consistent with the demands of cultural and technological progress, and hence pass the test of modern scientific reason and rationality.

Still, Khan was no sycophant. He was not looking to Westernize the Muslim population. He was looking to Islamize them. His ultimate concern was to ensure that Islam as a language of agency and history would once again flourish in this world. Modernity was another name for Islam, not a condition for judgment on Islam. This is a grand reversal! Here in the academy, questions of commensurability are near and dear to the hearts of theorists of the modern age. What religious systems are compatible with modernity, which ones have the right vocabulary, the proper pedigree, the nutritious historical flesh to serve as food for an emergent modern order? Islam usually comes up short in these discussions. Or, at best, its champions jump through hoops only to establish that it's not so foreign to core Western values after all. Sayyid Ahmad Khan renders these questions moot. The entire discussion of commensurability is the figment of divided imaginations. Divisions, dualisms, partitions. What else to expect from a Trinitarian God? The God of Islam is supremely One. The Muslim has no internal differentiations. Reason and science are aspects of an Islamic subjectivity, material progress and social development are internal to the unfolding of Islamic history. Khan challenges our received notions about modernity by describing it entirely in a reconstructed language of Islam. Liberal rationalism and Enlightenment progressivism are collapsed explicitly into the conservative aims of the preservation of religion. But what is this religion that Sayyid Ahmad Khan wants to preserve? It is neither the Islam of the *ʿulama* nor that of the Sufis. It is the religious dialectic of harmonization; it is Islam as critique.

All else is sham and masquerade.

Modernism and Humanism

A major lacuna in the study of British colonial India is what to call the events of 1857. Were they a mutinous uprising by British East India Company soldiers? A rebellion by Muslim elites looking to recapture the glory days of the Mughal rule? A war of "Indian" independence? Some combination or none of these things? And this confusion in historiography has a parallel in the historical record of the events themselves which were a bewildering cacophony of myriad actors, haphazard and sporadic eruptions of conflict bereft of any unified design, inexplicable alliances, and irresolute carnage amid a general perplexity about what was happening and to what end. If there is some unanimity among protagonists and scholars alike, it is on the point that 1857 marked the end of the old order and the beginning of high British imperialism in India. But even such a rendering of these events has the effect of ex post facto taming their diversity. The complexity of the old and the new is acknowledged, but marking 1857 as a *death* domesticates it and roots it in place as an *event*, localized and over with. In grasping unreservedly at 1857 as a historical event, as a "happening," scholars are often distracted from a true reckoning with its iconic character, its symbolic meaning as the *pivot* in a long and drawn out historical process by which the Muslims of India fell into modernity. The year 1857 was not so much an event as a sign. It was what Jean-Luc Marion calls a "saturated phenomenon" that overflows the limits of both time and space in its excess of meaning and significance.[1] Bell curved into both the past and the future, it was the tipping point at the top of the mountain that signifies the fact of a mountain without being the mountain itself.[2]

And the fate of no person is as emblematic of this falling into modernity down the other side of the mountain as that of the Lord Emperor Bahadur Shah Zafar who was tried in a British court like a common criminal, convicted of mutiny and sedition *in his own kingdom*, and exiled to an anonymous death in Yangon, the armpit of the British empire. Bahadur Shah's fate was iconic in the original sense of the term: it was a *sign* of things to come, a *primer* to a reality emergent but not yet fully constituted, a *window* into a strange, new, and unfamiliar world. Iconic also in the literal dismemberment of his sons, who lost their heads to the Company sword, and whose broken bodies were reputedly left out in the open to be consumed by street dogs in a piece of ghastly cautionary theater for the natives. What did these broken bodies signify? *Fragmentation.* As individuals and as a community, the Muslims of India were now like so many pieces of the princes' bodies. They too had gone to the dogs! In the same manner that much of Delhi was reduced to rubble by British cannon fire in the aftermath of 1857, the sense that Muslims had of themselves and of their place in the world, of belonging and being at home in their own skin had been atomized into a thousand pieces that no longer held together in a coherent narrative of meaningful identity.

It is this iconic obliteration, this falling into modernity that is the proper context for understanding and appreciating Sayyid Ahmad Khan as a modernist and humanist Muslim fully engaged with the complex realities of the modern age and of the Muslim's place in it. But the true measure of his modernism is not the trite designation of this or that moniker to him to make him appear more familiar to or in line with the West—this is why monikers like "liberal" that evoke a West-centered, forward-looking, and "progressive" orientation obfuscate more than they illuminate. No, his is what Marshall Berman called modernism as "any attempt by modern men and women to become subjects as well as objects of modernization, to get a grip on the modern world and to make themselves at home in it."[3] It is this sense of not being at home in the present moment, of being objectified by forces they could no longer control as subjects of their own history, that the Muslims of India needed rescue from after 1857. Having fallen into the present and lacking the control to guide its movement forward, Muslims were susceptible to making a reactionary retreat into their own pasts or to the opposing impulse of a future-oriented millenarianism. The kind of rescue Khan imagined then was neither progressive nor regressive but firmly rooted in attending to the reality of the present, the *jadid*, the novel contemporary. Khan's reformist theology, his new *'ilm al-kalam*, was an explicit repudiation of both the past-oriented and future-oriented impulses in the Muslim community of India. Against the obscurantism of the traditionalists and the progressive and regressive utopianism of the liberal and religious varieties, Khan therefore counseled a moral realism based on Shah Wali Allah's notion of *tatbi'a*, on the synthetic harmonization of these competing impulses to allow Muslims to feel at home in the present moment and to become subjects as well as objects of modernity.

Additionally, the true measure of Khan's humanism is not some anodyne ascription of liberal universalism to his work, or the kind of platitudes about religion one often encounters these days in vacuous interfaith dialogues and in the nauseating affirmations of each other's humanity as if such affirmation was an objective designation we can ply each other with. No, this is humanism of the sort that Hannah Arendt had in mind when she said that "the world is not human just because it is made by human beings . . . [rather] we humanize what is going on in the world and in ourselves only by speaking of it, and in the course of speaking of it we learn to be human."[4] The modernity that 1857 augured was deeply dehumanizing for Muslims of India not so much in political subjugation to the British but more importantly in their inability to meaningfully verbalize their existence either to themselves or to others. The discursive languages in which these Muslims historically spoke of their integrity and identity, and of their place in the world, were no longer coherent as a system of signs and symbols in this new reality. Khan's primary humanistic project was therefore an attempt to reconstruct these moribund languages, to make them fit for the modern age, and hence allow Muslims to once again effectively speak their humanity continuously into existence and to humanize the world around them by participating in public talk about it. Unlike many of his contemporaries, Khan did not prioritize political agitation but rather the laying of pre-political foundations for the salutary construction of a body politic constituted by an affirmation of one's humanity through deliberative speech-acts in the open *agora* of the modern *polis*. Sans a capacity for critical engagement with the common questions and concerns that Muslims now shared with all others as human beings, the dehumanized state of their contemporary existence would persist no matter who controlled the state. Khan's humanism was therefore not an ideological commitment to equality but an imperative to act and engage in the affairs of the world. And to deliberate its common futures and the nature and meaning of the good life with others.

But neither the dehumanized silences of modernity nor the falling into it without finding a home in it are experiences that are peculiar to Muslims or to the provincial context of India. In fact, these experiences are the universal corollary to the escalating transformations of the modern age. And as such, they have been experienced, theorized about, and dealt with in some form or manner by a wide variety of thinkers across the world over the last two centuries or so. Writing from their own corners of the world and hemmed in by the particularities of their own experiences, these thinkers all nonetheless engage with the common and universal conditions, and some may even say afflictions of modernity. Still, even as numerous thinkers have indeed engaged with this new reality, only Western ones have been allowed to contest the *general* meanings and ends of the condition of modernity in the global public mainstream. Folks like Sayyid Ahmad Khan usually only register as provincially relevant to India or to Muslims, while "philosophers" in Western metropoles speak about the human condition in the general universal sense. This discursive asymmetry means that although the modern age presents a superficial veneer of humanism embedded in abstract notions like freedom, human rights, and democracy, such notions are not rooted in genuinely humanistic foundations. The events of 1857, for example, unleashed an ever-expanding ripple of consequences in the ether of humanity at least as significant as those initiated by the French Revolution. Recent scholarship by Indian historian Seema Alavi has shown how "the mood of 1857" percolated far and wide in Muslim metropoles like Mecca, Istanbul, and Cairo as participants in the rebellion fanned out of India to escape their British inquisitors.[5] The nature of British imperial rule was fundamentally changed in1857, in India and elsewhere, as the civilizing mission and its relationship to a supposedly regressive, rebellious, and obscurantist "Islam" became more clearly sedimented in the everyday practices of empire.[6] The taxonomic practices of the empire in India, for example, that divided communities (and electorates) based on religion and the escalating production of knowledge about these communities by Orientalists all have had their proximate cause in the manner in which the events of 1857 were understood and explained by the British imperial authorities.[7] Yet, no proper accounting of 1857 as a world-historical event is on offer and certainly, no one has read Khan's intellectual reactions to the events of 1857 as having the same general relevance as G. W. F. Hegel's reactions to the French Revolution. It is high time that this discursive asymmetry be remedied and a good place to start, I believe, is in what Edward Said called a "contrapuntal" approach to the archive of modernity.[8] What Said meant by this was not conventionally comparative work but rather reading together the works of thinkers and writers that would normally not be found in the same archives or in the same autonomous fields. Said suggested, for example, that to read Jane Austen without also reading Frantz Fanon prevents us from properly affiliating modern culture with its engagements and attachments. This modern culture is not a Western creation but a product of what is for the first time in history a world in full. Which is to say that partly as a consequence of European imperial expansion, the story of no part of this world can now be properly told without reference to other parts, and to the whole. It is for this reason that to take a full measure of Khan's thinking and contribution, we must learn to read him not just with other Muslims but with other fellow moderns and intellectuals. This is the only way in to the significance of his work and to accounts and descriptions of a world made anew in the modern age.

* * *

The promise of reading Khan with his Western counterparts is the discovery of new terrain hitherto undiscovered. But the peril is illegibility. Sayyid Ahmad Khan's value lies in his Islamic distinction. Yet such distinction can also lead many to callously dismiss his work as provincially Islamic with little to offer to wider, more general conversations about the human condition. I will attempt to overcome this problem by deploying Said's contrapuntal approach to reading across difference in my treatment of Khan and his Western counterparts. If the purpose of comparison is an engaged critical re-evaluation of values and norms, then a contrapuntal study in fact necessitates both a conception of meaningful distinction and a common object of inquiry. The common object of inquiry here, of course, is modernity itself in the abstract. But for the purposes of comparison, this book focuses on a certain set of concepts that grounds a common experience of the modern age both for Muslim intellectuals like Khan and for their Western counterparts alike and yet also generates conflict between the two sides as to their meaning and significance. Ideas like freedom, sovereignty, progress, the human self, the meaning and end of history, "Islam" and the "West," and, of course, modernity itself are not settled in their meanings but constitute a shared arena in which contest about their meaning can and does ensue. Indeed, this contest is the very engine of modernity.

To this end, the next three chapters in this book contrapuntally juxtapose Khan's treatment of these and other master concepts of modernity with those of three major figures from within the Western tradition who have been allowed to engage critically with this tradition as "insiders": Reinhold Niebuhr (1892–1971), Hannah Arendt (1906–75), and Alasdair MacIntyre (1929–). The choice of the three main interlocutors for Khan needs some explaining. In my reading, Niebuhr, Arendt, and MacIntyre all critique universalist and triumphalist Western accounts and descriptions of modernity as constitutively defective and ethically untenable. The modern age as a whole often appears in their work as beset by internal contradictions. And in their own distinct ways, all three believe that these accounts and descriptions need serious re-orienting interventions.

Consider, for example, that Reinhold Niebuhr's Christian realism was a response to the overly optimistic accounts of human nature and of the

perfectibility of Man that were in vogue in the West in the 1920s and early
1930s. Liberal utopianism is a recurrent feature of Western modernity, and it
has taken many forms over the years. From Marxism to liberal internationalism,
to neo-conservatism, the West's continuing capacity for utopian thinking is well
documented. Niebuhr, an erstwhile Marxist himself (though never entirely,
and progressively less so), thought such optimism dangerous and misplaced.
Human history is precisely the movement of the human animal, in time, as an
imperfect moral being capable of moral praxis. For Niebuhr, moral praxis is the
very flow of time that utopian thinking seeks to interrupt and finally destroy in
the construction of a timeless Eden. But such timelessness cannot be attained
without the loss of humanity itself. A modern conception of *time* as continuous
progress is problematic for Niebuhr and Khan who both share a modernist
emphasis on the present to guard against fanciful flights into the past or the
future.

Hannah Arendt is also concerned with the dehumanizing aspects of the
modern condition. She suggests that the modern emphasis on instrumental
action is a perverse return to the biological existence of necessity. Truly human
action is free of such instrumentality, and it is only in and through such action
that human beings enact their humanity in a continuous struggle for becoming
human. This is what Arendt means when she says that "to be human and to be
free are the same."[9] Human existence, reduced to concerns of survival, becomes
animalistic, inhuman, bound not free. Arendt and Sayyid Ahmad Khan share
this concern with a reversion to animality in the guise of economic and political
progress. The recovery of a notion of freedom that accounts for the difference of
humanity is a project they are both invested in.

Similarly, Alasdair MacIntyre argues that the very concept of morality has
been rendered unintelligible in the modern West. The Enlightenment project
of discovering rational and universal foundations for making moral claims has
failed, and in its wake moral action has become conceptually intertwined with
notions of preference, utility, or interest. The West's rejection (and destruction)
of traditional modes of knowing has left the modern human being with scarce
resources for adjudicating between different moral claims. Rather than moral
argument being a means to ascertain the intrinsic value of a particular position
vis-à-vis a politics of just ends, it has devolved into a manipulative process
where the instrumental end of convincing others becomes the primary criterion
for moral legitimacy. MacIntyre refers to this as an "emotivist culture," where
emotivism is the opposite of true morality.[10] It is a rejection of morality. Or as
MacIntyre evocatively puts it in *After Virtue*, "the barbarians are not waiting

beyond the frontier; they have already been governing us for quite some time."[11] It is in this sense that the modern age is, in fact, a quintessentially immoral age. In their own ways, both Khan and MacIntyre seek to conserve traditional modes of producing "moral knowledge" while still accounting for the novelty of the present moment.

Sayyid Ahmad Khan comes from a very different intellectual tradition than these three thinkers. But they all share something very important: the moral, political, and epistemological consequences of modernity. And a new, emergent "World" that is the common context of their concerns. This is the ground on which they all stand. Yet it is also hard to ignore their differences. It is due to these differences that a standard comparison is difficult. Instead, by focusing on the problem of modernity, and their responses to it, we can build a common intellectual scaffolding in reverse. As MacIntyre himself points out, different traditions are most amenable to constructive engagement when each can offer viable interventions into the "epistemological crisis" that beset the other.[12] Each of these juxtapositions is in this sense a shared narrative engagement with common objects of inquiry that de-provincializes Khan's work while still maintaining its critical Islamic edge.

*   *   *

In the exposition of such a critical Islamic edge to Western accounts and descriptions of the modern world, Sayyid Ahmad Khan is hardly alone. There is in fact a long tradition in modern Islamic thought of engaged criticism that is neither a rejection of the West nor a wholesale acceptance of liberal or conservative principles. Muslim thinkers and activists have been generating complex responses to the novel conditions of modernity since at least the time of Napoleon's invasion of Egypt that augured a new world that was both frightening and exhilarating.[13] As is true for those working within any mature tradition, the work of these thinkers is polyvalent and layered with varied political and normative possibilities. But a feature common to this tradition across decades and continents is the recognition that while the old grammar of meaning-making must be leavened with the new language of modernity, the vocabulary of Islam still has a role to play in the construction of better futures for this world. And that the politics, epistemologies, and identities attendant to living in the modern age are all amenable to intervention from critical Muslim perspectives.

Consider, for example, that oftentimes "in [a] modern age deeply marked by the complex cultural, economic, and political processes of globalization, secularization, and cultural homogenization, religion appears to be the only refuge of difference, the true sanctuary of values and authenticity."[14] In the case of many Western born and/or educated Muslims, their Islam is therefore an obvious resource for fabricating accounts of the modern *demos* different from those offered by the secularized and hence ostensibly "neutral" public spheres that they inhabit. Contemporary Muslim intellectuals and activists like Tariq Ramadan, Malek Chebel, Ziauddin Sardar, and Fethi Benslama have all attempted to "manifest their faith as an open archive of knowledge, a metaphysical claim, and an open hermeneutic horizon of complex historical and cultural heritage" in their interventions in matters of common public concern in the West and elsewhere.[15] When Ramadan argues, for example, for civic (not legal) denunciation of willfully insulting behavior toward Muslims, he imagines free speech primarily as an attendant value to solidarity and discernment of truth in pluralistic societies, and only secondarily as a legal right to speak one's mind.[16] When it comes to building such solidarity in the various European publics, the primary problem for someone like Ramadan is to reimagine and hence reconstruct the very notion of *Shari'a* in order for Islamic *fiqh* to be a useful mechanism for Muslim participation in global debates.[17] This re-vision of Muslim conceptions of *Shari'a* therefore "presupposes the implementation of practical platforms for the inclusion of Muslims as citizens on the basis of a 'common good' shared with non-Muslim citizens. In other words, Muslim law should not define the dimensions of 'good' and 'bad,' only for Muslims; the law should be interpreted in a way that encompasses humanity in general."[18] Much like the Francophone Ramadan, the London-based Ziauddin Sardar believes that "Muslims have been on the verge of physical, cultural and intellectual extinction simply because they have allowed parochialism and traditionalism to rule their minds . . . [and that they] must break free from the ghetto mentality."[19] But he is equally critical of "culturalist" and postmodernist Western treatments of alterity that "by pretending to give voice to the marginalised, . . . in fact [undermine their] histories, tradition, morality, religions and worldviews—everything that provides meaning and sense of direction to non-western cultures and societies." As an alternative, Sardar advocates for what he calls "transmodernity" or the fruitful synthesis between a "life-enhancing tradition" like Islam and the particular novelties of the present modern.[20] In books like *The Future of Muslim Civilization* and *Islamic Futures: The Shape of Ideas to Come,* Sardar lays out in great detail what such synthesis entails, and what it demands from both Muslims and their Western interlocutors.[21] But Sardar, Ramadan, and the many other Muslims active in the public elucidation of critical Muslim perspectives are only the contemporary variants of a long tradition of making sense of the nature and meaning of modernity within modern Islamic thought.

Regarding this tradition of Critical Islam, consider, for example, the following "pearl" from Sayyid Ahmad Khan's rather remarkable exposition on modernity.[22] As he surveyed the desolation of the Muslim condition in India after 1857, Khan openly wondered whether there was even any hope of renewal, so complete was the devastation. But he responded by framing the problem as *loss* rather than as *lack*. Muslims lagged behind the West in technology and science, in political and social organization, because they were a sad shadow of their former selves. They were not lacking modernity; they had lost it, forgotten it! Khan's preferred term for modernity, *jadidiyyat* (novelty), is the same term he uses to describe the age of the Prophet. *Jadidiyyat* is contrasted with *jahiliyyat*, the age of ignorance and barbarity that preceded the Prophet's advent. The main feature of *jahiliyyat* was stagnation and stubbornness, an inability and unwillingness to change and to incorporate new forms of knowledge to move society forward. The Arabs were a backward people because they looked backward to the past for answers to all questions. The ways of the ancestors had become sedimented. Such sedimentation is the very condition of ahistoricism. Khan instead imagines Islam as a historical religion in the sense that it provides moral and epistemological mechanisms for moving human history forward by integrating the past with the future in the present. For Khan, the most important social aspect of the coming of Islam was that it had rescued the Arabs from their state of stagnation.[23]

In a book written as a response to William Muir's scandalous biography of the Prophet, Khan spends the first few chapters going over the details of pre-Islamic Arabian society in order to make this very point.[24] Khan argues that when Islam was revealed to Muhammad, the Arabs were a cacophony of warring clans and tribes. Blood feuds lasted for generations. The law of tribal solidarity was as if the law of nature itself. Enmity, the perverse underbelly of solidarity, was woven into the social fabric. Survival was sacred, revenge sacrosanct. Islam reconfigured much of this normative infrastructure through the proclamation of *tauhid*. Not just one God, but one community, with a unified purpose, and universal concerns. It provided the Arabs with a radical, hitherto unthinkable, sense of their own identity, their own humanity. In so doing, Islam both integrated a divided polity and re-oriented it to new ends. Fourteen hundred years on, the implications of this revolution reverberate down the ages. Khan quotes the British historian Thomas Carlyle who seems overwhelmed by the enormity of the transformation:

To the Arab nation [Islam] was as birth from darkness into light; Arabia first
became alive by means of it. A poor shepherd people, roaming unnoticed in the
desert since the creation of the world; a Hero-prophet was sent down to them
with a word they could believe; see, the unnoticed becomes world-notable, the
small has grown world-great; within one century afterwards, Arabia is at Grenada
on this hand, at Delhi on that; glancing in valor, splendor and the light of genius,
Arabia shines through long ages over a great section of the world. Belief is great,
life giving. The history of a nation becomes fruitful, soul elevating, great, so soon
as it believes. These Arabs, the man Mahomet, and that one century—is it not as
if a spark had fallen, one spark, on a world of what seemed black unnoticeable
sand; but lo! The sand proves explosive powder, blazes heaven high, from Delhi
to Grenada![25]

Khan suggests, wistfully, that "Muslims very quickly returned to that ancient
period (*zaman-e-qadim*) and closed their eyes to the light of modern times
(*zaman-i-jadid*) so that we were forced to extend the ancient period into the
thirteen-hundredth year [the nineteenth century of the Common Era] of the
Prophet's advent."[26] In this intriguing chronology, the modern exists in the past,
is followed by a traditional order that is akin to the ancient *jahiliyyat*, and then
it partially reappears a thousand miles to the west in the land of the Franks,
the quintessential barbarians! This reappearance is partial because European
modernity lacks the proper religious infrastructure to make itself whole. It is the
same species of novelty as that of the Prophet but it is burdened by Christianity.
Separation of spheres and a divided subjectivity are the natural state of affairs
for an incomplete religion. Secularism is therefore the appropriate normative
form for the modern body politic in Christian Europe. Only Islam combines
the ethical imperatives of faith with the progressive telos of reason through the
assertion of *tauhid*, unity, oneness. True Modernity is equivalent to Islam; there
is no distinction between the two.

Khan's critique of Western interpretations of the modern condition
rests therefore on a standard of judgment that takes *jadidiyyat*/modernity
as its main referent, where modernity and Islam are one and the same. Both
Western moderns and Islamic traditionalists need reform to harmonize with
the teleological imperatives of the human race. These imperatives are written
into the very structure of existence which is always *jadid*, novel, ever-changing,
modern. The constellation of norms, events, and ideas linked together to form
Khan's modernity is familiar enough to be coherent to a Western audience and
yet distinct enough to be uncanny and disturbing in its ethical implications.
For while the smoldering ruins of post-1857 Delhi may initially seem like so

many signs of European power and superiority, Khan cautions circumspection. Lacking the proper ethical framework to guide their progress, Europeans are doomed in the long run to crumble just as spectacularly as the Muslims. Like waves cresting on the ocean of history, nations rise only to fall back again into the anonymity of the sea. In this sense, Muslims are not the only ones who suffer from the loss of Islam. Khan saw in the disintegration of his own community a threat of universal catastrophe. Without the harmonizing influence of Islam, human history itself can begin to degenerate into the animalistic competition for survival and instrumental morality that are the hallmarks of *jahiliyyat*.

* * *

Constellations like Khan's modernity/*jadidiyyat* are in every corner of the modern Muslim sky. Pearls practically litter the ocean floor. I am thinking here, for example, of Muhammad Iqbal's notion of *khudi* (self or ego) as a reconstructive metaphor about the ills of modern Western individualism and his ameliorative formulation of an alternative Islamic form of individualism. Or of Sayyid Qutb's identification of serious philosophical deficiencies in certain modern conceptions of freedom and authority in his innovative treatment of *hakimiyya*/sovereignty in the Quran. Or even of Jamal al-Din al-Afghani critical reflections on *neichiriat* or naturalism as absolutely essential to scientific and material progress while still being the single greatest threat to continued vigor of the moral and ethical sciences in the Muslim world and beyond. These and many other such constellations in modern Islamic thought should engender interest not merely as provincial cultural artifacts of Muslim vintage but also as potential languages of critical Muslim engagement with the West. The Muslim-ness of these thinkers should have no more bearing on the legitimacy of their critical philosophical credentials in any such engagement than the often explicit influence of their Christianity on countless Western philosophers like Scotus, Leibniz, Pascal, Locke, Kant, Hegel (I could go on). But this is obviously not the case, neither in the academy nor out there in the "real world" where Muslims can be friends or foes, but not critics. This divestment of Islam from any critical posture toward mainstream Western ideas renders Muslims the perpetual outsiders to debates on the common good, on shared parameters of a communal existence, and on global norms. It depoliticizes Muslims and in so doing dehumanizes them. The distinctively Muslim voice needs an escape from this ghetto and a rehumanizing publicity in the global exchange of thoughts and ideas.

I believe this kind of publicity to have both global-democratic and epistemic value. In the age of globalized markets, internationalist institutions, and planetary concerns, Muslims now constitute about a fifth of the human population. And despite decades of re-education by some secularizing and modernizing regimes, most continue to insist on maintaining their Muslim identity. In communities everywhere, people are still animated by the possibility that Islam offers hope against the disorder, chaos, and corruption that has engulfed much of the Muslim world. The status of Muslims in Western societies also remains uncertain. This continuing disaggregation of the integrated edifice of Islam is a modern *fitna*, an overwhelming and chaotic series of events that threaten to rend asunder whatever still remains of a united fabric of Islam. Muslim societies are convulsing from the effects of a moral and political fragmentation that has little precedence in the history of Islam. And these convulsions are not just a Muslim problem but an imminent global concern. It is at times like these that the collective heart of suffering communities yearns for new prophets to speak into existence a world made fresh again. If such a new global order aspires to grow on genuinely universal foundations, the Muslim experience of modernity, expressed in the critical language of Islam, must be allowed a public hearing.

The idea that this world is strongly divided between the West and the rest is, in any case, a dangerous diversion from the globalized reality of an increasingly interconnected world and of planetary concerns. In recent years, there has been a plethora of scholarly writing from all sides advocating the thesis that there are insurmountable conceptual problems to imagining a meaningful critical engagement across cultures or religions. This "alternative modernities" thesis takes the form either of multi-culturalist, post-colonialist narratives on the left or of Western exceptionalism on the right. In either case, the issue of intellectual negotiation across these differences is deemed secondary to identity politics. Only the particularities of historical experience register as relevant. And yet, while the non-Western world is allowed to deal with this disaggregated modernity piecemeal, only Western thinkers have historically been allowed to deal with it as a whole. General theories of the human condition continue to be the exclusive purview of Western or Westernized thinkers talking about Western or Westernized men to Western or Westernized audiences about the world in general. The philosophical burden of dealing with the general problems attendant to living in the modern age naturally also falls squarely only on their resilient shoulders.

Now it is certainly true that the West pioneered processes and institutions that reshaped the world at large. As Carl Schmitt has pointed out, the very notion of a "world" as we know it today is an epistemological creation of the European expansion that began with the discovery of the New World.[27] This world has now evolved on a universal scale to include features such as the modern nation-state, the bureaucratization of political institutions, the globalization of economic and financial networks, the internationalization of rights discourse, and the primacy of scientific forms of knowledge. The rapid transformations and changes are an ongoing process. More important for our purposes are the ethical questions and debates that undergird and guide many of these changes. What is a human being? What is the ideal form of human sociality and governance? What is the meaning and end of history? What counts as knowledge? And in recent years the answers our intrepid generalists offer are beginning to grow ever more sedimented, inert, and opaque. The natural familiarity and matter-of-factness of the dominant Western moral lexicon has rendered it dangerously uninterested in the unfamiliar forms of knowledge that could aid its necessary evolution in an ever-changing world. Ever since the fall of communism, and especially in response to 9/11 and its aftermath, the West's values and norms have only hardened into their previously held meanings, refusing any re-arrangement, any new architecture (the answer to all problems, for example, is some combination of democracy, human rights, secularism, and free markets, variously understood). An orchestrated encounter with the distinct epistemological apparatus of Islam provides novel opportunities for re-thinking both settled and ongoing ethical disputes. Already in 1994, the sociologist Jose Casanova made the following intriguing (and still controversial) observation:

> Western modernity is at a crossroads. If it does not enter into a creative dialogue with the other, with those traditions which are challenging its identity, modernity will most likely triumph. But it may end up being devoured by the inflexible, inhuman logic of its own creations. It would be profoundly ironic if, after all the beating it has received from modernity, religion could somehow unintentionally help modernity save itself.[28]

Casanova points to the many contradictions that lie at the core of the modern project. Consider some of these: the overly instrumental rationality of modern bureaucracies; the privileging of intellectual discourse over tradition; the inability to build stable social solidarities in the regime of individualism; and the denial of religion as a legitimate repository for moral-practical reflection and of inter-subjective expression. Western modernity is broken and in thrall of its own contradictions. Casanova suggests that instead of decrying the "publicity" of modern religion, and its political consequences, scholars should instead acknowledge as fact the continuing relevance of religion in public life and focus on a different question: "What are the conditions of possibility for modern public religion?"[29] What would it mean to imagine religion as an active participant in modern public discourse rather than as a regressive force that seeks to destroy and undermine such discourse? The socio-normative stance against the "publicity" of religion is a re-iteration of an Enlightenment critique of religion that is based on a false premise. This is the secularization theory of religious decline that has as its normative core a mythical teleological account of "history as the progressive evolution of humanity from superstition to reason, from belief to unbelief, from religion to science."[30] It cannot account for the possibility that public religions may "contribute to strengthening the public sphere of modern civil societies" rather than destroying them.[31]

Casanova rejects the secularization thesis on both sociological and historical grounds. But he goes further. He argues that if the modern West refuses to engage meaningfully with those religious traditions that are now challenging its normative self-image, its own prejudices will ultimately serve to destroy it from within. Modernity needs religion to provide it with something akin to genetic diversity. Just as animal populations lacking a plurality of genetic traits are in constant danger of extinction, without such diversity, Western conceptions of modernity will eventually become inbred and fail. Critical Muslim perspectives may in fact be absolutely necessary in the long run to the healthful vigor of all modern societies, and of modernity as such for precisely this reason. In this reading, Critical Islam has greater affinity with feminism in its re-evaluation of the public/private distinction, or with nationalism in its re-configuring of older notions of community, or with the fight for civil and national rights for minorities and oppressed populations everywhere, etc., than with Islam as a religion in the conventional sense. From the election of Donald Trump in the United States to Britain's impending exit from Europe and the rise of right-wing nationalism on the continent itself, it appears that the West's own regnant paradigms for describing the world and its place in it are already hardening into a tribal identity that increasingly admits little in the way of adjustment to this world's emerging realities. In light of all of this, outsider traditions like Critical Islam will be essential to imagining this world's future. This is not just an intellectual imperative; the global moral contours of some common concerns could well require more ideas than the West can provide on its own.

The Meaning and End of Time

In the beginning, the Demiurge gives birth to his mother, Sophia, and becomes the father of the World. He is the Great Constructor. Overlord, the Law of the Land, the Fabricator of the Universe. But thinking himself the beginning, he fancies himself unborn. Eternal. Time-less. Mesmerized by his powers of Creation, he cannot recall the circumstances of his own birth. He cannot remember how he spilled out of Sophia's distended belly into the clouds of an atemporal fullness. It is this same fullness which he hungrily, unthinkingly, instinctively devoured and which now oozes out of him as the World. The hole in his memory manifests itself as a hole in the middle of his Creation. But this hole is not empty. It is filled to the brim with all accouterment of the Demiurge's supposed divinity, an unconscious attempt perhaps to hide from the World (and himself) the lack at the center of his own existence. Is it any wonder then that he names this hole paradise, Eden, *bihisht*? What better way to veil imperfection than by calling it perfect by definition?

The Garden knows no Law but the Demiurge. The flowers bloom, and the birds sing. The wind blows and the leaves rustle. Beasts roam the land. They devour and are in turn devoured. Mountains and plains, rivers and lakes, plants and animals, all exist in the rhythmic stillness of his eternal order. They move and are moved by the Word of their Creator. Like so many signs of his perfection, they are in seamless accord with his self-image. Eden is the manifest condition of unborn eternity; the circular cadence of biological life and the linear drone of materiality set to the music of the Demiurge's beating heart. Eden conforms to his will like a mirror conforms to the face.

To conform to eternity is to be out of Time. Without Time. Eden moves in cycles and straight lines. It is a construct of immense beauty, of transcendent order. But nothing happens in Eden. History is movement set not to the music of life or the metronomy of Law, but to the cacophony of events. It is the wandering path of planets in the night sky, not the rising and falling of a distant sun. The Demiurge thinks himself timeless. Unborn. Eternal. Eden is his refuge from the repressed memory of the event of his own birth. So Eden is to be devoid of events. Time is the antithesis of perfection. So what now, that the Man and the Woman have, accidentally, discovered Time. Are they doomed or to be destroyed? Are they to be cast out or be hemmed in? It will not take long for the Demiurge to notice the stench of imperfection emanating from their suddenly naked bodies. What will He do then? One thing is certain: He is the master of this World. He will think of something.[1]

* * *

Morality is the flow of time. This is the core, if obscure, insight that percolates through much of Reinhold Niebuhr's work. It is an insight shared by Sayyid Ahmad Khan. Human beings exist in historical time; they have a sense of the ebb and flow of history, because they are moral creatures. History and morality are complementary descriptions of the same underlying reality. What is this reality? That the human animal is a unique creation, and unique *in* creation, in experiencing the Law of God as contingent choice rather than as existential imperative. Morality is not Law. It is recognition of the existence of Law. The ontological distance between morality and Law is the voltage of human temporality. It makes time flow, where flow is not movement as such but meaningful movement, like a river flowing to the sea. A river is not a canal or an aqueduct. It is guided gently by gravity, as well as by the obstructions in its path. To equate morality to Law is to short-circuit this movement of time. To posit a morality completely independent of Law is to do the same. Either is to deny the meaning and end of the human condition, the meaning and end of Time.

Modernity is beset by such perverse denials. Notice, for example, that the two dominant normative tenses of modernity are *past-perfect* and *future-perfect*. To the first belong those social and ideological movements usually characterized as anti-modern: fundamentalisms of one sort or another, religious and racial revivals, and appeals to the values of a past golden age in a present beset by moral decay and existential crisis. The fascination of a certain segment of American society with "the good old days," the near realization of a racially pure society by the Nazis, and the attempt by modern-day Salafists to re-create a mythical seventh-century society in the present are all examples of the past-perfect sensibility. To the second belong utopianisms of all kind, although some more utopian than others: Marxism in its many political and philosophical varieties, liberal internationalism and its attendant hope of perpetual peace through global co-operation, neo-conservatism and other "end of history" programs that proclaim "joyful tidings of a golden future time."[2] The Shiʻi millenarianism of the Islamic regime in Iran, the Western attempts at social (re)-engineering on a grand scale through the export of Western institutions to Muslim countries, the liberal (over)confidence in international institutions, and, of course, Christian Zionism are all examples of the future-perfect sensibility. Both of these normative sensibilities are a reaction to the dominant sociological tense of modernity: the *present-imperfect*. Modernity is the epistemological, political, and psychological internalization of the present-imperfect as, in, and of itself, a normative problem. It is in this sense that contemporary fundamentalisms are no less modern in orientation than is Wilsonian liberalism, and scriptural literalism no less modern than scientific positivism. They are diametrically opposed reactions to be sure but opposed only in their conception of the sacred time of perfection, not in their proclamation of the need for perfection. In either case, they decry the inability or the unwillingness of the human animal to conform its morality to law-like states. And they seek to divest the human condition of the contingency that such unwillingness creates.

Jürgen Habermas, perhaps the greatest liberal internationalist of his time, suggests that "the philosophical formulation of the question of rational law—the question of how an association of . . . citizens can be constructed through the means of positive law—forms an emancipatory horizon of expectation within which resistance to what appears as an unreasonable reality becomes visible."[3] This "unreasonable reality" is the condition of inadequacy that generates "an emancipatory horizon of expectation." It is this horizon of expectation that has animated all great political projects of modernity.[4] Notice that the solution is posited in terms of the relationship between rational law and positive law. It is the distance between the two that creates the motive force for politics. Habermas, to his credit, is no utopian. He is a small "d" democrat. Seen against this backdrop of inadequacy, his understanding of society is precisely that condition of "tensions, contradictions and ambiguities that arise(s) from the realization of the ideals of freedom and equality."[5] In Habermas's post-Hegelian sociology, where there is no more recourse to the rationality of the real, or to a kind of self-steering history, but with the liberal normative backdrop of freedom and equality still very much intact, society reveals itself as both the problem (A) and the only source of steering-media for devising a solution (B) to itself as a problem. Politics, or the practice thereof, is shorthand for precisely this interminable project of trying to get from A to B, where B, being a "horizon of expectation," is both transformative (an *expectation*) and also ultimately unrealizable (a *horizon*).[6] For

Habermas, modern politics should always proceed from an acknowledgment of this emancipatory horizon as that normative ideal which stands in judgment of all our actions. Habermas counsels democratic humility in the face of such expectation. It is unfortunate then that this particular, quintessentially modern sense of inadequacy has also produced a fascination with utopia in all its disparate philosophical forms. Idealisms abound. Whenever such philosophy has bled unmediated into politics, it has produced revolutionary projects of tremendous power and scope. When it hasn't, it still continues to maintain a strong hold on the modern imagination in the West and elsewhere.

As an example of the said revolutionary projects, consider the case of the regime that has ruled in Iran since the Islamic revolution of 1979. Writing in exile, Imam Ruhullah Khomeini (the founder of this regime), noted that "if the nomenclature of an Islamic State could be labeled, it would be known as the government of Law," and it is for this reason that "Islam demands a Government at every stage that is obedient to the Law."[7] In fact, he goes on to claim that "Islam is the name of the Law that is incumbent upon the whole of Mankind to follow,"[8] and this Law is nothing other than "Reason, the Law of Islam."[9] Human reality has been rendered unreasonable because in "the period of absence" (the occultation of the twelfth Imam of the Twelver Shi'a) there is no one person capable of fully understanding and hence instantiating this Law in the affairs of men. This has led to political apathy among Muslims, and a rejection of Islam as the necessary basis for governance. Khomeini's radical new formulation of the doctrine of *Velayat-i-Faqih*, the guardianship of the jurists, into its contemporary, quasi-constitutionalist form was based on the then novel acknowledgment that the return of the invisible Imam is not an event to be awaited but a condition to be created by the efforts of Muslims themselves going forward: "The claim that the laws of Islam may remain in abeyance, or are restricted to a particular time and place, is contrary to the essential creedal basis of Islam."[10] Khomeini identifies the problem of the decline of Islam as the unwillingness of Muslims to continue to perfect their theological understanding of the Law and instantiating this Law in the political sphere. In this classic formulation of a future-perfect sensibility, he claims that the present-imperfect will be alleviated through the use of Law, because the Law "was laid down for the purpose of creating a state and administering the political, economic and cultural affairs of society."[11] The jurists are those with the requisite skills both to discover and refine the Law of Islam, as they have done now for a thousand years. Under the guidance of the jurists, when the positive law of the state conforms to the rational law of Islam—Law is Reason—the utopian parameters for the return of the Imam will have been met. Suffering and conflict will be at an end. All will be right with the world.

Positivism, the bastard child of Enlightenment scientism and Darwinian epistemology, is similarly concerned with seeking an end to the world's contingencies and miseries through the discovery of the "Laws of Man." One could reasonably call it the doctrine of *Velayat-i-daneshmandan*, the guardianship of the scientists.[12] In *The Moral Landscape*, the neurologist and self-proclaimed "New Atheist" Sam Harris contends that moral truth is not divine in origin, nor is it merely a product of "evolutionary or cultural invention."[13] One must think of it as one among the many other scientific facts that have been discovered and continue to be discovered through experimentation. Using data from brain imaging scans (and little else), Harris argues that "beliefs about facts and beliefs about values seem to arise from similar processes at the level of the brain," and that "the physiology of belief may be the same regardless of a proposition's content."[14] This being the case, it is only a matter of time before scientific knowledge concerning the truth claims of human values will ascend to the level of certainty and all debate about what is right and wrong will cease to be a matter of opinion or conjecture. Much like debates concerning heliocentrism, the structure of DNA, or the microbial roots of infectious disease, this debate too shall be resolved in the pristine certainty of fact. "The world of measurement," Harris claims, "and the world of meaning *must* eventually be reconciled."[15] Human conflict and suffering, be they social or psychological, are epiphenomenal to our lack of knowledge about the laws of human existence. The search and eventual discovery of such laws will render the human condition transparent, and the sources of suffering could then be engaged scientifically. Again, when our moral order conforms to the values associated with these laws, we will have reached the Eden of our existence.

Positivism had its heyday in the late nineteenth century during a period of intense optimism concerning the role of scientific progress in solving the problems of human society. After two technologically driven world wars that killed hundreds of millions, such optimism abated somewhat. But as the Harris's book suggests, positivism has been on the comeback trail in recent years. It has been fed, in equal measure, by the fall of communism and the unprecedented euphoric optimism that engulfed much of the West and its academies, and later by the events of 9/11 which provided right-wing, evolutionary positivists with a spectacular example of archaic, barbaric religious values to set up against the civilized values of the scientific West. Just as the Law of Islam has universal valence for Khomeini (the whole world must submit to it), the Law of Science is similarly universal. Both appeal to a conception of Reason that equates it to Law. Both identify ignorance and the lack of knowledge as the primary problem. Epistemology, not anthropology, is the root concern.

It is at the level of the sources of epistemological progress that different groups with a future-perfect sensibility differ. For the scientists, it is the scientific method and facts about material reality. For the Marxists, it is knowledge concerning the economic and material relations between groups of people. For the Shiʻi millenarians like Khomeini, it is the techniques of theological interpretations that have been honed by the *Usuli* school of Shiʻi jurisprudence over the years. All appeal to basic Reason and to natural states of human existence. Neo-conservatives are an interesting bunch, and they tend to mix and match one thing with the other. Liberals have similar tendencies. Many have been chastened and softened by the actual practice of politics. But in the ideal philosophical forms, both classical liberalism[16] and neo-conservatism are evolutionary paradigms.[17] And like all evolutionary paradigms they are forever in search of Eden. Or as Aldous Huxley famously, and ironically, put it, "Time must have a stop."[18]

*   *   *

When the Taliban took over Afghanistan in 1996, they were motivated by a different variety of utopian thinking. Afghan society had devolved into a state of anarchy after decades of war. It was the very definition of dystopia.[19] The Taliban sought to remake this society in the image of a historical fantasy that, after years of training in fundamentalist madrassas across the border in Pakistan, had the force of fact for them. What was this fantasy? That history has provided the human race with the blueprint for history's own destruction. A literal blueprint that once actualized renders the need for human intervention in moral affairs unnecessary, irrelevant, and dubious. It was in the early part of the twentieth century that Sayyid Abul Aʻla Maududi (1903–79) first imagined a return to a past golden age as a political program. Revival has been a perennial aspect of Muslim theological thinking, but this was different. Maududi was not a revivalist in any traditional sense of the term. He had extensive knowledge of Islamic theology and law. But lacking a formal education in the religious sciences or traditional training at a *madrassa*, Maududi's innovative reconstruction of Islam imagined it primarily as a political ideology.[20] He portrayed the nascent Muslim community at the time of the Prophet as an ideal state, governed by ideal laws, and in complete sync with the will of God as personified in the person of the Prophet and the government that he instituted. In those times, the vicissitudes of history and the contingency of human action had been thoroughly muted by the blaring of a divine horn. In a tract titled "The Fallacy of Rationalism," Maududi makes a claim that should be quite familiar to any scholar of modern fundamentalisms:

> Rationally, there can only be two positions of a person with relevance to Islam. Either he is a Muslim or a non-Muslim. If he is Muslim, it means that he has conceded that Allah is the Supreme Authority and the holy Prophet is the authentic Messenger of Allah. He has also committed to all injunctions conveyed to him by the authentic Messenger of Allah [in the Quran]. He has thus surrendered his right to demand any rational proof of argument for each and every injunction.[21]

Maududi was responding explicitly to the so-called Westernized liberals of his time who insisted on calling themselves Muslim even though they denied the absolute primacy of divine revelation and the *Shari'a*. These were the intellectual scions of Sayyid Ahmad Khan and the Aligarh movement which he founded in the latter half of the nineteenth century. Maududi found the supposed equivocation of his fellow Indian Muslims on these matters ridiculous, and their attempts to chart out a middle path seemed absurd to him:

> Reason and wisdom show only two courses open in such a situation, and a sensible person shall take any one of the courses when confronted with such a situation. But the difficulty with our learned writer and the like, brought up in west-oriented institutions, is that they do not have the courage to adopt the first course and feel ashamed of taking the second course. They have, therefore, taken to a middle course, which is quite illogical.[22]

Islam is an either/or proposition. While this in and of itself was not an innovative formulation, Maududi provided it with a peculiarly modern political valence. The Law of the Qur'an was akin to the Law of a state. Anyone who refuses to abide by the injunctions mentioned in the Qur'an is by definition a non-Muslim and a traitor. Moral reasoning not based on the Qur'an is dangerous and subversive since the exemplary moral framework for organizing an ideal society is already available in the form of the sacred book. The acknowledgment of this Law renders such extraneous moral reasoning superfluous.

There is a common misconception among the learned elites in the West that the Islamic Republic of Iran is a fundamentalist regime. It is for this reason that there is a general sense of confusion concerning the Iranian regime's implacable hostility toward ISIS (the Islamic State of Iraq and Syria), al-Qaeda, and the Taliban, and the brand of Islam that these groups represent. *Velayat* is social engineering based on expertise, not imitation. Fundamentalism is social engineering based on imitation, not expertise. Expertise is *bid'a*, innovation. God has already spoken, and the Law is clear, unequivocal. Anyone can read the book, and everyone should. Expertise, on the other hand, is progressive in its orientation. It imagines human knowledge about the mind of God (or the secrets of the universe) as gradually unfurling into a beautiful picture of perfection. It looks forward to a time when accumulating knowledge will reach this critical mass.[23] Modern fundamentalisms take the opposite approach. All relevant knowledge has already unfurled in its entirety. We are merely ruining the original by producing unnecessary sequels to a perfect film.[24] Let no man deny that which God has already confirmed.

It is for this reason that whereas future-perfect sensibility is almost always vanguardist, the past-perfect tends to produce populisms that are notoriously hard to control for any political party. When asked to describe the kind of polity he was imagining, Maududi suggested the term "theo-democratic," a quasi-anarchic society where everyone had access to the Law and hence everyone could hold everyone else accountable.[25] Maududi suggested that this is the way it was in the time of the Prophet: *amr bi l-ma'ruf wa nahy 'an al-munkar*—commanding what is right, and forbidding what is wrong.[26] The role of political leadership would be enforcement, not guidance. And if the political leadership fails to act, like it did in Mecca all those centuries ago, then individual Muslims must act to restore the Law: "The entire Muslim population runs the state in accordance with the Book of God and the practice of His Prophet."[27] The Prophet fought and defeated those Meccans, and contemporary Muslims must do the same with modern-day regimes that continue to resist the call of Islam.[28] This model of sacred action is seared into the historical memory of Islam. Maududi sought to re-activate it, and in so doing re-created the sacred time of the beginnings.

*   *   *

Reinhold Niebuhr once said that the Law of Love is never a simple possibility in the affairs of human beings. Note that he did not say that it was an impossibility but rather an "impossible possibility" but a possibility nonetheless.[29] The hope that human conflict and suffering could end decisively, and that power itself could be made to disappear from human relations is a misplaced and dangerous notion. The realization of such a hope, unequivocally and without exception, is a fantasy. The search for universal laws of human behavior and for overarching, un-contestable moral values is a dangerous diversion from the real work of being and acting as a human being. The human condition does not, cannot, and will not conform to law-like states in any simple manner without being divested of its humanity in the process. This is a tragic truth perhaps, but sadly the only truth that matters. It is in the very impossibility of its full realization in the affairs of mankind does the "law of love" gain its true relevance and essential significance, its "possibility" in the movement of human history.[30] Sayyid Ahmad Khan was similarly concerned about those who sought to make the Qur'an into a mere law book and the example of the Prophet into an ethical manual. It is for this reason that devotion to the Prophet was more important to him than mere adherence to his words and deeds. The "Islamic obscurantists" that he decried throughout much of his life sought to make of Islam a simple possibility as well, reducing it to rules and injunctions. The Sufi ambivalence with *shari'a* imagined as a "once and done" proposition, or as merely the legal precepts developed by the jurists, was instilled in Khan since early childhood, and it never left him.

But Niebuhr and Khan existed in sociopolitical milieus that were polar opposites in their normative sensibilities. Whereas the late nineteenth century was a time of intense optimism in the West and certainly also in America, Indian Muslims had just suffered their most devastating trauma in centuries. Not since the Mongols invaded and utterly destroyed the centers of Muslim power in the thirteenth century had a foreign force ended so decisively the primacy of Muslims in a great empire.[31] As the great biographer of Sayyid Ahmad Khan, Shan Muhammad (1937–) has pointed out that "the Muhammadan of the period before and after the mutiny was a wretched creature" for "the vitalizing energy for a vigorous life had departed from him, and a community which a few centuries before had occupied the supreme position was dwindling into insignificance."[32] Niebuhr faced the opposite problem in his community. In *The Children of Light and the Children of Darkness,* Niebuhr shows his impatience with the liberal enthusiasm for democracy by suggesting that "the excessively optimistic estimates of human nature and of human history with which the democratic credo has been historically associated are a source of peril in democratic society."[33] Niebuhr felt the normative sensibility of the West to be dominated by *moral optimism,* whereas Khan experienced the Muslim community of his day as beset by *moral pessimism.* Moral optimism is predicated on a belief in the capacity of human beings to ultimately perfect the human condition. It conforms, albeit imperfectly, to the future-perfect sensibility. In this worldview, the moral problem is epistemological; evil and suffering result from ignorance. For the Marxists, "false consciousness" does not allow the oppressed to comprehend fully the systematic nature of their oppression. For run-of-the-mill liberals, lack of education has the same effect. Lack of good knowledge lies at the root of both moral evil and suffering. Moral optimists look to the future for the ultimate realization of their aims. The past is a burden that needs to be overcome in the formulation of such a future. The present is the time of such overcoming. Moral pessimists also believe in the perfectibility of the human condition. But the same past that optimists seek to overcome is the reservoir of all that is good for moral pessimists. They are not pessimistic about the potential of reforming the human condition, only pessimistic about the human capacity to accomplish this in the present, on its own, without guidance from the past. It is for this reason that moral optimists valorize knowledge whereas moral pessimists valorize wisdom.

Moral optimists and pessimists have long existed in one form or another. But in the modern age they have become entangled in a peculiar feedback loop, one reinforcing the other in a perpetual-motion machine fed in equal parts by optimism and pessimism. The optimism of one side feeds the pessimism of the other. Back in the early aftermath of the events of 9/11, this is what Tariq Ali called "a clash of fundamentalisms" (in a book of the same name) when describing how the reductive certainties of both camps could end up fueling an endless conflict between Western hawks and their Islamist counterparts.[34] As the War on Terror grinds on under one name or another, Ali's words have indeed proved prescient. This is because the reductive certainties he described are characterized, first and foremost, by a flight from reality. In their normative emphases on the past or the future, both sides have lost their capacity to properly engage the present. The present is not a time to retreat into the past or to fly away into the future. The present is the condition of stitching the past into the future through the continuing practice of our humanity. This involves moral imagination not moral certainty. It involves movement not escape. Without a moral emphasis on the present, time itself is in danger of becoming disaggregated and undone and of history becoming fantasy. It is against these fantastic formulations of the modern age that both Reinhold Niebuhr and Sayyid Ahmad Khan counseled their different brands of moral realism. And it is with an exploration of their realism in the face of optimism on one side and cynicism on the other that the rest of this chapter is primarily concerned.

*   *   *

Reinhold Niebuhr begins an essay he wrote for *The Nation* in 1938 by noting that "one of the recurring motifs of Greek tragedy is the hero's deeper involvement in his own fate through his very efforts to extricate himself from it."[35] Niebuhr calls this "abundant proof of the profound insight [of the Greek dramatists] into human tragedy" and suggests that "they were [in fact] not writing melodrama but were interpreting history."[36] The essay was occasioned by Niebuhr's deep distaste for the unwillingness of democratic nations of the West to challenge the increasingly aggressive posturing of the various Axis powers in the years leading up to the Second World War. The war they seek to avoid, Niebuhr pointed out, will be thrust on them as a direct consequence of their inability to act. He found Chamberlain's assertion of "peace in our time" ridiculous, based as it was on a misplaced sense of trust in international treaties. In time such ridicule acquired a more universal following. In the meantime, "the history of our era seems to move in tragic circles," says Niebuhr with more than a hint of irony, "strangely analogous to those presented symbolically in Greek tragedy."[37]

In hindsight, it would appear that Niebuhr saw himself as a spectator of world events tragically unfolding before him much like an ancient Greek spectator of Oedipus's futile attempts to avoid killing his father by acting precisely in such a manner as to cause his father's death. The tragic point of view is always that of a spectator. Tragedy comes not from the plot in and of itself but rather is a function of the spectators' knowledge, or more correctly foreknowledge, that the protagonist's actions are from the beginning inevitably and fatally flawed. What gives Greek tragedy its special and unmistakable poignancy is the spectator's identification with the inescapable nature of the hero's fate.

Niebuhr is often assailed by his critics for being a relentless pessimist.[38] Such criticism, though sometimes needlessly acerbic, is not entirely unwarranted. Niebuhr himself would probably have preferred being called a realist or a pragmatist. But a thoroughgoing pessimism about the possibilities and limitations of human existence is certainly a part of his realistic appraisal of the human condition. Viewed from the proper perspective, such existence is ineluctably tragic in its inability to complete itself, to find a certain ground for itself. For Niebuhr, we are all "heroes" in the tragedy of human history. Niebuhr believes that Greek tragedy symbolically illustrates a paradox that was remarkably applicable to the politics of his day. But it also revealed something that lies at the heart of the human condition itself. History is revealed as paradoxical when it is viewed from, and against, the normative vantage point which gives history its meaning. This is what Niebuhr means when he calls Greek tragedy not melodrama but an interpretation of history. Taking full account of the tragic aspects of human history is critical for properly understanding Niebuhr's religious and political realism.

According to Niebuhr, history is the ongoing process of the development of human individuals and society through the mechanism of human action. The ineluctable tragedy of the human condition is fundamentally related to the inherently bifurcated nature of the subject who acts in history.

The essential nature of man contains two elements; and there are correspondingly two elements in the original perfection of man. To the essential nature belong, on the one hand, all his natural endowments, and determinations, his physical and social impulses, his sexual and racial differentiations, in short his character as a creature embedded in the natural order. On the other hand, his essential nature also includes the freedom of spirit, his transcendence over natural processes and finally his self-transcendence.[39]

Man is simultaneously both creature and creator.[40] His materiality makes him a creature not only bound by the physical laws of nature but also limited by his situatedness; to be finite is to be located particularly with respect to place, time, and perspective. To say that man is a creature is therefore to posit finitude with regard to man's knowledge as well as to the determination of his circumstance (both physical and otherwise) by the laws of nature. In addition to being a creature in nature, man is also the creator of history. "Freedom is precisely the natural capacity that persons embedded in the given circumstances of nature and history have to imagine and create a new reality in relation to the limitations from which they started."[41] The natural order and his concomitant materiality and situatedness limit man, but they do not determine him like they do the other entities and objects that exist within nature. Unlike a rock, or a tree, or a non-human animal, even man's nature, on account of its freedom, is never a settled matter. "[The human self] has the spiritual capacity of transcending both the natural processes in which it is immersed *and* its own consciousness. As consciousness is the principle of transcendence over process, so self-consciousness is the principle of transcending consciousness."[42] It is this freedom for which certain traditions like Catholicism, for example, prefer to use the term human dignity to distinguish its fundamental nature from the more qualified political freedoms given by governments.[43] It is the mark of being *imago dei*, being made in the image of God.

Niebuhr contends that theories of natural law make the mistake of imagining man too much a creature of this world or, at the very least, positing for his spiritual self a kind of truncated and reified "nature" which renders his spirituality merely another aspect of man's creatureliness. They do not take man's freedom of spirit seriously enough. It is on account of this freedom that man's nature itself is always in the process of being transcended by his inherent natural capacity to constantly transcend the limitations imposed on him by creatively imagining himself and his surroundings anew. "Human beings are," in some respects at least, "what they make of themselves, the product of their own freedom."[44]

Man's creative engagement of his own finitude through his natural capacity for freedom is what animates and drives history. There is no history in the natural order without the presence of a moral creature: man. It is in this sense that man can be said to be a creator of history.

Niebuhr is therefore obviously critical of the kinds of naturalism that drastically downplay man's freedom.[45] On the other hand, many idealistic philosophies make the opposite error of rendering man's finitude and creatureliness irrelevant with respect to man's ultimate nature. For Niebuhr, "the self is primarily an active rather than a contemplative organic unity" of its different aspects, and idealists "[fail] to recognize to what degree finiteness remains a basic character of human spirituality."[46] Reductive naturalisms and absolutist idealisms are therefore both implicated in attempting to philosophically undo this paradoxical unity of limitation and freedom by reducing man to one of his two natures. They seek to find a resolution to history by positing the possibility of the perfection (and perfectibility) of man according to whatever aspect they argue for as his true nature. But this kind of reductive perfection is not available within history precisely because man's finitude and freedom are inseparable. History is not perfectible, or completable, within itself and in and of itself, because history is ultimately the epiphenomenal description of this constitutive and irresolvable tension between man's different aspects and the inevitable consequences that issue from this tension. The impossibility of a resolution to this tension, and concomitantly to history, is the underlying problem for which the Christian doctrine of sin provides the most convincing explanation.

One must of course qualify that the doctrine of sin we are considering here is more correctly Niebuhr's version of it. Niebuhr is especially critical of those versions of the doctrine that identify sin with man's corporeality or with man's finitude. "The whole Biblical interpretation of life and history rests upon the assumption that the created world, the world of finite, dependent, and contingent existence, is *not* evil by reason of its finiteness."[47] Such an understanding of the created order has its roots not in biblical faith but rather in "the dualistic and cosmic faiths of the Hellenistic world"[48] and Niebuhr has no patience for what he sees as detrimental influences of classical philosophy and thinking on Christian doctrine.[49] Niebuhr identifies the problem differently and, in some ways, much more subtly. The problem is the human response to the condition of finitude, a response which the human subject is uniquely qualified to make.

> [Humanity's] partial involvement in, and partial transcendence over the process
> of nature and the flux of time . . . is not regarded as the evil from which man

must be redeemed. The evil in the situation arises, rather, from the fact that men seek to deny or to escape *prematurely* from the uncertainties of history and to claim a freedom, a transcendence and an eternal and universal perspective which is not possible for finite creatures.[50]

Freedom in the regime of nature is never freedom from limitation and situatedness; such a freedom is not possible within history because being a creature embedded in the natural order is part of man's essential nature as the creator of history. It is rather a freedom to transcend these limitations and enter into new situations, establish novel norms of action and transform one's self through the exercise of such freedom. There is no simple dualism between nature and spirit. "The relationship of freedom to the various determinations that Niebuhr lumps under the heading 'the natural order' appears at once in the fact that freedom is defined in relation to those determinations."[51] Man's freedom has the primary character of transcendence over himself and his historical and natural circumstances. It manifests itself in the human capacity to imagine and execute "indeterminate possibilities for higher levels of rational and moral insight, of technical and social development, and therefore of freedom and justice."[52] By virtue of their freedom, human beings are incurably creative. But freedom always "starts from somewhere and views the starting point in relation to other possibilities."[53] Human freedom is intertwined with human finitude and never offers up God's vantage point. Nevertheless, the fact of man's creatureliness, of his constant vulnerability to the laws of natural necessity, complicates and obscures man's self-understanding of his status as both free and bound, and tempts him to deny his finitude and exaggerate his freedom. It is the denial of this intertwined subjectivity, the bifurcated condition of man's essential nature that Niebuhr identifies as the precondition of sin.

> In short, man being both free and bound, both limited and limitless, is anxious. Anxiety is the inevitable concomitant of the paradox of freedom and the finiteness in which man is involved. Anxiety is the internal precondition of sin. It is the inevitable spiritual state of man, standing in the paradoxical situation of freedom and finiteness.[54]

Niebuhr claims that being in a liminal position, forever suspended between freedom and necessity, transcendence and finitude, has existential anxiety as an inevitable response. This is the same anxiety that prompts Augustine to posit the quintessential anthropological question, *quaestio mihi factus sum* ("a question have I become to myself"). The human subject experiences himself as a paradox with a leg in either world but being able to stand firm in neither. Anxiety operationalizes man's freedom, unleashes it, so to say, on the natural order as the concomitant phenomena of human change and social development, novelty and transcendence, imagination and creativity; in short, history. Man's freedom is therefore a very specific kind of freedom. It is the freedom of a finite creature that nevertheless has the capacity to engage with his own finitude by creatively imagining the possibility of change in himself and around him, a change to which he can legitimately lay claim to as its creator. Freedom is therefore the condition of moral and existential responsibility. History is the external manifest experience of man (whether as an individual or in a community) reflecting on himself, his thoughts, memories, and actions and those of others, in order to paint a coherent picture of his own temporal existence. But the desire for coherence is forever frustrated by the rational incoherence that lies at the core of the human condition. The fact that man cannot legitimately provide an answer to even the question of his own existence necessarily means that his judgments, either normative or empirical, about himself and the world around him can never be entirely complete, universal, or absolute. And yet it should be noted that this anxiety "must be distinguished from sin partly because it is its precondition and not its actuality and partly because it is the basis of all human creativity as well as the precondition of sin."[55] Sin is a very particular, and Niebuhr would claim ubiquitous, response to this anxiety and frustration—a response that seeks to alleviate such anxiety through a self-defeating delusion about the nature of freedom itself.

> Man is both strong and weak, both free and bound, both blind and far-seeing. He stands at the juncture of nature and spirit; and is involved in both freedom and necessity. His sin is never the sin of mere ignorance of his ignorance. It is always partly an effort to obscure his blindness by overestimating his sight and to obscure his insecurity by stretching his power beyond its limits. . . . Therefore man is tempted to deny the limited character of his knowledge, and the finitude of his perspectives. He pretends to have achieved a degree of knowledge which is beyond the limit of finite life. This is the ideological taint in which all human knowledge is involved and which is always more than mere human ignorance. It is always partly an effort to hide that ignorance by pretension.[56]

Sin is a pretension that accompanies all experiences of freedom within finite existence. But it is only in what Niebuhr calls the "liberal culture" of the modern West that this pretension has been raised to the level of dogma. A pretension that makes the capacity of freedom in the human condition into something it is not and can never be. Unable to reconcile his finitude with his freedom, man is liable to defer the question of finitude altogether by positing for himself a freedom from this finitude. This freedom (which is a mere hypothetical since it has no actual corollary in the human condition) allows man to make claims regarding access to knowledge of universals and the certainty of absolutes. To make of one's own point of view, one's own contingent normativity, and one's provisional identifications of meaning in history, a kind of standard by which all else can (and should) be judged is the paradigmatic sin of pride. Additionally, to reduce the conflicts and problems of history to merely a problem of imperfect but perfectible knowledge about history, or to posit for history a rationally accessible meaning embedded within the human experience of it is to disregard the fundamental nature of history. History is precisely that experience of temporal life which issues from man's anxiety about his *inability* to ever completely know the meaning of his own existence on account of the paradox of his particular bifurcated condition. It is the inability, so to say, to ever know right from wrong in any absolute sense. Moral certainty is an ahistorical phenomenon. It is reserved only for God. History does have a meaning and an end, but man cannot know it or conceptualize it or actualize it absolutely. One can know it only tangentially, as if looking awry. Pride is therefore a sin not of ignorance or error but of the inevitable desire of a free being to create an existential and normative foundation for its own being that is certain and absolute. It is the desire to know with certainty the answer to the anthropological question, "What am I?" and hence establish a meaning and an end to human existence.[57] It is a desire that can only be satisfied by willfully conflating man's relative freedom with the absolute freedom of God.

In the Niebuhrian worldview, this conflation is the original sin of which Christian faith and doctrine have spoken from the very beginning. This is the true meaning of the Genesis myth of the Fall: to seek to know the good, the meaning and end of his own existence and by extension that of existence as such, as only God can know it. And then to actualize this good in history to fulfill and complete it. "To suppose that we could create a good that was no longer particular and contingent, but somehow universal, permanent, and itself unsusceptible to further change and development would be to suppose that freedom could achieve its aims by destroying itself."[58]

In order to free himself from the problem of finitude by imagining his freedom to be limitless, pride is forever pushing man to destroy his freedom by making it into a thing, an object, a reified and unchanging absolute. It is in this way that the human condition can sometimes come to resemble the quicksand of Greek tragedy. Like Oedipus, man attempts to extricate himself from his finite condition and situated perspective through an exercise of freedom. But, in the regime of original sin, the death of freedom appears to man as the fulfillment of freedom's aims. It is an unequivocal tragedy for there is no easy escape from it. "The doctrine of original sin proceeds from a logical absurdity in the Christian conception of free will; sin proceeds from a defect in our will, but since the will presupposes freedom, that defect cannot be attributed to a defect in our nature."[59] Pride is one natural response to an anxiety that is internal to the essential nature of man as both bound and free. "Where there is history at all, there is freedom and where there is freedom there is sin."[60]

*   *   *

In describing the differences between realism and idealism, Niebuhr points out that whereas a "realistic" worldview takes "all factors in a social, and political situation, which offer resistance to established norms, into account, particularly the factors of self-interest and power," the "idealistic" worldview, on the other hand, is characterized by a "disposition to ignore or be indifferent to the forces in human life which offer resistance to universally valid ideals and norms."[61] According to Niebuhr, original sin is just such a resistive force in the human condition that was often ignored by the idealistic proponents of liberal Christianity and especially the Social Gospel movement of the late nineteenth and early twentieth century. This movement was predicated on the possibility and the desirability of the application of an undiluted Christian ethic to the affairs of men, and of "ushering in an era of international peace by the application of Christian love."[62] Perhaps the most important spokesperson of this movement, Walter Rauschenbusch, pointed out that "for the first time in religious history, we have the possibility of so directing religious energy by scientific knowledge that a comprehensive and continuous reconstruction of social life in the name of God is within the bounds of human possibility."[63] Niebuhr's Christian realism is a response to this sort of idealism in the liberal Christianity of his times. The value and applicability of the love ethic in human affairs can never be a simple possibility precisely because the human condition is so thoroughly subsumed within the regime of original sin. Self-interest and power are not aspects of individual or social life that can be eradicated merely by education or reform because they are in fact the manifest consequences of the condition of sinfulness. They do not follow from ignorance or error but rather from the fact of being human. To seek to alter fundamentally the nature of one's humanity is a most profound pretension. It is certainly outside the realm of human possibility.

Yet the modern age has made a mockery of the acknowledgment of such limitation. Niebuhr was a one-time president of the American Pacifist Society, and a self-proclaimed Christian Marxist. But the interwar years saw him gradually move away from such idealisms. Liberal Christianity of the Social Gospel variety was merely the Christian version of a general feeling among the learned elites that scientific, political, and sociological progress had put Enlightenment ideals well within the reach of practical possibility. Wilsonian internationalism and the founding of the League of Nations were predicated on the notion that "Never Again" was not an abstract hope but a workable aspiration. Economic development was merely a matter of working out the details of ideal systems of organizing the commercial and industrial activities of societies, and then letting these new systems wipe out poverty within mere generations.[64] Democratic idealists imagined increasing suffrage in the West and elsewhere as putting a final nail in the coffin of primitive monarchic systems of government and ushering in a new era of peace and prosperity for all. Niebuhr experienced the oozing optimism of his time with rising levels of anxiety. What was this anxiety? That the modern age had lost its moral compass. That it was too fascinated by ending things rather than dealing with them.

In his book *Reinhold Niebuhr and Christian Realism*, Robin Lovin provides an excellent account of Niebuhr's view on this variety of liberal utopianism by identifying three distinct yet interconnected "moments" in his thinking that together constitute a comprehensive description of Niebuhr's Christian realism. At the most basic level Niebuhr's ideas constitute a variety of *political* realism. Niebuhr's account of original sin is an understanding of human nature that precludes the possibility of moral argumentation as in and of itself sufficient to determine the course of human events. Niebuhr believes that man's curiously bifurcated nature, and its concomitant anxiety, introduces a level of complexity to the human condition that is not properly accounted for in language that takes account only of moral norms. This complexity is even more profound in human societies (as opposed to individuals) making the space for purely moral action and sentiment even narrower when dealing with groups of people.[65] Attending to such complexity requires a more inductive approach to the human condition that takes full stock of the social and political forces actually at play in given situations when formulating moral responses to them. Niebuhr believes that "to devote oneself exclusively to determining and proclaiming the right thing to do" no matter what possibilities are realistically obtainable in given situations "is most probably to render oneself powerless in the actual course of events."[66]

Niebuhr's political realism also has a normative bent that is informed by his experience with Marxist philosophy. Niebuhr was deeply suspicious of absolutist moralizing regardless of its feasibility. This suspicion stems from an understanding that moral ideals often have, and continue to, serve as justificatory discourses for exercises of the will to power on the part of individuals and societies. Moral idealism can thus function as an illusory mask for demands of moral rectitude behind which hide the interests of a political, national, economic, or social nature. This is the mechanism by which Marxists explain the ubiquity of class and the exploitation of the poor in capitalist societies, and Niebuhr is certainly cognizant of such possibilities. It is for this reason that Niebuhr's work is often associated with the desirability of maintaining balances of power within the national context and in the international arena since all power seeks to justify itself through normalizing and universalizing discourses that often have moral content. Such equilibrium may be a proximate and unsatisfying state of affairs for moral idealists, but in the social arena it may be the best that can be hoped for.

In addition to this Marxist variety of a political realism, Niebuhr's work also contains aspects of what Lovin suggests is a *moral* realism that furnishes it with a more nuanced understanding of the moral possibilities of the human condition. Unlike reductive naturalisms that make morality irrelevant by defining human action exhaustively with reference to the natural properties of the human condition, Niebuhr's moral realism is predicated on an ethical naturalism that grants the possibility of free, moral action that can transcend the limitations imposed by such natural properties.[67] Niebuhr's ethical naturalism is a variety of natural law thinking in that it posits morality as conformity with human nature. In the regime of original sin, Niebuhr calls for a rejection of perfectionist expectations within history. At the same time, however, the human subject is also free to imagine transformative possibilities for itself and for society, possibilities that have moral content which transcends the fact of human finitude and its concomitant limitations. The exact content of such possibilities is of course never certain and the dangers inherent in the use of destructive or counterproductive absolutes in the moral language of change can always be obtained. But the antithetical danger of a thoroughgoing moral despair is just as great. Niebuhr suggests this:

A free society prospers best in a cultural, religious, and moral atmosphere which encourages neither a too pessimistic nor too optimistic view of human nature. Both moral sentimentality and moral pessimism encourage totalitarian regimes, the one because it encourages the opinion that it is not necessary to check the power of government, and the second because it believes that only absolute political authority can restrain anarchy, created by conflicting and competitive interests.[68]

It is precisely this manner of moderation that Niebuhr's believes is missing from the perfectionist and idealistic strains of liberal Christianity. It is also missing from reductive naturalisms like Marxism and the "commonsense" realism of most political theory. The third aspect of Niebuhr's realism, his *theological* realism, provides the proper substantive moral language to create a space that mediates between these extreme positions. While it is certainly true that the undiluted ethic of Jesus is not a simple possibility in the realm of human affairs, Niebuhr still argues for the "relevance of an impossible ethical ideal."[69] Of course, it is not relevant in the simplistic manner of Christian idealisms. What separates Niebuhr's Christian realism from other forms of political realisms is this very emphasis on the relevance and meaningfulness of morality, even if moral language is never sufficient within the temporal human realm to create an ideal order of existence. Niebuhr's theological realism is an attempt to provide an account of this relationship between the love ethic of Jesus Christ and a realistic appraisal of what constitutes moral action in this world.

Niebuhr believed that all human conceptions of justice ultimately draw their valence from a source outside the reality of human sinfulness. The tragedy of the human condition is that such conflict is ineradicable. But the hope and struggle for justice that persists despite this state of affairs rests on an understanding that moral claims are somehow meaningful in an ultimate sense. Niebuhr suggests that "every truly moral act seeks to establish what ought to be, because the agent feels obligated to the ideal, though historically unrealized, as being the order of life in its more essential reality."[70] This ideal outside of history, and outside of reality, exists in the realm of moral imagination and religious faith. For the Christian, the Law of love is just such an ideal. It speaks of an ultimate unity and harmony of life with life that does not cohere with any realistic appraisal of the human condition. And yet without it the moral imperative of the "ought" would have no meaning except utility. But any accounting of human history suggests that the experience of the moral ought is not reducible to mere utility. This is what Niebuhr means when he says that "the law of human nature is love."[71] He means "nature" in the Aristotelian sense which is not the condition of human nature as it is (marked by original sin) but rather the condition in which such nature finds it ultimate end, its fulfillment, its completion.[72] The law of love is such an end not merely figuratively but rather literally in that human nature finds its fulfillment only in *ending*, so to say, in "a harmonious relation of life to life in obedience to the divine center and source of life."[73]

Just as Greek tragedy is not melodrama but a mythic interpretation of history, Niebuhr reads the theological and moral language of scripture less as a definite plan for moral action within history and more as a final interpretation of the human condition. Faith in God and belief in scripture is therefore an acknowledgment that history, though tragic in and of itself, has an ultimate end, a purpose conferred on it from outside of itself which provides moral action with meaning. "Though it cannot be denied that it is tragic because men always seek prematurely to complete it . . . from the standpoint of such a faith, history is not meaningless because it cannot complete itself."[74] It is in this sense that while Niebuhr's conception of history is undeniably a tragic one, he sees its end, beyond tragedy, in its fulfillment and completion through the grace of a loving God.

*   *   *

In assessing Niebuhr's realistic appraisal of the moral possibilities inherent in the human condition, Robin Lovin makes an interesting and instructive point. He points out that "properly understood, the Christian Realist claim that there are no limits to moral achievements within history is not an invitation to pride, but to politics."[75] To "seek prematurely to complete [history]" is a quintessentially anti-political attitude. Moral optimism is anti-political in this sense because it imagines an end to human conflict and suffering in the utopian institution of a final moral order in history. On the other hand, excessive despair and cynicism concerning the potential of moral development in human affairs is anti-political in its own way. Such a sensibility replaces politics with utility or instrumentality, and where Niebuhr sees the potential for moral action such cynicism sees only power. Neither attitude is properly political because neither accounts for the true nature of man, eviscerating either his finitude or his freedom. This is a kind of tragedy in itself.

In his famous 1952 tract, *The Irony of American History*, Niebuhr assails communism as quintessentially anti-political "in its pretension that its [vanguard] has taken the leap from the realm of necessity to the realm of freedom, and is therefore no longer subject to the limitations of nature and history which have hitherto bound the actions of men. It imagines itself the master of historical destiny."[76] He calls this vision "a very modern kind of religious apocalypse, for it contains the dearest hope of all moderns, Marxist or non-Marxist."[77] What is this vision? That "man may be delivered from his ambiguous position of being both creature and creator of the historical process and become unequivocally the master of his own destiny."[78] Niebuhr contends that this dream is a quintessential feature of Western modernity, so much so that even its most mainstream philosophy of self-definition, democratic liberalism, is informed by "a fanatic certainty that that it knows the end toward which history must move."[79] The liberal culture continues to be terribly impatient "with the seeming limitations of human wisdom in discerning the *total pattern of destiny* in which human actions take place, and the failure of human power to bring this total pattern under the domination of the human will."[80] The apocalyptic tendencies of the modern Western mind reveal themselves in such impatience and are unleashed on the world in the destructive political projects that it inevitably produces. Niebuhr asserts that all of this is predicated on a corrupt anthropology and a deeply troubling account of the nature of history.

History is the unfolding of moral promise against the grain of despair. But it is not rational in the Hegelian sense. It does not flow like a river to the sea, it is unable to bend, on its own, toward justice and love. It meanders. The aggregate disorder of countless acts of freedom in the regime of limitation, it often mocks human attempts at control and resolution. An invitation to politics is a call for engagement with this reality—not flight from it nor cynicism in the face of it. It is a call to see proximate solutions and compromises not as incomplete and morally unsatisfying but rather as the ever-evolving moral achievements of human freedom. It is still a river even if it does not make it to the sea. It still irrigates the fields. It still quenches thirst. It is still beautiful. To appreciate such unfinished beauty is to understand the true nature of justice and the essential meaning of the love ethic.

*   *   *

For Niebuhr, politics is the only access to justice available within the human condition. For in our "divided and sometimes chaotic reality, politics is the best approximation we have of a community of discourse in which our ideas about the human good could be tested against all the real human beings that the ideas are about."[81] Freedom as self-transcendence, the ability to see beyond one's situated condition, only becomes a concrete possibility in such communities of discourse. Niebuhr's ethic of realistic political engagement is ultimately born out of an acknowledgment of this fact. Engagement across difference and building communities of discourse in a "divided and sometimes chaotic reality" is also a good description of the task Sayyid Ahmad Khan set himself after the debacle of 1857. And for neither Niebuhr nor Khan is politics understood narrowly as contest for power but rather more broadly as discursive practices "in which our ideas about the human good could be tested against all the real human beings that the ideas are about." As the world shrank with the advent of European imperialism, such discursive practices became both harder to sustain on account of the escalating asymmetries attendant to colonialism and yet also absolutely essential to the continued well-being of people everywhere. This is what Khan meant when he identified the loss of a *voice* in matters of concern to them as the primary reason Indians in general, and Muslims in particular, rebelled against the Company Raj in the first place. And as the West has come to dominate the world to an even greater extent in the twentieth and twenty-first centuries, this Muslim voice has been muted even further in the global public sphere. Niebuhr's exhortations against the West taking excessive pride in its norms, values, and institutions and against excessive confidence in a progressively salutary future are therefore even more relevant today than they were in Khan's time or even in Niebuhr's own. Still, Khan was concerned as much about his co-religionists' response to the new world they found themselves in as he was with the behavior of British authorities. This is because excessive pride and confidence is only one end of a spectrum that extends on the other side all the way to an enervating stasis. The political constraints associated with being a subject people could well push Muslims toward an excessive cynicism about the future and a retreat into their own supposed past as a people of God. Khan attended to this danger by delving into this past and articulating an alternative account of the true meaning of the Muhammadan revolution and of the revolutionary potential of an Islamic anthropology.

It is to this end that Sayyid Ahmad Khan begins his refutation of William Muir's biography of Muhammad with a sustained analysis of the history of the Arab people from ancient times to the advent of the Prophet.[82] He complements this discussion with an assessment of the land and its geography, and their impact on the culture and society of the Arabs. With this background as contrast, he brings the enormity of the transformation brought about by the Muhammadan revolution into clear focus. As mentioned in the previous chapter, Khan even quotes the noted British historian Thomas Carlyle to make the case that the change Arab society went through in scarcely a generation has little precedent in human history. Still, it should be noted that Carlyle gets something very wrong in his assessment of Arabs when he suggests that they were "a poor shepherd people, roaming unnoticed in the desert since the creation of the world" before

Islam transformed them, within a century, into "world-notable" and "world-great." The pre-Islamic Arabs were not primarily desert Bedouins living on the margins of civilization and history. In fact, it is unlikely that nomadic people ever outnumbered settled populations in the history of human habitation on the Arabian peninsula.[83] The modern mind finds it hard to reconcile tribalism with more complex forms of social organization. The term "tribe" conjures up images of a wilderness populated by scantily clad savages, hunting or tending to their animal stock. Sometimes they are warriors, driven by honor and passion. Other times they are close to nature, attuned to the rhythms of the world. Noble perhaps, but primitive. There were desert Bedouins among the Arabs, of course. And some of them would have lived up to these stereotypes. But the milieu in which Islam was born was both tribal *and* urban. The material culture was more commercial than pastoral. While these urban Arabs did glorify the virtues of the desert nomad, this was not much different than a modern New Yorker's nostalgia for a simpler life. The desert was akin in this sense to the "American heartland," an abstraction that provided the Arabs with a sense of their "authentic" identity, but which bore little resemblance to their daily lives. Carlyle could only imagine fundamental social transformation in terms that were in vogue in the Europe of his time—from savagery to civilization. So he makes the Muhammadan revolution conform to this type.

I read Khan as arguing that the transformation was at once more subtle and more profound. Islam "civilized" the Arabs by radically reconfiguring their ethical subjectivities; that the transformation in their material culture was merely epiphenomenal to this more basic moral revolution.[84] Contrary to Sir William Muir's opinion that Islam has been injurious to human society,[85] Islam had transformed an "Arab nation [that] was in the dark ages, in a state of the most crass ignorance" into a world-altering civilization.[86] The Islamic term for this pre-Islamic society is *jahiliyyat*.[87] Commonly translated as "the age of ignorance," *jahiliyyat* also has more subtle connotations. In fact, the connotative domain of this term is panoramic. As ignorance, *jahiliyyat* is contrasted with *'ilm*, knowledge, and the coming of Islam is seen as bringing to the Arabs knowledge of virtues and ethics that they previously lacked. But in the Prophet's time, the word *jahilliyyat* also described the state of being easily and unreasonably angered. And as anger, it offers no easy epistemological remedies. Against this, the Qur'an and the Prophet counsel not *'ilm* but *hilm*, the state of being morally reasonable, of being stable and tranquil, of being humble. It is interesting to note here of course that the Islamic terms for knowledge and humility are so closely related.[88] *Jahiliyyat* was also sometimes equated with the pre-Islamic *muruwah*, the moral code of the Bedouin that emphasized the preservation of honor and valorized warrior virtues like self-assertion and aggression. As both anger and code, *jahiliyyat* is not so much an age or a period of time but a state of mind. It is clear that Sayyid Ahmad Khan imagined it as such. In fact, and more importantly perhaps, he imagined it as a state of mind *about* time. Consider, for example, the following verses from the *diwan* (corpus) of the great *jahili* poet 'Abid:

> You see man longing for length of life,
> Yet long life is the most chastising torment . . .
> And I live after them though I will not live forever:
> *Time is spiteful, the master of (many) colors.*[89]

Time, *dahr*, is a source of constant fascination and terror for the *jahili* mind, and a persistent theme in its register and archive that was *jahili* poetry. *Dahr*, often personified as Fate, is the master of all earthly gods, and the relentless destroyer of men. As another famed *jahilli* poet, Durayd b. al-Simma puts it, "then we, no doubt, are meat for the sword [of Time], and / doubtless, sometimes we feed it meat."[90] But perhaps the poet-king Imru' al-Qays puts it at its poignant best in this famous lament:

> Are we not subject to blind Fate,
> And allow ourselves to be fooled by food and drink?
> We are birds, flies and worms,
> And yet bolder than ravening wolves.
> The roots of my nobility reach deep into the earth,
> But Death robs me of my youth, and my life,
> And soon brings me to dust.
> How can I hope for compassion from Fate,
> Which spares not the solid mountains,
> Since I know it will shortly clutch me in its talons,
> As it dealt with my father Hujr and my grandfather?[91]

Imru' al-Qays's is a most nuanced description of the profound pessimism of *jahiliyyat*. Time lacks any moral quality, and history is merely a record of eternal destruction. Nothing survives. The nature and end of Time is the relentless grinding of all that exists into meaningless dust, be it mountains or men: "What are we, if not body and soul? / The body, we go down with it under the earth. / While the soul passes away like a gust of wind."[92] The only distinguishing quality of *dahr* for the pre-Islamic Arabs is its eternity. Time has no beginning, nor end. It marches on to the beat of its destruction for all eternity. It is the existential anxiety attendant to this conception of ahistorical time that provides *jahiliyyat* with its peculiar ethical subjectivity and its sense of (a)morality. *Jahiliyyat* is the condition of this existential anxiety operationalized into an idealized nightmare of self-assertion. This idealization is first a reflection of the physical geography of Arabia where the frailty of life is revealed in its most undiluted manner. But it is also a consequence of the combination of commercialism, tribalism, and an extreme form of self-reliance wedded to a potent traditionalism. This worldview valorizes self-reliance and freedom, independence. Yet the moral order is reduced to a mere regurgitation of ancestral virtues. And the highest virtue of all is survival, for the time being. Time will take everything away eventually. The *jahili* ethic is therefore an ethic of "in the mean*time*." In time without beginnings or ends, life ephemeral is end in itself.

*   *   *

Sayyid Ahmad Khan believed that this particular, intertwined moral subjectivity is not unique in human history but it rarely reaches the level of idealization as it did for the *jahili* Arabs.[93] And it is for this reason that Muhammad was sent to the Arabs in this place, and at this time, for a paradigmatic revelation of God's message. Their transformation is archetypical because the *jahili* Arabs, more than any before them or since, embodied the most archetypically disastrous response to the anxieties of being human. For their response is a reversion to animality, and the valorization of precisely those so-called virtues which are the antithesis of the human condition. It should come as no surprise to us then that what the Arabs found most disturbing about Muhammad's message was not monotheism (the dominant narrative in both scholarly and mainstream Muslim circles) but the idea of a *yaum al-qiyama*, a Day of Judgment, and an afterlife.[94] What fantasy! *Dahr* is terrifying precisely because it is eternal; there is no time after Time for an afterlife or for judgment. *Dahr*'s only judgment is destruction, and this it does at all times. The Qur'an was addressed to these Arabs, and its miracle is their transformation in the *particular*. Khan argues that the words of the Quran must be interpreted as speech addressed to and meant for Arab ears, for God himself has stated: "And we never sent a messenger save with the language of his folk."[95] It is for this reason that Khan begins his biography of Muhammad, and his defense of Islam against the likes of William Muir and Reverend Pfander, with a study of those to whom Muhammad was sent to deliver the message.

In Khan's reading of them, eternal time devoid of meaning would have rendered the *jahili* Arabs prone to two existential outlooks that should be all too familiar to modern Western audiences: intense individualism and a casuistic morality devoid of any overarching sense of Law and accountability. If time provides no standard outside itself for judgment of actions in time, then it becomes a mere stage for self-assertion. And the highest form such self-assertion took for the Arabs was a primitive form of utilitarian thinking. In his panoramic *History of the Arabs*, Philip K. Hitti (1886–1978) suggested that in the pre-Islamic Arab "individualism [was] so deeply ingrained that he [had] never become a socially conscious being. His ideals of devotion to the common good [had] not gone beyond that which pertain to the tribe."[96] Carl Brockelmann (1868–1956) similarly argued that "the Bedouin [was] above all a purely egotistic individualist."[97] This individualism was bred by an almost complete absence of any abstract conception of Law. The focus of the system of *lex talionis* (customary law) was, then, not justice according to law, but the restoration of tribal honor—that is, of social power.[98] "[At the base of Bedouin culture lay] an unrestrained individualism, a proud consciousness of oneself and an aversion to every authority and hierarchy which was, and is reflected in the anarchic particularism of the individual tribes."[99] It is in this sense that power relationships were simply a question of the strength of one individual or group against another, and they were hardly affected by notions of justice enshrined in a system of laws.[100] While these accounts by Hitti and Borckelmann are obviously highly Orientalized fictions that are no longer the standard for historical accuracy concerning the ways of pre-Islamic Arabs, they accurately capture both the nineteenth-century Western consensus on desert Bedouin culture and Khan's own understanding of a savage and uncivilized race requiring divine intervention.

In this reading, if there was a standard of valuation that rose above all else to provide a quasi-moral basis for judgment, it was life itself, and the preservation of this life, and a hedonistic enjoyment of this life. The three major interlocking emphases of Arab life and hence also of Arab poetry were the following: first, the *ghaziya*, the raid on the enemy; second, *al-haram*, the sacred truce in and around the *Ka'ba*; and third, a preoccupation with food, drink, and women. The *ghaziya* was a law unto itself, a perversely consequentialist law whereby success of the raid was the only standard for judgment of its righteousness. So ingrained was the *ghaziya* in the socioeconomic order that a *jahili* poet recorded the following with more than a hint of irony: "Our business is to make raids on the enemy, / On our neighbor. / And on our own brother. / In case we find none to raid, / But a brother!"[101] The truce in and around Mecca was similarly utilitarian since it provided a space devoid of violence to conduct business between enemies and friends alike. Like the modern stock exchange, it was designed to provide a context for commercial activity with no regard to the quasi-moral concerns of friendship and enmity. But it was in the obsession with food, drink, and women that the *jahili* mind revealed its essential pessimism in its most profound, and poignant form. Another poet captures this sensibility perfectly:[102]

> Come and give me a morning sip [of wine],
> For [though] man was not fashioned out of stone,
> He is pledged to stones and the dust of a grave.
> Come and give me a morning sip,
> For Fate is full of changes;
> It has destroyed Luqaima and destroyed al-Hirmas.
> Wine today! Tomorrow affairs will show their face;
> Fate is but a division of pleasure and hardship.
> So drink [from] a full [vessel] despite Fate's eventfulness;
> Worries cannot couple with the clanking of teeth against the [wine-] goblet.[103]

Life and its pleasures are raised in this worldview to the be-all and end-all of human existence. In meaningless, eternal time, yesterday, today, and tomorrow all bleed into one. In the eternal now, all man can do is enjoy and take pleasure in the fact of his life. Just as morality is the flow of time, amorality is the cessation of all movement in the present. It is in this sense that if history is development and becoming, the desert has no history. The almost complete impossibility of chronologically ordering the dates of the tradition concerning its guerilla wars and raids, and the thousand picturesque episodes of Bedouin life means there is little in the way of a historical record. Only occasionally there appeared on the surface some effort at overcoming the sterile anarchy which was the ordinance of desert life. The eternity of *dahr* is devoid of history and morality. In fact, to lack history and to lack morality is one and the same thing.

*   *   *

In their beautiful, poignant, and sad musings, the *jahili* poets point to the essential absurdity of the society to which they belonged. Niebuhr looked at the Greek dramatists similarly as shrewd spectators of the human condition and as interpreters of history. The *jahili* poet digs beneath the false bravado of the Bedouin and unearths the anxieties that lay below. Khan acknowledges the contribution of these poets, but he digs deeper.[104] The *jahili* anxieties are themselves only a second-order response to an even more basic set of tensions that is constitutive of the human condition. What is the source of these tensions? It is the fact that the human animal, like nothing else in existence, has a *composite* nature, constituted in, and as, a series of competing impulses and forms that can never be fully reconciled into a single, unified substance. All else in creation has a singular nature; it is what it is. Man alone lacks such unified, natural coherence. Man must constantly construct coherence out of the disparate elements that are internal to his definition. And the most basic obstacle to finding such coherence is the anxiety associated with the question of whether man is determined or determining, which Khan discusses with reference to the classical formulation of *jabr wa ikhtiyar*, or the question of predestination and free will.[105]

In literal terms, *jabr* means oppression or the condition of being under the sway of forces over which one has no control. *Ikhtiyar*, on the other hand, means ability, or capacity to control, or having power or responsibility over things, including oneself. In traditional theological discussion, the question of *jabr wa ikhtiyar* referred almost exclusively to the problem of reconciling human free will with the fact of an omniscient and omnipotent God. Khan extends the conceptual parameters of this discussion considerably, and reimagines the problem as an existential issue, not just a theological or philosophical one. In Khan's reading, *jabr wa ikhtiyar* refers to a whole set of dualisms in the human experience of reality. The first and most basic of these dualisms is between the material and non-material aspects of man. It is the existence of this dualism that distinguishes man from both other organic beings (like animals or plants) and inorganic matter. Man is determined, first of all, by what Khan calls internal causes of his material existence. Everything is created by God with a certain nature peculiar to it: "We see that inorganic things like stones and metals do not fly in the air, water does not exist above the air, and fish cannot live but in water, etc."[106] Similarly, a man whose eye is so made can only see objects lying near at hand and cannot see far-off objects.[107] Man is limited in his material capacities by the condition of being a material being. Yet, there is something in man that does not conform to such limitation:

> Among the many wonders of divine power the ideas of man are of extreme interest. We see that one kind of creature [animal] holds one and the same idea (*khayāl*). There are movements and actions in animals that derive from their being animate. However, you may name the mediate or immediate motive power (*muharrik*) of these actions and movements. They are the same thing that we call "idea" on the human level. . . . Yet we are amazed by the fact that whereas everywhere there is one kind of *khayāl* in one kind of animal and they all hold them to be absolutely certain, man, in spite of being a species of the animated beings, does not hold [like animals do] one kind of *khayāl* with one and the same degree of certainty. Why? At times, the thought occurs that the *khayālat* of all the animals [of one species] are identical because of their being limited, and that

the reason for the ideas of man being devoid of this quality [of being identical] is their being unlimited. . . . So the better acquainted we are with the ideas of men, the more we know about the wonders of divine power, and this advantage is not altered by [the ideas] being correct or incorrect; rather, the fact of their diversity adds to it.[108]

Khan often quoted the story of a man who once walked up to 'Ali ibn Abi Talib—the prophet's son-in-law and the fourth caliph of Sunni Islam and the first of the Shi'i Imams—and asked whether man was free or determined. 'Ali's answer is instructive:

> He asked the man to lift his right foot, which he did. Then he told him to raise both his left and right foot simultaneously which is, of course, impossible. By this example, he tried to convince the questioner that he is free to act in certain spheres and not free in others simply because his bodily organism is so determined.[109]

Another kind of dualism is that between the human being as an individual and as a socio-historical and communal creature. In addition to internal causes mentioned above, man is also under the sway of "external causes" of determination. These include the time period in which he is born, the society he belongs to, the particular knowledge he has acquired, the particular environment in which he exists: "A man is born in a particular society, and lives in a special cultural set-up, he undergoes a particular type of education and learns to respect certain moral values in his childhood—all these determine for him a particular set of activities and value judgments."[110] And yet, Khan contends that man is also clearly endowed with what he calls the "light of nature," a basic and amorphous moral sensibility that allows him to overcome the social constraints to which he is bound and discern right from wrong in spite of all determinations: "We have historical records of many persons who were brought up in a particular social pattern and witnessed people following a special moral code, and yet when they grew up and thought over the problems of life, they repudiated the accepted norms of moral and social behavior and tried to set up better norms for their compatriots."[111] The prophets, for example, are the quintessential repudiators of the social norms into which they have been born. In this sense, the individual experiences both *jabr* in his social relations and yet also has the *ikhtiyar* to transcend these limitations through the practice of moral imagination.

A third kind of dualism is that between two basic human faculties of *quwat-i taqwa* (faculty of godliness) and *quwat-i fujur* (faculty of iniquity). To put it more accurately, *taqwa* refers to the humility and thankfulness (*shukr*) that comes from the recognition of God and the constructive fear of the last judgment. Similarly, *fujur* has connotations of haughtiness, over-confidence, and lack of fear. "These two faculties," Sayyid Ahmad Khan explains, "exist in every man possessing reason."[112] And since someone not possessing reason is not, properly speaking, a human being, for Sayyid Ahmad Khan the dual-existence of these faculties is an internal feature of human existence. It is not something acquired or epiphenomenal but basic and essential. No human being is endowed with one without the other. And all human beings are endowed with both.

* * *

Jabr wa ikhtiyar provides Khan with the conceptual tools to embed his theological anthropology within the tradition of Muslim thinking concerning the question of will. The human will itself is composite, and it is this composite nature of the will that explains its freedom. It is free precisely in that it is also at the same time determined. But Khan goes further. He wants to turn the question of will into a byline, a mere afterthought to the more fundamental question of the nature of man. It is at this level that he makes his most profound and innovative, and also most controversial, contribution to Islamic thought: the equation of the faculty of reason (*'aql*) with the faculty of moral discernment based on a redefinition of both faculties in radically novel ways. The following excerpt from *Insan ke Khayalat* is instructive in this regard:

> Then I asked myself how reason can with certainty remain free from error. *I admitted that such certainty is not really obtainable.* Only if reason is used constantly can the error of the reason of one person be corrected by the reason of a second person, and the reasonings of one period by the reasonings of a second. Whereas as long as knowledge or certainty or faith are kept outside the reach of reason, certainty cannot be obtained at any period of time whatsoever. At that point a doubt arose in my heart. I held reason to be the paramount guide. Why did I not count on the possibility that there could be a greater guide than reason, a guide that could subdue even reason? The fact that we are not acquainted with it surely does not constitute a proof of its non-existence. But then I thought that to presume the existence of such a guide would not lead us any further. *What we need is knowledge and certainty about it. Since this is lacking there is no other guide but reason alone.*[113]

Reason is not, in Khan's reading, a mechanism for ending uncertainty about knowledge or about faith in the manner of moral formulas or indisputable scientific facts. Reason is in fact the peculiarly human experience of this uncertainty. One can never be more certain than the faculty of reason allows, and this faculty is itself conditioned by the determinations of one kind or another. Since the faculty of reason itself is predicated on the divided nature of man (harmony, not unity, between good and evil, and between freedom and determination), one can have no greater certainty than the certainty offered by reason. Like the speed of light, reason constitutes a final limit: "There is no other guide but reason alone" for no other "guide would lead us *any further.*" Additionally, there is no overarching "reason" to which all must bow, but rather the reasons of persons and reasons of age. And yet reason cannot be reduced to these limitations. Due to the curiously dual nature of man's existence, reason is always already that faculty of mind that opens human consciousness to unlimited *khayālat* (ideas), and to novel possibilities impossible for animals or other inanimate objects to imitate. But what is the source of this faculty? From whence does it arise? Or, in short, what is reason? For Khan, reason is nothing other than self-reflection. To use Heidegger's terminology, man is *dasein*, "that entity which in its Being has this very Being as an issue."[114] Man is the kind of being that asks the question of its own existence. Or, as per Socrates, all philosophy is properly in service of one imperative: know thyself. Self-interrogation is the source of man's reason and is identical to the experience of reason.

> In man there is not only this visible covering of flesh but another thing by which he truly can be called man. If man reflects on himself, he can become aware of the fact that in addition to this visible body there is something else in him through which he distinguishes between good and bad, and knows the inner reality of everything according to the measure of his reflective ability. If one reflects upon it more closely, one realizes that although this thing is somehow linked to the human body, it is yet independent of it. Man at times is so distracted that he forgets everything. *Himself, however, he does not forget.*[115]

A primordial, pre-conscious act of self-reflection already reveals to man his dual nature, and this revelation is the basis of his reason. It is also, simultaneously, the source of his anxiety. What is this anxiety? That man knows there are such things as "right" and "wrong," "true" and "false," but he cannot know them with certainty. He can imagine limitlessly, yet he is limited by his creatureliness. He seeks solid ground but he lives on shifting sands. He feels one, a single being, yet a unitary self-definition eludes him. He can neither forget himself nor understand himself entirely. It is this set of basic anxieties that Sayyid Ahmad Khan identifies with the theological concept of *taklif*, literally burden/obligation. In classical Muslim theology, *taklif* referred narrowly to the condition of humans being put under obligation of a binding law, the Law of God, by which they shall be judged on the Last Day. It has little or nothing to do with the capacity for reason or rationality. Khan's expands the theological scope of this concept by re-viewing it through his innovative analysis of the interplay between *naql* (transmitted knowledge) and *'aql* (capacity to reason) in determining the true *Shari'a*. While *naql* in Arabic refers to the reliance on transmitted knowledge and so does not require a suspension of *'aql* in its practice, Khan reframes *naql* as imitation (its primary meaning in his native Urdu) to imagine it as a conceptual opposite of *'aql*. In Khan's reformulation of the traditional relationship between *'aql* and *naql*, the burden of obligation can be said to be overcome by perfecting the imitation, not by employing one's capacity for reason. This is where Khan disagrees:

> Since man is made for worship, that is for religion, or religion for man, it follows that there should be something in man—*as distinct from other living things*—which can perceive the content and binding character of this obligation. This special thing or faculty in man is intellect *('aql)*. Whatever religion is given to man, therefore, cannot lie beyond the grasp of intellect (*'aql-i insān kē māfauq nah hō*).[116]

As with *jabr wa ikhtiyar*, Sayyid Ahmad Khan has a more expansive understanding of *taklif*. It is an unavoidable condition and cannot be wished away. To be burdened is as such to be a human being. It is this burden, this anxiety about the nature of his own existence that once turned outward exhibits itself as man's curiosity about the world he inhabits. It is the animating imperative of all human action, human knowledge, and human development. In short, of human history. Notice that Khan equates knowledge and faith in their relationship to reason in *Insan ke Khayalat*. In a different context, he makes this very explicit: "Reason alone is the instrument by which to acquire knowledge or faith (*'ilm yā imān*). Knowledge, certainty and faith are merely different words expressing the same reality, and this reality is confined to the reach of reason."[117] The same mental faculty that allows us to make good decisions, informed to the extent of our knowledge concerning material facts, scientific advances, and socioeconomic progress, is also the faculty that allows us to make better moral decisions. True rationality is the condition of modulating or coordinating between these dualities, which is also always already the nature of morality. Elsewhere (and like Niebuhr), Khan also reinterprets the story of the Fall to suggest that in Hebrew, the term "Knowledge of Good and Evil" has the dual meaning of "Knowledge of Everything" in much the same manner as saying "to look high and low" means "to look everywhere." Khan is arguing a profound point here. Moral curiosity about the right thing to do and scientific curiosity about the truth of the world are the same species of curiosity, have the same source, and are subject to the same faculty of judgment. Khan was often accused of being a moral naturalist in his insistence on reason as the final guide to all questions, including theological or moral ones. He is accused of this by many Muslims even to this day.[118] But in reality, this insistence is predicated on a rejection of the boundaries separating these supposedly different spheres of inquiry. Rationality and morality are not distinct spheres of discernment. They are merely different aspects of the reality of *taklif*, burden, anxiety.

It is this underlying unity of the experience of duality that, counter intuitively perhaps, leads to the diversity of reason(s) over time and space. This is what Khan means when he claims that the "advantage [of reason] is not altered by [the ideas] being correct or incorrect; rather, the fact of their diversity adds to it."[119] It is also with this in mind that Khan made his (in)famous proclamation that while religion (*din*) in the abstract is unitary, there is no such thing as a single *Shari'a*, or set of moral laws, once and for all time and place. Any prophet's great insight is in the manner he accounts for the determinations of his age and society to accommodate God's unitary message for particular human ears.

> True, to each one of them has been revealed a different *shari'at* that is the prescription regarding the service of the one God and the way He should be worshipped. This in fact is called "the *shari'at* of each prophet." When man's soul is afflicted by spiritual illness the *shari'at*, the method [*tariqa*] of service (*'ibadat*) by which this spiritual illness disappears is given to the prophet of that age. God almighty says in surah *al-Ma'idah*: "To each one of the prophets we have given an established order and a method." (cf. Q. 5, 48)[120]

Moral knowledge is subject to the same ebbs and flows as all other kinds of human knowledge. This is how Khan understood Wali Allah's imperative that *ijtihad* can, in fact must, be predicated on *al-masalih*, the sources of human flourishing, and on *al-fitrah*, human nature *and* knowledge about nature. The law must account for the condition and needs to whom it is applied. And it must rely on the production of accurate knowledge about the world man inhabits. Law is not merely a technical matter concerning the accurate representation of the Qur'an and the Sunna. It is the moral register of the flow of time and the diversity of space. It is "inherently flexible" precisely because the human creature obligated to follow it is itself flexible, plastic, and ever-changing in the tensions inherent in its many natures. The prophets know this implicitly, and so they use their reason, their intellect, to account for this, and to administer the necessary changes. They make time flow. The prophets realize implicitly that the *Shari'a* does not prescribe a set of rules extrinsic to the nature of man or his faculties, nor is it designed merely to test his obedience. On the contrary, it declares how man's innate faculties should be ordered toward his greatest possible happiness and thus in the service of God. Good and evil arise from the structure of reality. The *Shari'a* helps reveal existing structures and does not add any moral truth to them. Man's main duty is to achieve *tatbi'a* (harmony) between the opposing forces [in his nature]. Happiness and repose of the soul (*rāhat*) consists in achieving this harmony.[121] For Khan the *naql* of the prophets is not to be found merely in their deeds or in their revealed writings. It is also to be recognized in their motivations and their use of their own reason. In this sense, the *naql* of the Prophet is in fact the use of *'aql* by man. The distinction between the two imperatives (*'aql* and *naql*) is merely cosmetic, not constitutive.

In most respects, Muhammad is like any of the other prophets sent by God before him. What makes him special is the time and place in which he was born, and the people to which he was sent. For Sayyid Ahmad Khan, the problem of sin in human life is revealed not so much in man doing evil (which is a natural and unavoidable tendency) as it is by the unwillingness to develop one's moral sensibilities to the extent that they can be developed: "There is no sin to man over which he has no power; sin follows only when man does not put the tendency toward good to full use."[122] This unwillingness is one response to *taklif* and the desire to overcome the burden that it represents. And it usually takes one of two possible forms. Either man declares his freedom from obligation to be absolute and denies the presence of any overarching law to which he may be held accountable. Or man becomes completely subservient to a law that is simple, clear, and unchanging: a law written in stone. In usual circumstances, individuals and societies are susceptible to one form of sin or the other; the sin of hubris and pride, or the sin of sloth and quietude.

But in Khan's reading, *jahili* Arab society miraculously combined both forms of sin into a single, potent repudiation of their own humanity. On the one hand, they refused to grant any meaning to time except destruction, and in so doing rendered the idea of accountability to a higher standard outside of time inapplicable to themselves. In this they declared their freedom from the burden of any obligation to anything other than to themselves and to their own lives. But, on the other hand, they clung to the ancient so-called virtues of their ancestors as if these were the laws of nature itself. The *ghaziya*, the demands of the *muruwah*, their absolute adherence to their ancestors as the only source of guidance stood in stark contrast to their supposed sense of independence and freedom. God Himself points to their intransigence and their refusal to accept Muhammad's message: "What! Have We given them a scripture prior to this, / To which they are holding fast? / No! They say: 'We found our fathers following certain religion, / And we will guide ourselves by their footsteps.'"[123] What kind of creature is both averse to change and yet counts himself entirely unfettered and free? How did the pre-Islamic Arabs manage to hold this contradictory state of mind? They had disaggregated the idea of tradition from the idea of morality. Additionally, they had reduced their moral sensibility to mere utility, lacking reference to anything other than their own base needs. They had also reduced tradition to mere imitation of the ways of the ancestors. And tradition repeated ad infinitum is the antithesis of true morality, which is adaptive and ever-changing. In doing all this to allay their anxieties, they had accomplished an existential feat of incredible complexity. Their denial of *taklif* was profound and extreme at all levels. They instantiated the paradigms of the denial of *taklif* perfectly. In so doing, they provided an ideal circumstance for a paradigmatic revelation. Khan argued that this incredible confluence of factors made Muhammad's ministry special and made the Qur'an a superior manual of religious instruction than any of its antecedents. A rare confluence of factors indeed. But, to Khan's dismay, not so rare as to be impossible to repeat. Khan saw these factors gradually coalescing, once again, in the world of his time. A nightmarish scenario, but as always, also an opportunity for a restatement of the *din* (religion) of Islam in a new *Shari'a* for the modern age.

*   *   *

For much of his life it appears that Sayyid Ahmad Khan casually held to the Ptolemaic view of the universe, with Earth at its center and the heavenly bodies revolving around it.[124] The debate between heliocentric and geocentric views of the cosmos had a long history among Muslim astronomers dating all the way back to the medieval period.[125] But the Ptolemaic view continued to be the dominant one among most Muslims even into the early modern period. Translations of Copernicus's particular heliocentric model had already appeared in India by 1807. As was clear from its original reception in the Christian West, "a heliocentric view of the world was never just a mathematical concept . . . [but] serious reflection required a radical transformation of one's mode of thinking—not only in philosophical terms (inasmuch as Aristotelian postulates were dumped), but also in religious terms."[126] When Khan was finally convinced of the Copernican worldview and sought to popularize it in Muslim circles, he was attacked relentlessly by even many of his erstwhile friends for abandoning the "Muslim" view of the universe for a foreign one. It was in response to these attacks that Khan first developed his mature conception of the scientific method and its relationship to Islam. He pointed to the absurdity of thinking of science as belonging to this or that people. In fact, what his detractors were calling "Muslim" sciences were of Greek origin. The fact of their foreign-ness did not render them any more false back when they were integrated into Islamic theology and philosophy and did not make them any truer now that they were clearly being refuted by modern science. When Muslims were first confronted with Greek philosophy and astronomy, these sciences represented a body of knowledge for observing and understanding the world far superior to anything they possessed at the time. The well-meaning among them correctly intuited the need to reconcile this body of knowledge with the truth of Quranic revelation. More importantly, they did not understand this as a defensive move or an acceptance of inferiority. They saw a proper understanding of nature and the world as internal to their Islam. There was nothing foreign about knowledge. There was one God and one universe, and both these were common to all. Khan's contemporaries had fundamentally misunderstood the nature of knowledge and its relationship to their faith. Quoting a passage from Fakhr al-Din Razi's *Tafsir al-kabir,* where the author explains how the heavens break *physically* open whenever an angel descends from heaven, Khan comments (with more than a hint of irritation):

> My Reverend Maulwi Sahab, by reaffirming such absurdities you are not at all a well-wisher of Islam but quite clearly harm it and denigrate its name by [attributing to it] things which do not correspond to the truth . . . [instead] true love of Islam is this: not to care for derision or for death—but simply to remain a lover of Islam. And however many wrong traditions and opinions have been mixed up with Islam which in truth are not Islam, remove them from Islam as you remove the fly from the milk.[127]

What was this fly in the milk? The notion that a thirteenth-century consensus on knowledge about the world was somehow an incontrovertible fact of existence and an internal part of Islam. Mankind makes progress in knowledge. The *rouhani haqiqat* (spiritual reality) is not threatened by the fact of such change. "The work of God, namely the laws of nature (*qānūn-i qudrat*) is a practical covenant (*'amali 'ahd*) and the promise and threat (of revelation) a verbal one (*qaulī mu'āhadah*). And between the two there can be no contradiction whatsoever."[128] Not only is moral and spiritual development not threatened by the study of nature, but one also cannot do without the other. Anyone who claimed otherwise was peddling absurdities and nonsense. His critics should be elated that all this new scientific knowledge would now allow them to understand the nature of God's existence better than before and provide new investigative tools for re-interpreting the Qur'an and the Sunna. They could go back to the Qur'an, and in light of this new knowledge, determine through a renewed *ijtihad* which passages in the Qur'an need to be read through *ta'wil* (interpretive reasoning) and which others literally. To move Islamic history forward, so to say. Instead, they were stuck in the morass of their own traditionalism, appealing to their ancestors as the *jahili* Arabs had once appealed to theirs. This was a pathetic reversion. And a dangerous one. For to call the antithesis of Islam, Islam itself, is the worst kind of apostasy. Its pessimism, cynicism, a lack of faith.

Once Khan had become better acquainted with the modern scientific method as practiced by his European contemporaries, he began to realize how perfectly it matched the Islamic emphasis on the production of knowledge about God's creation. There are, literally hundreds of references in the Qur'an proclaiming that *all* of existence is Muslim in that everything is, in one way or another, involved in constant praise of God and is in a state of worship of God.[129] God's practical covenant with creation is a necessary corollary to his verbal one with *baniAdam* (the progeny of Adam). It is for this reason that the Qur'an constantly exhorts Muslims to look at all of creation, all its movements and rhythms, as *ayat*, signs of God.

> Lo! In the creation of the heavens and the earth, and the difference of night and day, and the ships which run upon the sea with that which is of use to men, and the water which ALLAH sends down from the sky, thereby reviving the earth after its death, and dispersing all kinds of beasts therein, and *in* the ordinance of the winds, and the clouds obedient between heaven and earth: are signs of God's sovereignty for people who have sense.[130]

Creation is like a grand icon, a window into God's mind, and into the purposes attendant on existence in being obligated to Him. Nature's rhythms, but also the rhythms of human life, of human history, are all signs of God "for people who have sense," who have eyes to see. Khan believed that modern science's emphasis on observation, verification, and experiment was an ideal mechanism for revealing the mysteries of nature, as well as the social realities of man. As a method for producing new knowledge about nature and man's place in it, modern Western science appeared without equal in human history. Whereas the Greek sciences had functioned through the use of logic and analogical reasoning (as had Greek philosophy), "the proofs of modern science had not remained merely analogical (*qiyāsī*) and hypothetical (*fardī*); rather, experience and practice (*tajribah aur 'amal*) had definitively given them the status of observation (*mushāhida*)."[131] God in fact calls Himself *al-Muhit*, the All-encompassing, the All-pervading.[132] It is the same term that is used to denote the environment in Arabic. So, to understand God, one must understand the environment in which one exists. The study of nature and its laws is necessary and obligatory. The Prophet is said to have remarked that "Seeking knowledge is obligatory upon every Muslim."[133] The West had stumbled upon a method of unveiling definitive facts about God's practical covenant, the laws that governed His creation. Under these circumstances, any religion that continued to resist the advances of science or which refused to account for knowledge so produced risked being destroyed "in the same way as frost kills tender plants."[134] The intransigence of his fellow Muslims was suicidal apostasy.

Still, there was one fundamental problem with modern science. The peculiar history of the Scientific Revolution in Europe had pitted its advocates, almost from the beginning, against Christian clerics. As a result, the advance of reason represented a break from religion, and its advocates imagined increasing rationality in matters of knowledge as ipso facto representing decreasing religious sentiment. Science had become the nemesis of religion in the West. Epistemological reason had become disaggregated from moral reason as a consequence of this historical battle. As this battle hardened into dogma, the modern West had unwittingly re-created the conditions of *jahiliyyat* in the present. What was the character of this re-creation? Khan believed that in setting itself up as independent of moral concerns, modern Western science had created a perverse incentive for religion to set itself up as independent of epistemological concerns. This had certainly happened in the West, despite valiant attempts by some European scholars of the late eighteenth and early nineteenth century to hypothesize the parameters of reconciliation.[135] Now Khan feared that this unnecessary battle between secular rationality and religious faith, between science and religion, was repeating itself in the Muslim world. It was creating a new breed of Muslim, the strident, reactionary, conservative who dealt with the superiority of Western science by declaring Islam independent from its influence. What was one in the *jahili* mind was now two, but tied into a Gordian knot of mutual reinforcement. One side proclaimed the absolute freedom of knowledge production, the other an unswerving commitment to moral tradition. To Khan this was akin to the two sides of the brain proclaiming that they were independently conscious. Consciousness is a feature of the entirety of the brain. Moral and epistemological concerns ought to be intertwined for they have a common mental faculty of discernment. The process we call history is in this sense the constant working out or adaptation that comes from our uncertainty about what is right and what is true, while at the same time we desire to know what is right and what is true. This desire is the same desire as the desire to know oneself. The so-called is/ought fallacy is correct only insofar as it claims that moral questions cannot be reduced to epistemological questions. But in the final analysis, this lack of resolution does not, and should not, lead us to a rejection of the mutual relevance of epistemology to morality. No ultimate reconciliation is possible within history. Still, both Niebuhr and Khan look to an ultimate reconciliation outside of history in the coming Kingdom of God or in the Day of Judgment. It is then that the essential nature of history, its meaning, and purpose will be revealed in the resolution of these dualities through divine grace and judgment. A spectacular revelation of moral unity and epistemological certainty.

*   *   *

We are now far removed in time from both Khan's nineteenth-century India and Niebuhr's twentieth-century America. And yet some things remain eerily constant. Consider, for example, that the world we now inhabit is still as in thrall of its competing optimisms and pessimisms as it ever was. On the one hand, the promise of emerging technologies like AI, virtual reality, nanotech, and genetic sciences to fundamentally alter and enhance our experience of the world generates tremendous hope in the future of humanity. On the other hand, the pace of change associated with these technologies engenders enormous anxiety about what they may mean for the very nature and meaning of our humanity. And this anxiety often provokes not just a fear of science and reason but a generalized suspicion about the very nature of truth itself. Consider also that while the flow of goods, people, and information in the age of the internet, and of rapid transport, makes it possible for the first time in human history for each of us to have information about the others in the palm of our hands, this interconnectivity produces not only beatific visions of our common humanity but also fierce tribalisms and enormous conflict. The dueling temptations to either ascend into the perfect freedom of our universal imaginations or descend into the comforting constraints of our myriad particularities are as verdant as ever. And together they constitute a pathological feedback loop, a futile back-and-forth that is the perpetual-motion-machine of relentless struggle.

It is against these kinds of pathological feedback loops that both Reinhold Niebuhr and Sayyid Ahmad Khan counseled their different brands of moral realism. This realism was based in both cases on a re-interpretation of foundational theological principles in response to the peculiar conditions they found themselves in. Niebuhr reimagined the Christian concept of sin as excess confidence and pride in the human ability to overcome the constraints of finitude and to perfect the human condition through the deployment of freedom, reason, and rationality. His realism sought to put the brakes on utopic visions of a future-perfect society that were not sufficiently attendant to the fractured realities of his contemporary moment. But fractured though it may be, Niebuhr did not counsel escape from this reality but engagement with it. Khan similarly reinterpreted the Qur'anic concept of *taklif* as not just the condition of being put under obligation to the binding command of God but also the source of man's curiosity about what such command entails and about the world in which God has placed humanity. And as the basis of man's faculty of reason. Against the past-perfect visions of his co-religionists, Khan counseled that the anxieties and imperfections of their present was an opportunity to rethink their place in the world and to engage with it in the full actualization of their humanity. A realistic appraisal of their contemporary backwardness was cause for reflection, not for lashing out in unreasoned violence. There was no other way to get a grip on this rapidly transforming world and to feel at home in it.

Today these same pathologies are on display in so much of what we see happening between the Muslim world and the West. The cartoonish confidence of some in the West to thoroughly transform the Muslim world using the salutary deployment of freedom and reason (and, of course, bombs and boots on the ground) is often matched on the other side by a frustrating intransigence on the part of many Muslims to ascribe any value to all to the West or Western forms of knowledge. Instead of what Niebuhr called a "community of discourse in which our ideas about the human good [can] be tested against all the real human beings that the ideas are about," we have a fractured global reality in which it is far more common to talk past each other than to each other.[136] This fractured reality is of course also evident in the incessant debates between men of science on the one hand, and men of faith on the other, and in the perpetual conflict between reason and religion. But what if these fractures themselves are what causes the conflict and not the other way around? Having first imagined constraint and freedom, religion and reason, faith and science as distinct categories of human experience and knowledge, an agonistic dualism appears to be built right into the structure of Western modernity on account of the history of its origins. This is the same agonism projected onto categories like "Islam" and "the West" as either perpetually and naturally in conflict with each other or having nothing to say to the other. In this age of fractures and conflict, what would it mean to imagine science as a religious vocation? Or religion as a scientific vocation? To imagine secular reason as an ally of religious commitment, and rationality as an aspect of faith? And to imagine constraint as the source of freedom, not a denial of it? These kinds of questions demand ways of looking at the world and of speaking about it that fully acknowledge the bifurcated unities that actually constitute it rather than the fractured dualities that so often inhabit our speech about it.

Sayyid Ahmad Khan had precisely these kinds of concerns in mind when he created the Muhammadan Anglo-Oriental College as a conscious alternative to the incessant bickering about religion or science and Islam or the West. The naming of the college was itself a vivid act of reconciliation, integration, of *tatbi'a*, harmonizing. The furious antagonisms of our contemporary present demand a similar sensibility from all those who seek to secure it against the history-ending dreams of both moral pessimists and moral optimists. In their humble recognition of this world's fractured realities, and even separated by creeds and continents, Khan and Niebuhr were indeed kindred spirits. As they were also in the hope that attended their engagement with this imperfect reality and not despair in the face of it. For the meaning and end of time is not to be found in dreams of pasts or futures but in engaging this reality in the present with humility and hope. Between the limits of freedom and the freedom of limits is the middle space of our humanity. It is only by inhabiting this space actively and with vigor can the flow of history be sustained as a moral adventure without end.

The *Viva Activa*

Some seventy odd years ago, in what was then colonial India, a young girl was discovered in the woods near the small village of Changa in the northeastern state of Assam. To say that she was "discovered" is perhaps somewhat euphemistic. She was captured while trying to evade a British hunting party, a capture that was necessitated by the fact that she was being protected by a pack of no fewer than twelve wolves. During this capture, five members of her "pack" were killed and she herself put up one hell of a fight, biting and scratching to the last. Later, in a university hospital in Calcutta, anthropologists and biologists carefully scrutinized this rather peculiar specimen of the human species. It was established early in her examination that this young girl was in fact a child that had been missing from the village of Changa for some twelve years and who had been, according to what was till then the stuff of myth and legend, abducted as an infant by a female wolf. It would appear that the legend was at least in part true. But after twelve years of co-habitation with wolves in a jungle, the child presented a strange taxonomical puzzle for the researchers. She was entirely incapable of speech, and after months of attempts to teach her the rudiments of language, still could not utter a single word that made any sense whatsoever. Additionally, she continued to walk on all fours, with her callused knuckles serving as paws. Any attempt to clothe her was met with furious resistance and she refused to eat cooked food. Unable, and seemingly unwilling, to communicate and incapable of meeting the demands of basic social life, could this child still be reasonably called human? In a fictional retelling of these events, a Bengali anthropologist is said to have responded to this question with quite a bit of trepidation:

> How can I possibly answer that? She is not human; she is not a wolf. If we were to approach her in terms of her intelligence, then certainly we would say that she is closer to the wolves. But a wolf's intelligence is a completed thing; in other words, a wolf is just as intelligent as a

wolf should be. Whether she is as intelligent as a wolf should be, I don't
know. Presumably a wolf with her cranial capacity would be capable of
a great deal of learning. She, on the other hand, is not capable of the
kind of learning we would expect from this theoretical but nonexistent
wolf with a super-large cranial capacity. What, then, is the poor child?
A human being? No, I don't think she is a human being. A wolf? Quite
obviously she is not a wolf. We can conclude this: she has been denied
the opportunity to be a human being?[1]

The girl died within a year or so of being rescued and many are said to
have remarked that this was just as well. The girl was an abomination,
and in any case appeared to have been in constant pain during her ordeal
with the humans. With her death, order was restored at the sacred
boundaries separating the species, and anthropologists could return once
again to the study of human beings. In a final, if sentimental, gesture to
her lost humanity, her father held a traditional cremation ceremony for
her, complete with priests and the singing of Sanskrit hymns. A tenuous
link perhaps but a link nonetheless to the world of human beings she
never had the opportunity to inhabit. There is of course also her story
which persists to this day.[2]

*   *   *

In an article fantastically titled "Goodness, Savage Style" (*Wahshiyānah Nekī*)
by translator John W. Wilder, Sayyid Ahmad Khan relates a fictional story of
two men who have grown up together and share a deep personal bond.[3] In
modern parlance, we would call them blood brothers. Unfortunately, they both
fall in love with the same woman. Deducing, correctly, that this endangers their
bond, they sit down together to talk it over and figure out a way out of this
vexing problem. Not long after, they come up with what seems like an ideal
solution. They go over to the woman's house and murder her, thus removing
the one thing that threatened their bond to each other. Satisfied and happy with
this good resolution of their problem, they pat each other on the back. What
was Khan's purpose in relating this perplexing story? What's goodness to the
savage is not the same as goodness to a human being. To even call it goodness
is perhaps to misstate the nature of the savage's actions. The savage is savage
precisely because his moral discernment lacks human maturity. Morality is
merely an overdeveloped sense of instinct to him. In this case, the instinct for
the preservation of their near familial bond clarified a course of action for them,
and on which they then followed through. The two men of this story act from

pure intentions. They are not evil men. They lack the capacity to tell good from evil. And, in the end, such action merely confirms their savagery.

The savage is an interesting, in-between, entity that allows Sayyid Ahmad Khan to point to something essential about the human condition. The savage is not an animal and not fully human. He is the middle term in a tripartite taxonomy that overlays the division between animals and human beings. He is either unable or unwilling to be human. Khan is suggesting that being human is more a verb than a noun, something one chooses or enacts, not merely something one is. To be born a human being is no guarantee of one's humanity. The existence of the savage proves this proposition. Additionally, the savage also reveals something profoundly disturbing about the human condition. This is the temptation of reversion to animality that has stalked mankind from the very beginning. It is to prevent such reversion that God has sent His prophets, time and time again, to remind human beings of the moral nature of their existence. It is for this same reason that Muhammad was sent with the Qur'an to the *jahili* Arabs, the archetypical savages.

The case of the *jahili* Arabs also reveals that the condition of being savage should not be confused with the condition of lacking an advanced material culture or social refinement. The Arabs did not lack in either, and yet their normative sensibilities showed clear signs of savagery. What does savagery signify? That the normative arrow is pointing the wrong way. While the human being is clearly bifurcated, this duality is asymmetrical. Necessity cannot be escaped; it must be accounted for and dealt with. But it is in acts of freedom that the human being enacts its humanity. Similarly, the burden of moral obligation, of *taklif*, demands that man do the right thing, the good thing, though evil can never be wholly made absent from human affairs. Acknowledgment of duality is not a surrender to it. As with Niebuhr, Khan's realism is not neutral. Duality provides us with the capacity to reason, but the asymmetry also presents us with the necessary distinction to be good. We share our necessity with everything else. Our freedom, on the other hand, we do not share. And in this sense, to act like a human being is ultimately to act in freedom.

The struggle to be human, to remain human in the face of temptation to savagery is the ongoing reality of a life well-lived. And inasmuch as this aspiration to righteousness represents an inner battle against one's own baser impulses and inclination toward animality, one term that can be associated with this struggle within the Islamic tradition is "jihad."[4] This term often appears in the Qur'an within the broader formulation *al-jihad fi sabil Allah* or striving in the path of God, and has been understood by many Muslims throughout the ages as that active principle in Islam through which Muslims are required to struggle for greater self-knowledge and better moral discernment.[5] Though by no means definitive of the tradition itself, these conceptions of a *jihad bi-l qalb/nafs* or a jihad of the heart—a struggle against the evil persuasions of the devil—and of a *jihad bi-l lisan* or a jihad of the tongue—speaking the truth of Islam to others— have existed alongside the more commonly recognized notions of a *jihad bi-l saif* or a jihad of the sword and of a *jihad bi-l yad* or a jihad of the hand, the active, even militant, interventions into the affairs of the world and struggle in the path of God through war.[6] It is with these former two formulation of the meaning of jihad in mind that some modern Muslim scholars like Fazlur Rahman, Mahmoud Ayoub, and Ayesha Jalal have argued that "if the triad of submission (*islam*), faith (*iman*) and good conduct (*ihsan*) is constitutive of Islam, its moving principle is the notion of *jihad* as a spiritual, intellectual and moral struggle."[7] It is in this sense that jihad in the writings of these modern scholars often becomes epistemically indistinguishable from being and acting like a human being. It is obligatory, not optional. In this reading, Islam without jihad would be like a car without an engine or a route that leads precisely nowhere. If morality is the flow of time, jihad is the arrow that points it in the right direction. It is the kind of action that affirms and confirms one's humanity. Without constant struggle, man is in danger of reversion to savagery. The savage is a completed thing, static and sure. The human being is an active entity, like a shark that must keep swimming to keep itself from sinking to the ocean floor.

Of course, inasmuch as it is deployed in global public discourse, the term "jihad" has very different connotations in the world today. Already by the middle of the nineteenth century, it had acquired its synonymy with "holy war" in the minds of many Westerners. This was certainly true in post-1857 India when a plethora of articles and books by British authors accused Islam of being an inveterate and violent religion that demands its adherents fight a never-ending religious war against all infidels. Back then, jihad was often thrown into Muslim faces as a verbal spit. It still is today. It should be noted though that this association of jihad with warfare against the enemies of Islam is hardly unknown within the Islamic tradition itself. In fact, it was probably the dominant public meaning associated with the term as the Arab conquests of the early Islamic period matured into a full-fledged empire.[8] Jurists of this emerging Muslim empire quickly co-opted the qur'anic concept of jihad and tried to reduce its scope to the matter of making war against non-Muslims. In the affairs of the state, at least, it was largely stripped of its religio-ethical, its spiritual and ideological centrality in the practice of Islam and directed outward instead, at the enemy or the non-Muslim. Far from being a moving principle internal to the practice of

Islam, jihad in this juridical, "statist" formulation became a marker of political or religious difference. Because of the close relationship between jurists and the emerging Muslim state, this legal conception of jihad was, paradoxically, more in line with the secular or political aims of Muslim rulers than with the broadly religious aims suggested by alternative readings of its theological significance. In a manner of speaking then, the concept of jihad was secularized in the affairs of the state. Like the writers of the torture memos in the Bush administration, the jurists could be relied on to declare even other Muslim enemies as infidels and hence sanctify the struggle against them as a religious duty.

This "statist" conception of jihad acquired great significance in India where Muslim rulers had to deal with a majority non-Muslim population, and with local kings and maharajas who often resisted their economic and political domination. By the time of the Mughals, jihad had clearly come to mean two very different things to different groups of people. At the popular level, and especially in Sufi circles, it maintained the connotations of an everyday struggle for the acquisition of truth and of moral discernment, to know and to act in a manner right with one's nature as a servant of God.[9] Matters were very different at the level of the *'ulama* closely aligned with the state. Here, "an emphasis on the material rather than the spiritual aspects of *jihad* was symptomatic of a much broader collusion between secular authority and the would-be guardians of the sharia."[10] In the hands of these jurists, jihad often came to resemble a Muslim version of Just War Theory, pertaining to both the justification of going to a war and a guide for conduct during and after a war. It became a theological instrument for the legitimate assumption of political power over any polity that contained even a modicum of Muslim population.[11] Ayesha Jalal points out that such transparently cynical use of the concept "makes a parody of the Quranic idea of jihad."[12] The Qur'an makes a clear distinction between a war fought for worldly (*dunyawi*) interests, called *harb*, killing or violence, called *qital*, and jihad. This is not to suggest that the theological significance of jihad does not apply to other aspects of human life, to war and violence, etc. But jihad reduced to the conduct surrounding war and violence completely neuters the panoramic potency of the term. It is for this reason that in popular parlance in Mughal India, the jurists and *'ulama* who carried out such neutering at the behest of their rulers were pejoratively called *'ulama-i-duniya* (worldly scholars) and differentiated from the righteous, *'ulama-i-rabbani* (godly scholars) or *'ulama-i-akhirat* (scholars concerned with the hereafter and not this world.).[13]

This tension between jihad as a broad ethico-moral orientation and jihad narrowly defined as armed struggle has thus been a feature of Muslim theological thinking from very early on. The delicate equilibrium that allowed jihad to be understood and utilized differently in different circles could no longer hold as Muslim political power began to fade in India. From the middle of the eighteenth century, the "statist" conception of jihad began a gradual rise to prominence in the popular masses and even in militant Sufi circles. As ever-increasing numbers of Muslims became subjects to non-Muslim powers (Sikhs in the North, Marathas in Central India, and the British in the East), the idea of a righteous, armed struggle to regain lost glory and power became more appealing to many. So it was in the early nineteenth century that we see the first instance of non-state Muslim actors declaring jihad on a non-Muslim state power in the name of Islam. This was the jihad of the aforementioned Sayyid Ahmad Shahid and his *mujahidin* movement that declared the Sikh kingdom of Punjab *dar al-harb*, and then proceeded to wage relentless war against the Sikhs and the British. We are so well acquainted with Muslim fundamentalists throwing around the term "jihad" and declaring religious wars on this or that entity, that the novelty of such a formulation is lost on many of us. The idea that an individual or a ragtag group of Muslims could just "declare themselves an institution" and use a quasi-legal conception of jihad to justify their attacks on anyone was profoundly innovative and flew in the face of centuries of established jurisprudence and social precedence.[14] Even notwithstanding its suspect theological standing, the statist conception was designed precisely to limit the authority of waging war in the name of religion to rulers, and not to allow any Muslim subject to declare war on their own. But it was as if a Rubicon had been crossed with the jihad of Sayyid Ahmad Shahid. And the Muslims of India, and elsewhere, would now have to deal with this new and powerful idea that jihad as armed struggle could be understood as a personal obligation.

Sayyid Ahmad Khan was deeply troubled by the idea of jihad as armed struggle, and even more so by the notion that the assumption of state power was the primary raison d'être of the theological obligation of jihad.[15] It is with this in mind that he vociferously opposed any kind of agitation or armed resistance against the British government in India. Such agitation was based on false assumptions. The desire for overarching state power, or worldly sovereignty, should not be confused with the demands of creating a Muslim polity. These two different ends had become conceptually intertwined in the age of Muslim empires that followed the death of 'Ali, the last of the *Khalifa-i-Rashidun*, the rightly guided Caliphs. This was unfortunate. For a Muslim polity was a very different sort of thing than empires and countries. It is not a state, or a private home, but rather an egalitarian space of public discourse on moral issues or on matters of importance to the Muslim community. It both underlays and overlays the usual *dunyawi* communities, of nation and empire and tribe or family. The rightly guided caliphs knew this very well. Those who followed after 'Ali began to equate the *umma* with empire, and the caliphate with kingship. The open *agora* of the early caliphate gradually disappeared under the morass of worldly and secular concerns of these so-called Muslim rulers. Through his educational work, in publishing numerous journals and scientific gazettes, and in his speeches and other activism, Khan was clearly involved in the recovery of what he called *zaman-i-jadid*, the novel humanistic age of discovery that the Prophet augured but which was so quickly overwhelmed by the resurgence of *zaman-i-qadim*, the old regressive ways of savagery, among Muslims.[16] This new emphasis on jihad as an offensive war against the British (or other non-Muslims) was merely the latest iteration of an assertive animality among a certain subset of Muslims in India and had little or nothing to do with the obligation enjoined by the Qur'an.[17]

What needed emphasis in Muslim life instead was a different kind of jihad, a reconfigured and reconstructed version of the classical notion of *ijtihad*, or the exercise of one's discretionary opinion (*ra'y*) on the basis of knowledge (*'ilm*) of legal opinion. *Ijtihad* shares the consonant cluster J-H-D with, and hence is a variation on the root term jihad, implying struggle or exertion in the way of such knowledge. In its traditional use, *ijtihad* referred to the process of legal reasoning and hermeneutics through which the jurist-*mujtahid* derives or rationalizes law on the basis of the Qur'an and the Sunna.[18] But Khan (and some of his contemporary "modernists" like Jamal al-Din al-Afghani and Muhammad Abduh) expanded this term's narrowly juridical meaning to also include new forms of scientific and intellectual knowledge as the basis of reform not just of Islamic law but also of Muslim life as such.[19] Khan pointed out, for example, "what a great pity it is that the Muslims of this age have not only failed to discover any way to preserve the exercise of intellectual scrutiny, but have even discarded those methods which had been discovered in the past."[20] The Muslims' willful reversion to an ignorant state of existence, devoid of intellectual curiosity about the new world and rising antagonism toward those in it, augured a tragic decline into savagery that could only be avoided by humanizing injection of *ijitihad* into their lived reality.

But as usual, Khan's exhortations for an open-ended engagement with the new reality attendant to being Muslim in British India faced severe headwinds. Consider that after the disastrous events of 1857, Khan was faced by two opposing camps among his co-religionists. On one end were the so-called *mujahidin* mentioned above, many of whom fought in the mutiny against the British, and who insisted that Muslims could not legitimately practice their religion in any polity that was not led by a Muslim and governed by the laws of Islam. They equated jihad with the struggle to create a Muslim society through the capture of state power, and the thorough reorganization of society as such along Islamic lines. In this sense, theirs was a "socialist" conception of Islam, where jihad was not about moral discernment but about enforcement of a social order based on the rules and regulations contained in the Qur'an. On the other end were the traditionalist conservatives, most closely associated with the 'ulama of Dar-ul-Ulum in the north Indian city of Deoband (from which the movement associated with these 'ulama takes its popular name, Deobandi). They had largely reconciled themselves to the loss of political power by proclaiming that the fundamental obligations of Islam were to purify one's heart and to organize one's private life in a manner that most closely resembled the example of the prophet. British imperial rule in India represented a grave danger to the pure practice of Islam and therefore required Muslims to recommit to the original teachings of Islam as contained within the four major schools of Sunni jurisprudence. In time, Deobandis also became associated with proselytizing (*da'wah*) movements inside and outside India under the auspices of the Tablighi Jamaat (Missionary Party).[21] And in more recent years, their close theological connection with militant movements like the Taliban in Afghanistan, and Sipah-i-Sahaba and Laskar-i-Jhangvi in Pakistan has rendered the term "Deobandi" a casual designation of radical Islam or political resistance to the West. But in its earliest iteration, the Deoband movement was a rearguard action against further erosion of Islamic norms among the Muslim population of India and its teachings were almost entirely moralistic, focused on living a virtuous life, maintaining proper decorum of dress and food, praying five times a day, and organizing the private relations of marriage, property, parenthood, and family along Islamic lines. As the historian Barbara Metcalf points out, "the brutal repression of the so-called Mutiny of 1857 against the British had fallen very hard on north Indian Muslims [and in its] aftermath, the 'ulama, not surprisingly, adopted a stance of a-political quietism."[22] In contradistinction to the jihadis, these 'ulama largely decided to opt out of political engagement with the powers that be altogether. Instead, they were interested in creating a parallel society of virtuous Muslims. The struggle to preserve Islam in these times of great existential danger was the primary obligation of their jihad. After the devastation of 1857, everything else was secondary.

Khan naturally drew the ire of both these camps because he believed in neither the private moralistic conception of jihad among the Deobandis nor the overly statist idea of the jihadis who equated it strongly with the assumption of political power. Sieved through the notion of *ijtihad*, Khan's version of jihad more closely resembled a humanistic struggle for greater knowledge and discernment both about moral matters and about the world of human beings. Like those Christians that decry Constantinianism, or the corruption of original Christianity due to its involvement with the machinations of state power, Khan was of the opinion that worldly concerns had overwhelmed the discursive focus of jihad and turned it into an instrument of political power. And with the loss of political power, this instrumental understanding of jihad had now infected the larger body politic of Muslim societies. This explained why Muslims in India were either constantly clamoring for the end of British rule through forceful violence or were retreating into their ghettos and *madrasas*, advocating political quietude in deference to narrowly moral concerns. But neither of these attitudes conformed to the properly righteous focus on struggle, exertion, engagement, and action. What was this righteous focus? That Muslims seek to live in sociopolitical contexts where they can continue to develop their capacities for moral discernment and for seeking knowledge and truth as only human beings can.

* * *

Later in his life, Sayyid Ahmad Khan began to see the hand of divine providence in the loss of Muslim state power in India and elsewhere. On his (in)famous trip to Europe, Khan experienced a world of open discussion, of magazines and salons, newspapers and journals, of scientific communities and political debates. He realized that the loss of political power had in fact opened up a new space of deliberation in between concerns of standard governance and the private household.[23] This is what we now call the sphere of civil society, of free association and freedom of opinion. The modern West had stumbled upon the kind of egalitarian space of communal deliberation that Khan imagined the early Muslim community tried to create in Medina and then in Mecca during the time of the rightly guided Caliphs.[24] As discussed in the previous chapter, Khan believed that the *jahili* Arab society lacked such a space. Their speech was assertive, not deliberative. Truth was a function of either power or sedimented tradition. Islam had broken through this sedimentation and freed the *jahili* mind to explore the possibilities of discovery through communal discourse rather than by diktat or imitation. Of course, the Qur'an provided much guidance on important matters, and during the life of the Prophet, his conduct and example were sacrosanct. But in the Prophet's absence, Muslims were instructed to guide themselves. And the mode of such guidance was to be deliberation.[25] It should be noted that Khan did not imagine such deliberation as a democratic free for all. In fact, (taking a cue for John Stuart Mill) he explicitly argued that since "India [had] not attained the status of an advanced society, a pre-requisite for representative government . . . the concept of election based on democracy or universal adult franchise" must be opposed until the Indian body politic was sufficiently ready.[26] For Khan, the closest Western analog to the mode of rule in the early Muslim community was probably the Roman republic in the years before it gave way to empire. The council of electors, *majlis* or *shura* of learned and important men of the community served much the same function as the Roman senate, not only electing the caliph but also debating important matters on the open floor.[27] As the community rapidly expanded in those early years, new groups of people would have become important members of the *majlis*. But soon enough, the self-professed egalitarianism of this early community gave way to an imperial order.[28] All Islamic polities since that time had been imperial societies of one sort or another. Now suddenly, after all these years, Muslims had come to find themselves in a rather novel situation. The imperial aspect of the *umma* had been swept away by superior political powers. And Islam's strong association with state power on the one hand and with private moral conduct on the other now had the potential to be reconfigured to reflect its core deliberative roots.[29]

It is with such a reconfiguration in mind that Khan first advocated the learning of foreign languages, and especially English, to bring Muslims out of their shells and communicate vigorously with their British overlords about their concerns. Speaking to an audience at the Muhammadan Literary Society in Calcutta (which Khan co-founded), he argued that "no religious prejudices interfere with our learning any language spoken by any nation of the world. From remote antiquity, we have studied Persian and no prejudice has ever interfered with the study of that language. How then can any religious objection be raised against our learning and perfecting ourselves in English."[30] To attain this objective, Khan founded the Scientific Society of Ghazipur in 1864 to both translate works from foreign languages into Urdu and begin the process of acquainting the Muslim community with English and other European languages. These works included texts in the natural and human sciences, philosophy, literature, and political economy. The idea was to improve the status of the Western sciences in the Muslim population and also provide this population with an adequate familiarity with European language and life for a fruitful conversation going forward. Ignorance on both sides about both sides had done enormous damage to the relationship between Muslims and the British in the years before and after the mutiny of 1857. Khan was adamant that such ignorance not be allowed to undercut a relationship he took to be essential to the future progress of Muslims.

It is for this same reason that Khan strongly advocated for native voices in the colonial legislative councils that deliberated regularly on issues of law and public policy in India and were tasked with making recommendations to the colonial administration on such matters. As I have already noted, Khan believed that the fundamental cause of the revolt was the inability or unwillingness of the native population to adequately voice their opinions and their concerns in open forums. In the absence of engagement, Muslims had either retreated back into their households or taken up arms against the British. Both the British and Muslims now needed to be coaxed back into deliberative, communicative interactions. And Khan was certainly up for this task. In speech after speech, he exhorted his fellow Muslims to be more engaged in "[pointing] out to the defects of the government and the shortcomings they experience in its workings. If the subjects fail to do this they cannot be considered as loyal subjects."[31] On the other hand, he consistently demanded that the colonial government listen to the voices and concerns of its Muslim subjects, "for they *must* have the opportunity to criticize and their criticism will be helpful to the government."[32] In founding numerous societies and associations that brought Europeans and native Indians together for discussion, deliberation, and frank conversation, Sayyid Ahmad Khan positioned himself squarely in the middle, as a conduit, a medium, for just the kind of communication he advocated for throughout his life.

What was Khan's philosophical basis for this strong advocacy of both the legitimacy of the British colonial government *and* the ability of its subjects to criticize it? It was the belief that freedom of opinion, and not political self-determination, was the most basic and natural human right. Khan was so taken by John Stuart Mill's work that he paraphrased and expanded Mill's famous formulation in his own writing:

> Suppose, all men, except one, agree upon one thing, and only that particular man maintains a different opinion; in such a case, all those men do not have the right to condemn his views. There is no reason to hold that whereas any five men have a perfect right to contest the correctness of the opinion of five others, one man does not have the right to challenge nine others. . . . If it is possible that the opinion of nine is correct in comparison to one, it can also be possible that the view of one man is correct in comparison to nine.[33]

The role of the state should be limited to providing order and security, and social conditions adequate for the continuation of conversations among its subjects, and between itself and its subjects. A state ruled by a Muslim has no different basis for legitimacy than a state ruled by a non-Muslim. An Islamic polity is one in which the *ijma'* of its inhabitants, be they Muslim or non-Muslim, is allowed to coalesce into sound public opinion through debate and discussion. In fact, the original constitution of Medina, the document which provided the early Muslims with the template for how to run a government, was forged in conversation not just among Muslims (who were a minority) but between the followers of Muhammad and the local Jews, Christians, and all other tribes of Yathrib. In this it resembled the constitutional republics and monarchies of the modern West much more than the kingdoms and empires of latter-day Islam. Muslims who clung to the notion of Islam as a state authority enforcing the laws of the Qur'an were peddling the *bida'at* of kings and emperors, which were designed to serve their own secular interests and ends and not the religious ends for which Islam was revealed to mankind. And this religious end was nothing other than providing the basis for a proclamation of one's humanity in the exercise of one's freedom:

> Liberty is a natural right of the individual which is not to be interfered with, as such interference is destructive of the human self. God may be said to be the author of this right. Freedom is the essence of human life, and it is the condition for the realization of all that man has been made capable of by God and Nature.[34]

Every issue of Khan's *Aligarh Institute Gazette* bore the inscription, "To permit the liberty of the Press is the part of a wise government, to preserve it is the part of a Free People." British rule in India was benign and legitimate as long as it allowed for the free expression of all opinions. Khan claimed that "liberty of the Press is the prominent duty of the government and a natural right of the subjects. People have every right to express their views and the government that checks them is not a civilized one."[35] The free press was, bar none, the modern West's greatest creation. The notion that all can speak was so powerful to Khan that he claimed it was the most basic of all human rights. Indeed, was this not what Muhammad was denied in Mecca, and the main reason he and his followers had to leave their homes for Medina?[36] And the first mosque was the Prophet's home in Medina where people would gather to listen to him speak and to talk to each other about both religious issues and matters of importance to the well-being of the community. This was the model for both the communal mosque and the *majlis* of the early caliphate.

*   *   *

Sayyid Ahmad Khan founded numerous institutes and associations and was the organizing force behind at least a dozen journals, gazettes, and magazines. But his single, self-professed, and greatest achievement was the Muhammadan Anglo-Oriental (MAO) College in Aligarh. Founded in 1875, it brought together the multifaceted foci of his entire mission in one place. Khan modeled the college on the educational institutions he had seen in Europe, where young men lived in a community of discourse rather than being taught by a single teacher or learning merely from books. Speaking to a gathering of Muslims in Meerut on the nature and value of education, Khan laid out the reasons why a university set up in this way is essential to the creation and sustenance of a Muslim polity:

> [What] I wish to see established in our people is national [*qaumi*] feeling and sympathy; and this cannot be created unless the boys of our nation [*qaum*] read together. At this moment we all of us have come together the assembly itself has an effect on our hearts, and an involuntary emotion gives birth to the thought— "Our Nation! Our Nation!"—but when we separate the effect vanishes. This is not merely my assertion; I trust all here will acknowledge its truth. If you will reflect on the principles of religion, you will see the reason why our Prophet ordered all the dwellers in one neighborhood to meet five times a day for prayer in the mosque, and why the whole town had to meet together on Fridays in the city mosque, and on *Eid* all the people of the district had to assemble. The reason was that the effect of the gathering should influence all, and create a national feeling among those present. . . . Hence it is necessary for the good training and education of the Muhammadans that they should gather together into one place to receive it; that they may live together and eat together, and learn to love one another.[37]

The mosque, the *majlis*, and the university are in this sense all different versions of the same kind of space. They are spaces where individual human beings leave the comfort of their own homes and gather together in communal spirit. It is not without significance that for the first headmaster of MAO College, Khan's choice was neither himself nor another Muslim, but rather a Christian and an Englishman. The communal spirit he sought to elevate among the Muslims of his time was not imagined narrowly as the spirit of Muslim solidarity. The word *qaum* that Khan often used to describe community has elicited much controversy over the years. This is because it has often been translated as "nation" and has therefore picked up all kinds of connotations that Khan never intended. In fact, nationalism of the sort that we are now familiar with was one of the banes of Khan's intellectual existence. The political association of Islam with a kind of nationalistic, statist enterprise was the primary focus of Khan's most celebrated and vociferous modernist critic, Sayyid Jamal al-Din al-Afghani.

In many ways, Afghani and Khan were kindred spirits when it came to the importance of the modern sciences, and on the idea of jihad as a constant struggle for better moral discernment and for the acquisition of new forms of knowledge. Afghani claimed that God made man in such a way that the ends of man's existence could not be attained without struggle. At the same time, God has endowed man with the capacity to think and to reason, which were the prerequisites for the attainment of ever greater knowledge about himself and the world around him. Wisdom for Afghani was the natural corollary of man's acquisition and use of his knowledge to overcome the obstacles in his path, be they natural, social, economic, or political. According to Afghani, success or failure are merely consequences of the level of knowledge one brings to the problem. It is this understanding that made him proclaim that "the king of the world is science," and that "the military conquests are not of the French or the English but it is knowledge projecting its magnificence and glory, and ignorance has no other way except its inferiority and servitude to science."[38] The importance of the sciences and the acquisition of knowledge notwithstanding, Afghani did not share Sayyid Ahmad Khan's confidence that such knowledge could in fact lead to the betterment of the Muslim people while they continued to exist in a state of servitude to the West. Afghani pointed out that "while the utility of the modern sciences, the urgency to popularize them among the Muslims is indisputable," such a task "cannot be accomplished unless it is supported first by a sovereign political power and secondly by sound finance."[39] In the regime of European imperialism, Muslims had neither. Afghani accused those like Khan, and other modernist reformers in Egypt and Turkey, who believed that by opening a few schools in the European mold and educating some members of the Muslim elites they could bring about a renewal of Muslim society as grossly "miscalculating the trends of the prevailing conditions."[40] At its core, the fundamental and most urgent problem of the Muslim world was a political one, and for Afghani, the solution would need to be political as well.

Afghani had no delusions about the sorry state of the Ottoman Caliphate in his time, but he saw it as a strategic nexus around which he could rally the Muslim community as a whole. Additionally, he saw the *Khilafat* (Caliphate) as providing the centralizing core for his plans to bring the *'ulama* of the entire Muslim world together in order to forge an informed consensus on Islamic *ijtihad*. He understood resisting the imperial ambitions of the West in religious terms, and war against them a religious and holy war that was critical to the continued survival, development, and progress of the Muslim people. It was with reference to these aims that Afghani vociferously, and mercilessly, attacked

Sayyid Ahmad Khan, calling him the pejorative *niechiri*, a doomed naturalist who failed to understand that social and political cohesion and sovereignty were as critical to the advancement of Muslim society as scientific development. "The sect of the *Neichiris*, among whatever people they appear, try to nullify those beliefs [of universal bonds of cohesion] and those qualities [of love of the nation]. From them destruction penetrates the pillars of the social order of the people and heads them toward dissolution, until they are suddenly destroyed."[41]

But Sayyid Ahmad Khan believed that Afghani and his ilk had fundamentally misunderstood the true nature of Islamic politics. Khan did not see himself as anti-political. He just did not buy into the agitational politics that many of his co-religionists were bent on calling jihad. In fact, Afghani's ideas appeared more in line with the Western notion of ethnic nationalism than with the kind of Islamic polity that Khan envisioned for the Muslims of India. If the idea of free speech and press, or open inquiry and discussion, were the West's great gifts to the rest of the world, nationalism and statism were the great evils. The idea that the be-all and end-all of political identity was in the nationalization of political discourse, instantiated in the demands for state power, was anathema to Khan. The calls for the renewal of the caliphate rang far and wide in the Muslim world. But this renewal had as its template not the rightly guided caliphs of the early Muslim community but the nationalistic movements sweeping across Europe in the nineteenth century. Islam was like Germany, Italy, or Spain to these folks, to be cobbled together into a single political unit in a wave of nationalistic fervor. This was tribalism by another name. Modern Western states had assumed a kind of familial model where the government functions as an overarching mechanism providing for the needs of the people much like a tribal chief is responsible for his kin. Such a situation is ripe with the possibility of confusion between non-instrumental moral concerns and the narrower national interests of self-assertion and survival. Nations go to war for much the same reason that the two savages murdered the poor woman who they supposedly loved; to serve their own interests at the expense of others. It is in coming up with the moral justifications for their self-interested, instrumental actions that they muddy the waters and obfuscate moral truth. Nationalist sensibility confused with morality ("my country, right or wrong") makes the task of moral discernment much harder. It is an obstacle to the practice of *ijtihad*, not a boon to it. Yet, Muslims everywhere were buying this nationalistic and statist conception of Islam hook, line, and sinker. The caliphate imagined as a modern state was a dangerous diversion. Those aspects of Western sociality (intellectual pluralism and freedom of opinion) that were in fact in line with the obligation of jihad were being ignored, while the most troubling forms of sociality (nationalism and statism) were being valorized as the very meaning of Islam. And these confusions and conflations were a grave danger to the practice of Islam and to the Muslims of India.

The underlying reasons for this myriad of confusions were the series of historical accidents by which the right to free speech had become intertwined with the twin notions of self-determination and toleration in the West. When it came to scientific advancement, free exchange of ideas was considered essential to progress. As was the free exchange of goods considered instrumental to economic success.[42] But in many other spheres of public activity, freedom of opinion was imagined as merely a negative right, not productive toward anything in particular but necessary to keep the peace. It was imagined as a narrowly political right assuring that people be allowed to say what they want concerning religious or moral matters and be allowed to voice their opinions in the public sphere and allow others to do the same. Khan disagreed with this formulation. Intellectual pluralism and free exchange of ideas are an "epistemological" right no matter what sphere it is applied to. It is productive toward better discernment of the truth value of propositions, be they scientific, economic, moral, or political. This is the true value of the right to free speech.

Khan suggests that unwillingness to admit to the possible correctness of an opposing opinion is to claim that "our conviction holds the position of infallibility, and to forbid conversation and argument about [the opposing opinion] is to consider oneself greater than the prophets: incapable of error."[43] Furthermore, this does even more damage to one's own viewpoint that to that of our opponents. For "if the opposing viewpoint is correct, then [one] would miss the correct idea. And if the opinion is wrong, the refusal to debate it removes the opportunity to compare the false with the true and thus to obtain an excellent benefit of strengthening the correct view and making the influence of its truth greater."[44] Khan was a great admirer of Sir Isaac Newton and uses his example to make this point:

> If Newton's wisdom, his astronomy and his Theory of Gravity, were not admissible to criticism and discussion, the world could not have placed such firm confidence in their truth as it now does. Is there any opposition that people have spared toward this wise philosopher? And what religious taunt has not been made against that wise man and the bearer of true views? But we must ponder over the result of this opposition: Today all the world, both wise and foolish, both learned and prejudiced followers of religion, all acknowledge him, all admit him to be right, and *his truth has become more firmly established in people's hearts than religious creeds.* (Emphasis added.)[45]

The final line is, of course, the most important one. And this development, that while science advances in its ability to discern material truths about nature and God's creation, religion has been retreating for years into a shell, not admitting to any competition, worried Khan no end. Khan believed that it is for this reason that religion was losing ground in Europe and would eventually lose ground among his own community as well if they do not break the shackles of their own obscurantism. Instead of debating with their European counterparts, and even with those of their co-religionists who disagreed with them, too many Muslim scholars, leaders, and ordinary folks were digging themselves an epistemological hole from which they would never emerge. They may even take the whole community down with them. They were more interested in self-preservation than truth, for if "an opinion cannot be discussed fairly, fearlessly, and boldly, it will be judged a dead and decaying opinion, and not a living, true reality and that it will never be able to find acceptance as one of those truths whose influence permanently affects the outlook of the people."[46] This is because "truth does not possess any miraculous power by which it may take possession of the mind by itself. It's only miraculous to the extent that it possesses no fear of discussion."[47] The truths of these obscurantists were dead and decaying truths and lacked any ability to frame an effective conception of the good life for Muslims of their age. They were possessed of fear and denial, and no truth can survive that. This is because human truth, be it scientific, moral, or any other kind of truth, has no other means of production and refinement over time than through such a method. For "wisdom may not be attained through any other method than this." Indeed, the distinctive feature of human intelligence is that it cannot become cultured and reasonable any other way: "No other basis can be considered for placing confidence in any matter, but the basis of a permanent habit of comparing one's opinion with that of others, and then reforming and perfecting it."[48] This process, this constant struggle for greater refinement and perfection, depends on the courage to admit to one's fallibility and the persistence to make this a "permanent habit." And the cultivation and practice of such a permanent habit is nothing other than the obligation of jihad.

* * *

Sayyid Ahmad Khan makes two interlocking claims about truth in light of the nature of human intelligence and the demands of human reason. First, that truth of propositions has an internal relationship to the demands of human sociality. Khan suggests that "it is pleasing, but fallacious to say that even without debate and the presentation of reasons, a correct opinion will enter and take root in people's minds."[49] He was responding here directly to the Doctrine of Conformity (*taqlid*) to one of the four schools (*madhahib*) of Sunni Islamic Law (and generally discouraging inter-school eclecticism) popular among the run-of-the-mill Muslim legists and prominent conservatives of his time.[50] This doctrine stated that Muslims should conform to their traditions and should disengage from open discussion about "settled" matters. But while conformity may have preserved some semblance of theological stability, it also had the effect of making Muslim youth completely disinterested in theological matters. So Khan asks, "Now Muslims should look at their condition in a fair spirit and see if, because of this very opposition to free opinion because of Conformity, their entire theological structure, whether derived from traditional or rational disciplines, is actually fallen into [a state of decline] or not."[51] The reason for such a decline has to do with the way in which the human mind interacts with ideas, internalizes them as ethical imperatives, and is convinced of their rightness not merely in a formal sense but also in an active sense. Do beliefs and ideas lead to actual praxis or only nominal acceptance? Khan believed that once ideas have become sedimented as a given tradition,

> the creed or doctrine that [past] leaders established with such great labors begin to decline. Then all the holy people who are counted as leaders begin to complain that they find in the hearts of believers no effects at all of those beliefs, which the latter have accepted in name only. And although the believers outwardly accept those beliefs and doctrines, their conduct, morals, habits, and culture fail to be actually influenced by them.[52]

These believers "accept the customs of their forefathers or religious preceptors as though they were sacred relics," not as ethical injunctions.[53] And truth devoid of action is no truth at all.

Second, truth in the regime of the human condition has an internal relationship with it being exposed constantly to discussion and debate. This is as true of moral truths as of any other. Even correct opinions, if not frequently challenged and confirmed, begin to lose the quality of "correctness" over time. This is because the quality of correctness is not an objective quality that resides in a proposition independent of its reception in the world. It is a feature of its existence in the world. It is with this in mind that Khan makes the following claim:

> When people are forced to hear arguments on both sides of a matter, there is always hope for justice, but when they hear only one side, falsehoods become

obdurate and turn into prejudice. *Even truth does not retain the effect of truth because it tends to get more and more exaggerated until it turns into a lie.* The virtue of justice, which resides in mankind, comes to useful effect most clearly when, at the time of the public hearing of each case, the contenders and supporters of both sides are present face to face, and both are forceful enough to present their arguments and reasons compellingly to the people. Apart from this procedure there is no way of attaining the truth.[54]

Truth becomes falsehood, and the correct incorrect, if it is not reliably tackled in the *agora* of open discussion. This is not toleration of opposing points of view, but rather the desire to know the truth as best as a fallible creature like a human being can and must. Without the cultivation of this habit, of this desire, human beings become savages. They lose their humanity, either to the serenity of mere toleration or the obduracy of stubborn conviction. Khan saw his fellow Muslims going the latter route, and the West often going the former. And neither route was a route fit for human travel.

*   *   *

The modern age is a mess of contradictions. With one hand it gives, and with the other, it takes away. Khan struggled all his life to trim the hedges, so to say, to clear out the weeds from this garden of modernity. Like Gandhi after him, he warned of the ruinous danger of accepting Western modernity wholesale.[55] Why was there such danger? Because in far too many ways, the emerging Western order could be deeply dehumanizing. Khan saw much of this first hand: the overly bureaucratized nature of Western governance; the propensity to count and taxonomize all aspects of national life; the persistent attempts to turn every aspect of public life into settled law; the homogenizing tendencies of nationalist sentiment; the equation of agonism with politics, where the search for truth is made secondary to winning the argument. Whereas Western civil society was clearly a boon to the humanistic impulses of Islam, the Western nation-state, and its concomitant institutional and political infrastructure, was a serious problem for Khan. It was as if the Western mind suffered from a deep-seated schizophrenia. It was the kind of mental illness that Muslims could and should do without.

What was the source and nature of these dehumanizing aspects of Western modernity? Khan lists them in passing but makes no rigorous attempt to explore the nature of the problem. He was too busy laying out a plan for Islam to take in the best and avoid the worst of what the West had to offer. And in any case, his knowledge of Western political and intellectual history was inadequate to the task. Writing a good half-century after Sayyid Ahmad Khan, Hannah Arendt engages with this question in a manner that Khan may well have approved of. In a collection of essays titled *The Promise of Politics*, Arendt gives an evocative account of the dangers of the modern condition that is strangely reminiscent of Khan's take on the *jahili* Arabs of the desert:

> The modern growth of worldlessness, the withering away of everything *between* us, can also be described as the spread of the desert. . . . Modern psychology is desert psychology: when we lose the faculty to judge—to suffer and condemn— we begin to think that there is something wrong with us if we cannot live under the conditions of the desert. Insofar as psychology tries to help us, to help us adjust to those conditions, taking away our only hope, namely that we, who are *not of the desert though we live in it*, are able to transform it into a human world. . . . Precisely because we suffer under desert conditions we are still human and intact; the danger lies in becoming true inhabitants of the desert and feeling at home in it.[56]

This "worldlessness" prompts two kinds of responses in the suffering human being. These are the storms in the desert of Arendt's metaphor. The first is "totalitarian movements whose chief characteristic is that they are extremely well adjusted to the conditions of the desert. In fact they reckon with nothing else, and therefore seem to be the most adequate political form of desert life."[57] The second danger, the more common one, is "escapism: to escape from the world of the desert, from politics, into . . . whatever it may be, is less dangerous and more subtle form of ruining the oases [of humanity] than the sandstorms that menace their existence, as it were, from without."[58] It is out of these

> conditions of worldlessness that first appeared in the modern age—which should not be confused with Christian *otherworldliness*—grew the question of Leibniz, Schelling and Heidegger: Why there is anything at all and not rather nothing? And out of the specific conditions of our contemporary world, which menace us not only with no-thingness but also no-bodyness, may grow the question, why is there anybody at all, and not rather nobody?[59]

Just as Khan decries the opposing impulses of totalitarianism and isolation among Muslims of his day, Arendt identifies these impulses as internal to the modern condition as such. And she offers a remedy that Khan himself embodied throughout much of his life: "Only those who can endure the passion of living under desert conditions can be trusted to summon up in themselves the courage that lies at the root of action, of becoming an active being."[60] Only such an active being can transform the desert into an oasis fit for human existence, much like Muhammad and his followers did in seventh-century Arabia.

What is this "worldlessness" that besets the modern age? In the aptly titled *The Human Condition*, Hannah Arendt offers a tripartite taxonomy similar to Khan's.[61] First, *animal laborans* is the kind of entity that finds the entirety of its meaning in the condition of *labor*, which is that set of activities which corresponds to the biological processes of the human body; metabolism and eventual decay are bound to the virtual necessities produced and fed by life.[62] Second, *Homo faber*, on the other hand, is the kind of entity that finds the entirety of its meaning in the condition of *work*, which is that set of activities which corresponds to the unnaturalness of human existence, and which fabricates an "artificial" world of things, distinctly different from natural surroundings.[63] The primary standard of normative preference for *animal laborans* is necessity, and for *Homo faber*, it is instrumentality. The former exists in nature as a natural thing, whereas the latter is a destroyer of nature, using it instrumentally for the creation of the World. But who inhabits the World? For Arendt, the ascent of consumer culture and mass society in the modern age is the valorization of an *animal laborans* mode of being, as is the Marxist conception of labor as the fundamental human activity. The rising tide of commercialism and international market capitalism of the voracious variety is an indication of the rise of *Homo faber* and his instrumental use of nature (which includes *animal laborans*) for the endless construction and acquisition of things.

Finally, it is in such circumstances that "*action*, the only activity that goes on directly between men without the intermediary of things or matter," begins to disappear from the world.[64] When human beings cease to inhabit the world that *Homo faber* has created and that *animal laborans* sustains, when it becomes devoid of human action, worldlessness becomes the condition of human existence. For action is that mode of activity which "corresponds to the human condition of plurality," and "this plurality is specifically *the* condition—not only the *conditio sine qua non* but also the *conditio per quam*—of political life."[65] Action is the mechanism by which human beings engage with the fact of their plurality, the fact that "we are all the same, that is, human, in such a way that nobody is ever the same as anyone else who ever lived, lives or will ever live."[66] It is this condition of plurality that the modern notion of equality (as opposed to the ancient notion which I discuss below) undercuts in the valorization of mass society. What is mass society? It is that form of society that "equalizes under all circumstances, and the victory of equality in the modern world is only the political and legal recognition of the fact that society has conquered the public realm and that distinction and difference have become private matters of the individual."[67] It is for this reason that the modern age sees the rise of two supposedly opposite forms of governance which are in essence equally anti-political: the despotisms of one-man rule (or ideologically driven single system rule) and the various tyrannies of no-man rule (bureaucratic states and nationalisms of one sort or another). Arendt can be faulted perhaps for not making enough of a distinction between the limited tyrannies of liberal democracies and the ghastly regimes that seek to "normalize" their populations through the use of coordinated force. But with regard to her underlying premise, the distinction is not as clear as it may appear from a different vantage point. Her claim is that mass societies of the liberal West are just as dehumanizing as any other in the modern world. That they do not kill their citizens with impunity, and they do maintain a certain degree of tolerance for differences of personal opinion, is a different matter altogether. Arendt's pessimism can be quite relentless. In this at least, she and Sayyid Ahmad Khan are very different indeed.

*   *   *

Aristotle was always the explicit frame of normative reference for much of Hannah Arendt's mature work. She was often mocked as a conservative Grecophile by many of her liberal contemporaries. Others found her fascination with the past perplexing in an age where the *sensis communis* of the West was so clearly future-oriented. Some called her anti-modern and obscurantist, and later in life, anti-woman. These were unfair critiques. She did not fit a mold. She was deeply uncomfortable with the priorities of the modern West. Central to this discomfort was her belief that far from expanding political participation to the masses (as the triumphalist liberal democrats contended), Western modernity was in the process of radically depoliticizing the public sphere. And the champions of modernity were so in thrall of all its many attendant projects that the death of politics appeared as the triumph of freedom to them. They had fundamentally misconstrued the nature and meaning of politics and of human freedom. Political action and participation is not something that human beings do; it is humanizing action, the practice of our humanity. It is that specific form of moral praxis that distinguishes us, and our freedom, from the world of necessity and law. Arendt saw this distinction fast eroding in the modern world as the needs of necessity were being discursively elevated to the demands of freedom. And it is with the preservation of this distinction that she was most concerned. She feared that humans would gradually devolve into glorified, self-satisfied animals without the maintenance of such distinctions. And that would be tragic indeed.

It was in Aristotle's distinction between the polis, the city, and the *oikia*, the household, that Arendt found an excellent philosophical scaffolding for the construction of a monumental critique of such modern depoliticization. The polis is fundamentally different from the *oikia* in several important ways for Aristotle. First, the ends that constitute the natural reason for their existence are different. The household exists primarily as the means of securing life itself. "The family is the association established by nature for the supply of man's everyday wants."[68] It is the context for economic and productive activities that aim at accounting for "the bare needs of life."[69] The polis has an essentially different character than the *oikia* because "a polis exists for the sake of a good life, and not for the sake of life only."[70] A good life is the life "of noble and just actions, a life of ethical and intellectual virtue,"[71] and "the political society exists for the sake of noble actions."[72]

Second, the subjects that constitute the polis and the *oikia* are different. The household is composed of masters and slaves, fathers and sons, husbands and wives, where the head of the household necessarily exists in a position of absolute and unified authority over the others. In fact, the Greek word for the head of household is *despotikon*, from which the modern term "despot" is derived. "The rule of a household is a monarchy," according to Aristotle, "for every house is under *one* head."[73] For Aristotle, the rule of the master over his slaves (and his sons who are not yet of age) is natural, necessary, and just with regard to the constitutive ends of the household, for "no man can live well, or indeed live at all, unless he be provided with necessities," and the slave or servant is "a kind of instrument for maintaining life."[74] The relations between the *despotikon* and his slaves, sons, and servants is one of possession, the most acute kind of inequality, for the slave is by nature "a living possession."[75] The polis is not constituted by the end of seeking and preserving life, and therefore, the subjects which compose it are not marked by the natural inequality that marks the household. "For there is one kind of rule over subjects who are by nature free, another over subjects who are by nature slaves."[76] The polis has an essentially different kind of rule, a "constitutional rule," which is by definition "a government of free men and equals."[77] The good life is a life of virtue and noble actions, of reasoned speech. And the development of a sense of justice and sufficient equality are necessary preconditions for these ends to be realized concretely. As Aristotle puts it in the *Nicomachean Ethics*, "[political justice] is found among men who share their life with a view to self-sufficiency, men who are free and either proportionally or arithmetically equal, so that between those who do not fulfill this condition there is no political justice."[78] A plurality of equal and free men who are ruled by a constitutional order, "whose mutual relations are governed by law," is the necessary context for the realization of the good life.[79]

Although the ends of the polis and the *oikia* are distinct, they are nonetheless also related. Aristotle clearly believes that there is a natural developmental relationship between the family or household and the city-state, and that this relationship also establishes the hierarchy that operates between them. Groups of families designed by nature to provide for life come together to form villages which are more self-sufficient than single households, and on and on it goes until it culminates in the ideal, most complete form of society.

> When several villages are united in a single complete community, large enough to be nearly and quite self-sufficient, the state comes into existence, originating in the bare needs of life, and continuing in existence for the sake of the good life. And therefore, if the earlier forms of society are natural, so is the state, for it is the end of them, and the nature of a thing is its end.[80]

What Aristotle is clearly suggesting here is that the *nature* of the household, from the very beginning, is the state. It is the end for which the household exists. And by extension, life itself, which is the end associated with the activities and structure of the household, is merely a provisional end. Just as the *oikia* is the means to the end of the polis, "life has its primary value as a ground for the attainment of the good life."[81]

What separates the household from the political association is also what connects them in a natural teleology of priority. The polis only emerges as, and through, the association of those who have become self-sufficient through the natural development of their prior associations to this end. This emergence, although naturally related to the previous associations, nevertheless constitutes a break from them because self-sufficiency makes possible a fundamentally different kind of life that is no longer merely occupied with the instrumental concerns of sufficiency and necessity. This is what Aristotle means when he says that "the state is by nature clearly prior to the family and to the individual, since the whole is of necessity prior to the part."[82] The family or the individual are parts in relation to the whole of the polis because the ends of securing life are only sufficiently realized in the self-sufficiency that undergirds a city-state. "The proof that the state is a creation of nature and prior to the individual is that the individual, when isolated, is not self-sufficing; and therefore he is a part in relation to the whole."[83] The whole is that particular form of association in which the goals and ends of all other forms become actualized but in so being actualized they are thoroughly transformed. The end for which the provisional end of sufficiency, security, and preservation of life is a means is the good life, the way of life made available in the polis which assumes self-sufficiency for its members. So while the political realm may be "last in the order of becoming . . . it is first in the order of nature."[84]

As with the ends of the household and the political realm, the constitutive elements of each are distinct, and also related in a teleological framework. The key to understanding this relationship is Aristotle's much quoted assertion that "man is by nature a political animal (*zōon politikon*)."[85] As a consequence, if there is someone "who by nature and not by mere accident is without a *polis*, [he] is either a bad man or above humanity," a beast or a god.[86] In the realm of nature, man alone is by nature a political animal because he

> is the only animal whom [nature] has endowed with the gift of speech. And whereas mere voice is but an indication of pleasure or pain, and is therefore found in other animals, the power of speech is intended to set forth the expedient and the inexpedient, and therefore likewise the just and the unjust. And it is characteristic of man that he alone has any sense of good and evil, of just and unjust.[87]

The master of the household may appear at first glance to be in a political relationship with the slave. But Aristotle is clear on the point that, although the master may have power over the slave and others within his household, this power is in and of itself not yet political, but rather a pre-political form of rule. The instrumentality of the *oikia* is inherently incapable of actualizing politics. It is only when the *despotikon* leaves the private sphere of his household (hence liberated from the direct concerns of life maintenance) and enters the polis that he becomes a citizen. A citizen is the true political subject, the end contained within man's nature as a political animal. For Aristotle, the distinction between political life and good life is indeed merely a linguistic distinction, not an essential one.[88] Man becomes fully human so to say, a completely realized actuality of his political nature, only by developing his potential for reasoned speech, his ability to distinguish between "the just and the unjust," and his capacity for noble and virtuous actions. Only the polis, the "whole" of which all other forms of political associations are merely "parts," is the self-sufficient (*autarkeia*) and perfect (*entelechia*) context in which man's nature is fulfilled. Only the citizen can enjoy the good life because, ultimately, no other kind of subject is in fact ever fully human at all.

The essential differences between the private realm *(oikia)* and the public realm (polis) are indicated in Aristotle's work through the formulation of a series of intertwined dualisms and distinctions. The *oikia* is both the household realm associated with the distinct activities appropriate to the maintenance of life and the means for the development of the polis. The polis is both the political realm of free and equal citizens distinct from the despotism of the *oikia* and at the same time also the "whole" of which the *oikia* is merely a part. The *oikia* can be said to be subsumed within the polis in a certain sense. But this sublimation is only comprehensible within the Aristotelian teleological schema of means and ends if the distinction between that which is the whole and that which is part is strictly maintained. The unity of Plato's *Republic* is inherently different from this kind of sublimation because it is based on equivalence between these different realms of human life. The unity of the city-state in Aristotle is of an altogether different order, undergirded as it is by a firm distinction between notions of the good and the just in each realm, and between activities that are appropriate to each.

*   *   *

Hannah Arendt appropriates Aristotle's distinction between the polis and the *oikia* as the basis for her novel articulation of a distinction between the public and the private in human affairs. She regards the fundamental value of this distinction to be a clarification of the differences between a realm of freedom and a realm of necessity. Insofar as the ends of household existence were the maintenance and continuation of biological life, the *oikia* was "born of necessity, and necessity ruled over all activities performed in it."[89] In this sense, it was the highest, most advanced form of animal existence, but not much more. On the other hand, while "mastering of necessities in the household was the condition" for the existence of the polis, the polis itself was a "sphere of freedom,"[90] and "as far as the members of the polis [were] concerned, household life [existed] for the sake of the 'good life.'"[91] The nature of the polis is best defined by its finality as the natural end of all forms of human association. And this finality has the special character of "self-sufficiency" because the "final cause and end of a thing is the best, and to be self-sufficing is the end and the best."[92] The "good life" is the best, most complete form of life; it is what has the possibility of emerging from the actualization of this self-sufficiency. It is in this sense that the polis is "not a means to the good life, or one among several conditions necessary for its possibility, but the arena in which this life occurs."[93] Unlike the *oikia*, the polis is an end in itself, "the actuality *(energeia)* contained only potentially in prepolitical forms of community."[94] For Arendt, freedom is precisely that aspect of human existence and activity that reveals itself as a possibility in a sphere which is end-constitutive like the Aristotelian polis, and in actions that are self-contained and undertaken for the sake of the activity itself and not for some end beyond them. This is what Aristotle means when he claims that "those activities are desirable in themselves from which nothing is sought beyond the activity,"[95] and that these "desirable" activities are naturally more perfect than actions "where there are ends apart from the actions, [for] it is the nature of the products to be better than the activities"[96] that produce them. For Arendt, the fundamental difference between freedom and necessity is *ateleis*, the non-teleological character of free action, which is revealed with such marvelous clarity in Aristotle's discussion of the polis and the *oikia*.

This discussion has an obvious and pertinent parallel in Aristotle's distinction between *praxis* (acting) and *poesis* (making) in the *Nicomachean Ethics*. Poesis is productive activity, designed to produce a result or a product which is its end and is hence more perfect than it. Such activities include not only the household functions of preserving life, and the fabrication of goods and structures of human habitation, but also *technai* (artistic activities) in general.[97] The defining characteristic of poesis is its instrumentality. Praxis is "action," which for Aristotle is an activity of an altogether different order. "While making has an end other than itself, action cannot; for good action itself is its end."[98] This is why "making and acting are distinct," and "the reasoned state for the capacity to act is different from the reasoned state for the capacity to make."[99] Praxis lies outside the category of means and ends; it is *ateleis*, perfect and complete in and of itself. "The good or distinctively human life cannot be characterized by the instrumentality that is the essence of poesis, since this would rob it of value."[100] For Aristotle, the "good life" is a life lived in the performance of good and noble actions (*eupraxis*). Such a life has "no further need of pleasure as a sort of adventitious charm, but has its pleasure in itself."[101]

Arendt uses this Aristotelian distinction between praxis and poesis to parse out the differences between the public and the private, the political and the non-political, which are ultimately also the differences between freedom and necessity. What the polis makes available is the possibility of politics, of the political way of life, the "good life." It makes available the possibility of freedom and free action. For Arendt, the fundamental problem of modernity is precisely that this distinction between praxis and poesis has become muddled and confused, such that the "instrumentalization of the world," the schematization of the world into means and ends, has become "the ultimate [standard] for life and the world of men."[102] Productive and instrumental activity is certainly an aspect of human existence that cannot be wished away nor should it, for the continuation of the humankind, and the very existence of the polis, depends on it. But the problem is that for genuinely human life to be a possibility, this cannot be the sole content of human activity nor the sole standard by which such activity is judged. When poesis becomes indistinguishable from praxis, and in fact becomes the content of praxis, political life, genuinely human life disappears from the world. For when "the 'in order to' [becomes] the content of the 'for the sake of,'"[103] then instrumentality and utility become the sole reservoirs of meaning. And "utility established as meaning generates meaninglessness."[104]

Arendt calls this modern "depoliticization" of the public realm "the rise of the social," which is the rise of concerns of necessity and instrumentality, of the general interest in economic self-production of society, into a position of "unquestionable priority."[105] This inevitable correlate of such priority is bureaucracy, "the most social form of government,"[106] where the ruler is inchoate and abstract, a system rather than a person. But this rule of nobody is "not necessarily no rule; it may indeed, under certain circumstances, even turn out to be one of its cruelest and tyrannical versions."[107] Arendt is certainly not suggesting that concerns of economic self-production are not important concerns, or that the necessary activities like feeding and housing oneself and others are somehow irrelevant. But they are ultimately not political concerns, per se. When they appear in the public sphere, as such, and claim to be the standard and content of the practice of political action, they drive genuine politics out of this realm. The entire sphere of human society then reveals itself as a kind of "national household," an all-encompassing *oikia*, where normalization of behavior and the instrumentalization of all activity is necessarily the norm. It is the naturalization of this model of political community in the modern age that has led fundamentalist and nationalist groups of all kinds to demand state power and then remake the polity in line with their own normative or nationalist agendas. This is what often counts as legitimate political ends in the regime of modernity. The Aristotelian notion of the plurality of the polis, and the *ateleis* of the good life, is replaced by the unity of the Platonic *Republic*, "like harmony passing into unison, or rhythm which has been reduced to a single foot."[108]

*   *   *

Using Aristotle as both an inspiration and a guide, Arendt seeks an alternative paradigm for defining political action as distinct from the instrumental logic of contemporary politics. The question for Arendt of course is exactly this: "What conception of politics results from the rigorous application of the Aristotelian standard?"[109] As noted above, this is just another way of asking what a non-teleological, non-instrumental, and "self-contained politics looks like?"[110] Arendt considers and dismisses many possible candidates for such a conception of politics. Revolutionary action, for example, has at times provided glimpses of such politics, but in the modern age, such revolutions have always also had anti-political content, "unleashing the tremendous 'natural' forces bred by hunger, poverty and exploration."[111] The French Revolution, for an example, began (the historical memory of it notwithstanding) primarily as a revolutionary demand for the rights of people to "dress, [for] food and [for the] reproduction of their species," and it was precisely this priority of necessity that "unleashed the terror and sent the revolution to its doom."[112] Representative democracy is encumbered by the obvious instrumentality inherent in the very notion of representation, for it is designed primarily to free the constituent to pursue his or her private economic or other interests while the job of representing such interests in the public sphere is performed by a so-called politician. Arendt's critique of this system is pointed and direct: "What we today call democracy is a form of government where the few rule, at least supposedly, in the interest of the many."[113]

Arendtian politics turns out to be a much simpler sort of thing, and so much more significant because of that simplicity. She goes back to Aristotle's definitive claim that man "is the only animal whom [nature] has endowed with the gift of speech," and that "the power of speech is intended to set forth the expedient and the inexpedient, and therefore likewise the just and the unjust. And it is characteristic of man that he alone has any sense of good and evil, of just and unjust."[114] Political action for Arendt is nothing other than a particular variety of reasoned speech for it is the capacity to speak that makes man (uniquely) a political animal and enables him to "ascend from mere expression of appetite or aversion, or the perception of pleasure and pain, to the expression of *judgment*."[115] Arendt puts it rather more evocatively in an essay on Lessing when she points out that "the world[116] is not human just because it is made by human beings," but only becomes human when "we humanize what is going on in the world by speaking of it, and in the course of speaking we learn to be human."[117] Reasoned speech is also what takes place between citizens in the polis, for such speech is the only appropriate means of persuasion in a sphere that is by definition populated by free and equal men, and is hence free of coercion. "In the Greek self-understanding" as manifest in Aristotle's writings, "to force people by violence, to command rather than persuade, were prepolitical ways to deal with people characteristic of life outside the *polis*,"[118] or inside the *oikia*. It is in this respect that speech is praxis, it is action, or rather action without speech is not properly speaking action at all, because "it fails to express [the] capacity of judgment."[119]

Additionally, it is not any kind of speech that meets the standard of self-containedness, of *ateleis*, but only a particular variety of reasoned speech which can properly be called political. For Arendt this is deliberative speech, the "talk and argument," and the "persuasion, negotiation and compromise"[120] that is about the world of people, concerning some matter of interest that is shared by such people. Again, Arendt follows Aristotle on this point. Political deliberation is end-constitutive when a "man of practical wisdom (*phronēsis*) [is] able to deliberate well about what is good and expedient for himself, not in some *particular* respect, e.g. about what sorts of things conduce to health and strength, but about what sorts of things conduce to the 'good life' in *general*."[121] The "good life" is the shared premise and the general condition of the polis, and deliberation about its content is its very actualization in the lives of men. Such use of *phronesis* is excellent in the "unqualified" sense of constituting its own end in its performance.[122] It is in this respect that the public realm in Arendt's thinking is revealed as that "space of freedom and action [which is] primarily an arena in which this unconstrained exchange of opinion can take place."[123]

A common criticism of Arendt's rigorous Aristotelian emphasis on the self-containedness and self-sufficiency of action, which in Arendt's formulation reveals itself as deliberative speech, is the question of what exactly is the content of such speech. This is more than mere rhetoric on the part of the critics. If in fact the proper standard for praxis is its lack of instrumentality and utility, and if it is the case that matters of economic, personal, or the necessary nature are not political matters per se, then what is it that political speech is about. Hannah Pitkin, a neo-Marxist critic of Arendt puts it best perhaps when she asks, "What keeps these citizens together? . . . What is it that they talk about in the endless palaver of the *agora*?"[124]

The most interesting, and also perhaps the most enigmatically tautological, answer to this question is provided by the Arendtian scholar George Kateb when he suggests that "for political action to be valued for its own sake . . . the content of political action must be politics in the sense that political action is talk about politics" itself.[125] The enigmatic circularity of this formulation resolves into clarity when one considers that the most critical lesson Arendt draws from Aristotle is the maintenance of the distinction between the public and the private, and its corollary, the preservation of the public realm as the proper context for the realization of one's genuine humanity. For Arendt, the great crisis of our age is the slow yet inexorable erosion of this distinction, and the consequent extinction of a truly pluralistic public sphere to serve as the context for the practice of human freedom and action. Political action is speech concerned about itself insofar as it is ultimately concerned with "the creation of the conditions that make [politics] possible or with the preservation of those conditions."[126] It is in this sense that Arendt finds the debates surrounding the creation of the American republic quintessentially political in that they were about creating a constitutional framework for the maintenance of the kind of political deliberative speech that went into the writing of the constitution. In a similar vein, paradigmatic acts of civil disobedience of the kind performed in modern history by leaders like Mahatma Gandhi and Martin Luther King Jr. are examples of political speech-acts insofar as in their very performance, in their resistance of an unjust authority, they enact the conditions which are being sought as the ends of such actions. What they seek (freedom) and what they do (acts of freedom) are identical. For Arendt, this participatory and deliberative spirit is divested of its power and influence in modern societies caught in the vicious cycle of utilitarian reasoning and instrumental cycles of means and ends. The possibility of "noble and just actions" by "free and equal men" is inextricably tied to the continued existence of a "space for the appearance of freedom." The fundamental value of the public sphere is that it provides the means for its own existence, and in being so, for the existence of "indefinite future possibilities of political action."[127]

The public sphere is ultimately a "space of appearance" for Arendt, a space where human beings appear to each other and in such appearance actualize their freedom, which is equivalent to their humanity. There is nothing in the nature of man that makes him human. It is a function of the spaces that we fashion ourselves in order to actualize our freedom through the practice of politics. This is the critical, if somewhat pedantic, corollary of the notion that our freedom, no different from our human selves, is a flimsy and tenuous affair, forever in danger of being taken from us by our own indifference to the continued creation and preservation of properly public spheres. To guard against the extinction of humanity, an idea that on its face appears so outlandish in this age of overpopulation, is not merely a philosophical or hypothetical exercise but rather a responsibility that we all share just as we share the world. Arendt's enduring message is that to think any less of this responsibility, to ignore it, to deny it, or to merely note it in passing, is after all just another kind of death. It is a death of a world grown so old and so jaded that ultimately nothing will mean very much to us except the continuation of our own petty lives, and the instrumentalization and naturalization of all our activities to the point that such lives would already be dead to their humanity. Her "Greek fetish" is an attempt to access the very earliest iterations of man's recognition of himself and the possibilities of who he could be. Back when the world was still young.

*   *   *

This time of beginnings, when the "world" was still young, is important to both Sayyid Ahmad Khan and Hannah Arendt. This marks them as conservatives of a sort. But they are not anti-modern. Seyla Benhabib calls Arendt a "reluctant modernist."[128] This moniker could apply just as well to Khan. They are reluctant to accept modernity as necessity but are eager to engage the spheres of freedom it has also created. At issue of course is the definition of freedom they adhere to, and the manner in which such freedom is to be realized. In a piece he wrote warning against political agitation against the British government, Khan derides his co-religionists for buying into Western concepts of freedom without fully comprehending what such freedom entails Islamically: "They learnt the word 'liberty' and understood it to mean that they might say what came on their tongue or what passed in their mind; whether it was right or wrong, suited to the occasion or not, whether there were sufficient reasons in support of it or not."[129] Freedom is not a condition of being, per se, but the opportunity, and the capacity, for good judgment. Freedom understood as the mere proclamation of one's preferences, or the liberty to say and do whatever comes into one's mind, represents a rather impoverished conception of its relationship to the human condition. Arendt similarly derides Westerners for prioritizing Kant's *Critique of Practical Reason (CPR)* as representing the epitome of his political philosophy, when it is actually the least political of Kant's mature work. *CPR* proceeds from the Platonic imperative that "since I am one, it is better for me to disagree with the whole world than to be in disagreement with myself."[130] The categorical imperative is ultimately a theoretical construct designed to eliminate rational contradiction, but its conception of rationality is centered on the individual mind as a universal category. Arendt takes *The Critique of Judgment*, the least well known of Kant's three critiques, as his political tract par excellence. For here, Kant proposes a very different way of thinking, "for which it would not be enough to be in agreement with oneself, but which consisted of being able to 'think in the place of others' and which he therefore called 'enlarged mentality.'"[131]

In the condition of plurality, the capacity to engage sympathetically with others, literally "to learn to love others" as Khan put it in his speech at Meerut, is the gift of freedom that only humans possess. It is this freedom that allows us to refine moral judgment and make good decisions regarding our common life together. Against the solidarities of nationalism and the disarray of rampant individualism, such freedom is only actualized in communities of sympathetic discourse. For

> the power of judgment rests on a potential agreement with others, and the thinking process which is active in judging is not, like the thought process of pure reasoning, a dialogue between me and myself, but finds itself always, and primarily, even if I am quite alone in making up my mind, in an anticipated communication with others with whom I know I must finally come to some agreement.[132]

It is in this sense that both Khan's conception of jihad and Arendt's notion of action provide us with an alternative reading of the nature of human freedom than the common liberal understanding of freedom as a negative right. Kant took moral judgment to be inherently different from aesthetic judgment, which is why he initially called the tract *The Critique of Taste*. Still, he recognized that the fact of social existence required a different sort of engagement than the one a person can have with his or her own rational faculty. Arendt claims that

> the capacity to judge is a specifically political ability in exactly the same sense denoted by Kant, namely, the ability to see things not only from one's own point of view but in the perspective of all those who happen to be present; even that judgment may be one of the fundamental abilities of man as a political being, insofar as it enables him to orient himself in the public realm, the common world."[133]

Khan imagines jihad as the cultivation of those discriminating, discerning, and judging elements of habit that are attendant to an active love of truth. And such cultivation demands both the capacity to speak to others, a voice, and a language of engagement. Without such engagement, human beings revert to savagery, or to the proto-human states of *animal laborans* and *Homo faber*.

* * *

Suppose the "wolf-girl" of the story recounted at the beginning of this chapter had been abducted not by a wolf but rather by a German tourist. And having been taken to Germany, and despite much effort, could find no facility with the

German language or culture. Unable to speak to her peers, she could understand them only vaguely through the motions of their heads and gestures of their hands. The limitations on her opportunity to be a human being, an opportunity that was obviously denied to her by being raised by animals in the jungle, would not, at least on cursory examination, appear as severe as was the case where and when she was found. She would be clothed and healthy perhaps, cared for and loved by her abductee parents, able to enjoy nice cooked meals of potatoes and meat. She would walk on two feet, not on all fours. She would look human. But her humanity would have been denied to her as much as if she was in the jungle. She would have little ability to actualize her natural freedom as a human being through the development of her faculty of judgment in conversation with others.

Muslims of Khan's day were in the same sort of predicament. To a great extent, they still are today. In the larger discourses about the world which they inhabit with all others, they appear to lack the capacity for engagement with the myriad abductee parents they have acquired over the years. Such abductee parents include both the West and those of their co-religionists who speak in modern apostasies. Most Muslims are dumb and mute. But at least they feel the suffering of life in the desert. At least they appear to know that their humanity is gradually being extinguished by forces over which they have little control. Arendt's pessimism, on the other hand, is a reaction to the exuberant optimism of the West, and the attendant "danger of becoming true inhabitants of the desert and feeling at home in it." Khan was more optimistic, of course. He clearly believed that the intervention of the West had rescued Muslims from apathy and malaise and had opened up the possibility of an Islamic renaissance through engagement with Europe. This he imagined as a re-politicization of Islam in the Arendtian sense. And he was successful in at least clarifying the parameters of what such re-politicization would actually entail; not state power or private morality but discursive spaces of freedom's appearance. But for his project to be successful in the long run, both Muslims and the West would need to develop an "enlarged mentality," and cultivate a habit of engagement without which proper moral discernment and good judgment concerning our common world are impossible. Additionally, Muslims would need such engagement internally as well, to reknit the broken fabric of their own social and communal existence. Both tasks are an ongoing struggle. But to struggle is to be human. And to struggle *to be* human is most quintessentially human. As the great nineteenth-century Indian poet Mirza Asadullah Ghalib put it, "Alas, not all things in life are easy / Even man struggles to be human."[134]

Knowledge and Wisdom

The evaluative infrastructure of Western modernity is defective because knowledge has become disaggregated from wisdom. What is knowledge? Knowledge is information that begets information. It is information that has become alive. What is wisdom? Wisdom is an artifact of knowledge.[1] As knowledge accumulates, it sediments into layers of meaning that provide evaluative foundations for further accumulation. This is wisdom. In the beginning, information was merely instrumental to the needs of biological survival. Or at best it concerned the menial work of hunting and gathering, and such information did not yet have proper human value. A primordial accumulation of surplus information first produces the faint outlines of wisdom, of self-reflexive knowledge. This is information that has no good use, like drawings of animals on cave walls, or the first fleeting sense of compassion, or the feeling of elation when surrounded by others. This is something akin to "collective effervescence" perhaps, an emergence of a communal evaluative sensibility, of something deemed sacred as opposed to merely useful.[2] It is in the evaluative regime of such wisdom that information is no longer merely replicated from one generation to the next but reproduced in the sense of being directed through such reproduction. Knowledge both grows on the foundation of wisdom and constantly produces new wisdom as an artifact of such growth. When a certain kind of animal becomes self-consciously mimetic in its relationship to information, both knowledge and wisdom are co-produced. For to mimic is not to repeat, but to *re-present* the original. This is the beginning of proper human societies. If knowledge is brain matter, then wisdom is consciousness. And in this metaphor, tradition is narrative self-awareness. It is identity.

In modern societies, knowledge production has become unmoored from the direction of wisdom. Wisdom no longer properly sediments as a function of the growth of knowledge. This is the condition that Alasdair MacIntyre so plaintively describes in his landmark book *After Virtue*. What binds knowledge and wisdom together is tradition; a constantly evolving yet coherent narrative of the norms of collective identity and its attendant cosmologies. MacIntyre believes that the origins of Western modernity lie in what he calls a "moral calamity."[3] This was the calamitous breakdown of a tradition of moral thinking that had earlier provided a philosophical mechanism for imagining societies as coherent and meaningful wholes. With the loss of this tradition, incoherence enters our moral thinking and societies become fragmented into mere collections of aggregated individuals and of free-floating spheres of judgment. What was this tradition? MacIntyre describes it as a system of norms, signs, and symbols based on a broad Aristotelian normative sensibility, though in *After Virtue* he does not yet lay out in detail the goods associated with the particular form of Aristotelianism he himself identifies with (this task is undertaken in his next book *Whose Justice? Which Rationality?*). The moral calamity was the slow unraveling of this culture and the tradition of moral thought associated with it. Modernity is the fruits of this unraveling. In *After Virtue*, MacIntyre sets himself the task of explaining the nature and content of this unraveling, and how the emergent culture has handled its consequences. The short answer to the latter inquiry is, of course, not very well. One particularly vexing aspect of modernity is the manner in which the very concept of "tradition" has been reconfigured. So MacIntyre provides a general account of the un-reconstructed concept of tradition (as traditionally understood) and hence attempts to rescue the notion of tradition itself from the modern meanings (mis)ascribed to it. What are these meanings? And what are the problems associated with understanding tradition as associated with these meanings?

The two dominant modes of understanding tradition in the modern age broadly correspond to the definitions provided by liberal individualists and Burkean traditionalists. According to MacIntyre, these two positions essentially provide the same definition, but more on this later.[4] Taking the latter first, Edmund Burke was famously perturbed by the goings-on in France during the revolution. In his *Reflections on the Revolution in France*, Burke counseled "wisdom without reflection."[5] The political and social order of late eighteenth-century England was the apotheosis of stability to Burke. Any "appeals to theoretically grounded principles purporting to have an authority independent of that conferred from within" this order were prima facie corrupt.[6] Appeals to universal reason or to "A Declaration of the Rights of Man and the Citizen" to radically reconfigure an existing order clearly mischaracterized the social nature of Man and the function of authority in human societies.[7] Burke and those theorists of tradition who have followed him continue to contrast the authority of "tradition with [that of] reason, and the stability of tradition with conflict" bred by such appeals.[8] The authority of tradition is only properly conferred by established social and political orders that embody in their very stability the legitimacy of their own norms.[9] If any appeals are to be made, they can only be "to values already acknowledged within the exchanges of benefits and satisfactions which partially constituted [an] already existing order."[10] Traditions that persist over time have only managed to do so because they correspond to the peculiarities of the societies for which they provide normative scaffolding. If the scaffolding is disturbed, the further construction and growth of such societies cannot continue. And the whole house is liable to collapse. This is what Burke saw happening in France, and, needless to say, he was not impressed.

Perhaps MacIntyre mischaracterizes some of Burke's positions, and perhaps he also obfuscates others.[11] But I believe the crux of the argument is secure. Burke accepts a dualism that is central to most quintessentially modern accounts of tradition. This is the notion that appeals to rationality are essentially different from appeals to tradition, and that the two proceed from opposing conceptions of the manner of authority that corresponds to human flourishing. "Wisdom without reflection" is an acknowledgment that a sociopolitical order, and not rational reflection, is the proper source of authority. Reflection here obviously, if not explicitly, refers to something like what Kant had in mind with his account of practical reason and of the categorical imperative; the idea that man is a rational animal that can and *ought* to give law to himself.[12] But how should one choose which particular sociopolitical order to pledge allegiance to? For Burke, there is no such thing as personal choice in such matters. The existence of a stable order is itself choice enough. It is in this sense then that "Burke's own allegiance tried to combine adherence in politics to a conception of tradition which would vindicate the oligarchical revolution of property of 1688 and adherence in economics to the doctrine and institutions of the free market."[13] Thus a particular sedimentation of knowledge, at a particular time and place, becomes the wisdom for all ages for a particular society.

Of course, Burke's brand of traditionalism has its origins in what he saw himself as resisting. These were the then-nascent and now-dominant paradigms of liberal individualism. But MacIntyre contends that this resistance, then as now, is illusory on two levels. First, the particular tradition Burke pledged allegiance to, and some version of which modern conservatives that have followed him are often engaged in conserving, is "only older rather than [a] later version of liberal individualism. Their own doctrine is as liberal and as individualist as that of self-avowed liberals."[14] To establish the second sense in which such resistance is illusory requires unpacking the main tenets of liberal individualism's understanding of tradition. From such a perspective, the autonomy of the individual is sacrosanct. Tradition is that set of social constraints which holds the individual in a straitjacket and prevents a free exercise of judgment that is the most basic aspect of its rationality. "The self is thought of as lacking any *necessary* social identity," and moral agency ultimately rests on being "able to stand back from any and every situation in which one is involved, from any and every characteristic that one may possess, and to pass judgment on it from a purely universal and abstract point of view that is totally detached from all social particularity."[15] As with the Burkean conservatives, liberal individualists contrast the demands of reason with the authority of tradition. Human rationality is independent of and prior to the formation of the social self, which is a secondary sedimentation that prevents the true self from realizing its potential in freedom from tradition.

Questions regarding the nature of the self's moral autonomy have produced two broad philosophical strains within liberalism which, in the final analysis, are mere inversions of each other. First, the Enlightenment project insisted that moral "truth is guaranteed by rational method and rational method appeals to principles undeniable by any fully reflective person."[16] The most famous instance of such a formulation is, of course, Kant's categorical imperative which applies not only to human beings but also to any rational being whatsoever (be it here on Earth or elsewhere in the universe!). Individuals do not need traditions to tell them what is right or wrong, good or evil. It is written into the very structure of our consciousness in the form of the self's rationality and its capacity to reason. Traditions obfuscate this truth since they emerge from contingent processes of society formation, and hence often mold themselves around the contours and configurations of particular interests. Morality becomes a front for power.[17]

But Friedrich Nietzsche's critique of the Enlightenment suggested that even the progressive morality of the Enlightenment was itself a front for the will to power. Nietzsche was responding to all the different iterations of continental idealisms spawned by Kant in the nineteenth century, from Bentham's theory of Utilitarianism to the fast-multiplying adherents of the theory of moral sentiments first put forward by Adam Smith in 1759 (in which self-interest aggregates to produce morally beneficial results for all).[18] The entire substance of Nietzsche's critique need not concern us here. According to MacIntyre, "Nietzsche jeers at the notion of basing morality on inner moral sentiments, on conscience, on the one hand or on the Kantian categorical imperative, on universalizability, on the other" and "in five, swift, witty and cogent paragraphs [in *The Gay Science*], he disposes of what [MacIntyre] called the Enlightenment project to discover rational foundations for an objective morality."[19] But if there is nothing to morality as such except expressions of will, what remains? It is the proclamation that "we, however, want to become who we are—human beings who are new, unique, incomparable, who give themselves laws, who create themselves."[20] It is this notion, of a human self as radically individuated and radically free, that spawned the second dominant philosophical strain within modern liberalism. These are the twin challenges to the notion of universal, rational morality posed by post-Enlightenment moral relativism and perspectivism. Moral relativism (of both the modern and the post-modern sort) proceeds from the assumption that there is no possibility of rational debate between rival traditions, whereas the perspectivist position goes one step further and "puts in question the possibility of making truth claims from [even] within any one tradition."[21] The contemporary champions of "pluralism" are the philosophical heirs of these kinds of positions. But both the Enlightenment project and these post-Enlightenment challenges to it are identical in at least two important ways. First, they ascribe to a broadly Cartesian notion of human rationality; it is a function, and a confirmation, of one's individual existence, of a rational self. One does not need society to affirm one's existence. One has to merely think and reflect on one's own existence in the quiet of contemplation. Second, and relatedly, "neither [position] was or is able to recognize the kind of rationality possessed by traditions. In part this is because of the enmity to tradition as inherently obscurantist which is and was to be found equally among Kantians and Benthamites, neo-Kantians and later Utilitarians, on the one hand, and among Nietzschean and post-Nietzscheans, on the other."[22] Morality understood either as an expression of the self's freedom or as a universal, timeless formula requires no guidance from the past. There is no need for wisdom. It is mere social sedimentation, like mud covering the pristine self. It must be stripped away.

*   *   *

The self-images of modernity, however they may be constituted, mirror each other in their understanding of tradition. But MacIntyre believes the whole project is based on a willful miscomprehension of the true nature of traditions. The supposed champions of tradition, like Burke and the many others that have followed him, do the most positive harm by merely regurgitating the liberal position that tradition is opposed to reason, and that stability and order necessitate that rational conflict be made subservient to acceptance of given authority, to the practice of "wisdom without reflection." Against these self-images, MacIntyre contends that "when a tradition is in good order, it is always partially constituted by an argument about the goods the pursuit of which gives to that tradition its particular point and purpose."[23] Such traditions do not demand blind acceptance to authority. This is merely a caricature. "Traditions when vital embody *continuities of conflict*. Indeed when a tradition becomes Burkean, it is always dying or already dead."[24] The modern conception of tradition is a strawman and a scapegoat. It is a notional sacrifice on the altar of modernity for the supposed sins of nonexistent fathers.

So what is tradition in the traditional sense? In a faint echo of the tautological logic of the Arendtian notion of politics, MacIntyre claims that "a living tradition is a historically extended, socially embodied argument, and an argument precisely in part about the goods which constitute the tradition."[25] Tradition's primary points of normative reference, and the objects of the tradition's continuous (re) constructions, are both the tradition itself. It is for this reason that the catalog of virtues in the Aristotelian schema must include

> the virtues required to sustain the kind of households and the kind of political communities in which men and women can seek for the good together and the virtues necessary for philosophical inquiry about the character of the good . . . the good life for man is the life spent in seeking for the good life for man, and the virtues necessary for the seeking are those which will enable us to understand what more and what else the good life for man is.[26]

But tradition understood in this manner does not, in fact cannot, proceed from outside the social reality which underlies the tradition's own existence. There are no abstract universals, no views from no-where, no original positions. Like the "thick" morality that philosopher Michael Walzer talks about in his work, traditions are socially embodied, historically specific, and particular.[27] And yet a living tradition is not so much bound by its particularity and specificity but rather set free from delusions of its own universality.

> Without these moral particularities to begin from there would never be anywhere to begin; but it is moving forward from such particularity that the search for the good, the universal, consists. Yet particularity can never be simply left behind or obliterated. . . . When men and women identify what are in fact partial and particular causes *too easily* and *too completely* with the cause of some universal principle they usually behave worse than they would otherwise do.[28]

It is this ease and this comfort with universals that allowed European imperialism to thrive and grow at precisely the same time as Europe was undergoing its supposed Enlightenment. The natives were derided for their primitive traditions, their barbaric practices, or at best romanticized as noble savages from an age already long past in civilized Europe.[29] To civilize them in the knowledge of universals was the white man's burden. On the other hand, the de-historicization and de-socialization of the self allows well-meaning individuals to wash their hands of any social or historical guilt associated with living in societies often enriched by the exploitation of others. It is in this sense that modern American individuals can deny any responsibility for slavery ("I never owned any slaves") or an Englishman can deny any lingering social culpability for colonialism ("I never did any harm to the Irish") and even a young German can "[believe] that being born after 1945 means that what the Nazis did to Jews has no moral relevance to his relationship to his Jewish contemporaries."[30] The past lives in the present as a moral category and the moral relevance of the past is enacted in the present through the construction of a better future taking account of such a past. Morality is historical, social, and embodied. This is as true for morality as it is for natural science or any other mode of empirical inquiry. It would be absurd to claim that Einstein could have formulated his theory of gravity without reference to, or absent a critical conversation with, that of Newton. The problems faced by modern physics are a reflection of what our scientific ancestors did or did not adequately address, the mistakes they made, the things they left undone. But the opportunities afforded to contemporaries are also a function of the historical development of science. Still, the modern mind accepts material facts as having a historical character, and a social context in and through which such facts emerge and are perfected. No such luxury is afforded the realm of moral inquiry. Here the "fact-value distinction" is deployed to sever tradition from precisely that mode of rational inquiry that is designed to produce "moral facts."

MacIntyre points out that the modern notion of fact, as either a kind of sense-datum or an experimentally verifiable thing, is of recent origin; "like telescopes and wigs for gentlemen, [facts] were a seventeenth century invention."[31] The Latin root word *factum* means a deed or an action, and the Scholastic interpretation of it carries the suggestion of an event or a happening. In this sense, one could legitimately judge facts as good or bad. The term "fact" acquired its current meaning during attempts by early modern scientists to protect their findings from the contingent judgment of others (including but not limited to the clerical authorities) by positing for them a different kind of ontological reality. Experience and experiment were "events" of an altogether different quality, immune to moral judgment. In a perverse reversal, moral claims were henceforth rendered by these social renegades as a function *only* of contingent judgment as opposed to the facts that they had discovered. It is to rescue morality from such contingency that Kant, in particular, and the Enlightenment project, in general, sought to provide a rational foundation for moral judgment. But by this time the association of reason with the scientific method was so pervasive that the only rational mechanism they could find to carry out such a rescue was to make moral judgment independent of the social order altogether. The notion of tradition as an arena where values predominate as so many signs of historical contingency and personal preference based on irrational beliefs or social edicts can be traced back to this period when facts first became facts.

The rationality of tradition proceeds from a very different conception of facts. Against the Cartesian notion of the mind, it posits the idea of "mind as activity, of mind as engaging with the natural and social world in such activities as identification, collecting, separating, classifying, and naming and all this, by touching, grasping, pointing, breaking down, building up, calling to, answering to, and so on."[32] To understand facts in this sense is to make claims regarding the adequacy or inadequacy of re-presentations of the social and natural reality that one inhabits. It is precisely because the rationality of tradition deals in re-presentative facts that "one of the great insights of tradition-constitutive enquiries is that false beliefs and false judgments represent a failure of the mind not of its objects."[33] The standard of what constitutes an adequate or inadequate representation is the tradition itself. But a well-ordered tradition, a living tradition, does not represent the kind of authority ascribed to the caricatures of it in the modern Western worldview. In any given tradition, "the weakest form of argument," which only prevails ultimately in the absolute absence of all others, "will be the appeal to the authority of established belief, merely as established."[34] A mature tradition has already done the important work of exposing the beliefs, scriptures, or authoritative texts from its contingent beginnings to all manners of theorizing, enhancement, and deliberation such that *they make sense.* Contrary to popular modern opinion, mature traditions are never irrational. They exist and persist because they make sense to a vast majority of their adherents.

* * *

Because every rational tradition begins with the contingency and positivity of some set of established facts, rational justifications in tradition-constituted inquiries are always, simultaneously, dialectical and historical: "They are justified insofar as in the history of this tradition they have, by surviving the process of dialectical questioning, vindicated themselves to their historical predecessors."[35]

To claim one's propositions as true is to claim that they have been so vindicated. Even when such claims are made as being universally applicable, these truths are claimed for, on behalf of, and in, one's tradition, not with reference to one's individual self or to some abstract universal standard of evaluation. The rationality of traditions is also historical in the sense that "an adequate sense of tradition manifests itself in a grasp of those future possibilities which the past has made available to the present."[36] So, "there are constraints on how the [tradition] can continue *[but]* within those constraints there are *indefinitely many ways that it can continue*" (emphasis added).[37]

"Some core of shared beliefs, constitutive allegiance to the tradition, has to survive every rupture," but the fact of ruptures is constitutive of traditions imagined as continuities of conflict.[38] The sources of such conflict are many. Some of these are internal to the traditions themselves, others emerge from the social and natural environment within which all particular traditions exist. MacIntyre describes the greatest challenge to traditions as the threat of an "Epistemological Crisis." Such a crisis is precipitated by the sudden appearance of some set of social or natural facts that threaten the rationality of the tradition; its capacity to offer intelligible, convincing, and justifiable propositions about the world. One could just as easily call it a moral crisis (as MacIntyre himself does, a "moral calamity") or a crisis of judgment. In such circumstances, the language provided by the tradition becomes deficient and inadequate to making sense of the world. Something akin to an "Epistemological Crisis" is precisely what befell the Muslims of India after 1857, for example, and which has plagued Muslims in general ever since. It is a world turned mysterious and ineffable, and the face in the mirror rendered unrecognizable. Such crisis usually occurs when "hitherto trusted methods of enquiry have become sterile," and the tradition is faced with "hitherto unrecognized incoherences, and new problems the solutions to which there seems to be insufficient or no resources within the fabric of established belief."[39] In the Muslim case, Wilfred Cantwell Smith described the nature of the crisis in *Islam in Modern History*:

> The fundamental malaise of modern Islam is that something has gone wrong with Islamic history. The fundamental problem of modern Islam is how to rehabilitate that history: to set it going again in full vigor, so that Islamic society may once again flourish as a divinely guided society should and must. The fundamental spiritual crisis of Islam in the 20th century stems from an awareness that something is awry between the religion that God has appointed and the historical development of the world He controls.[40]

This feeling, that something is awry and yet a solution does not present itself, is emblematic of an Epistemological Crisis. In fact, it is almost always also the case that one does not even have the language to describe the nature of the problem much less offer reasonable solutions to it. Muslims knew that this particular crisis had something to do with their political domination by European powers and with their increasing irrelevance in the production of new forms of knowledge. But the specifics escaped most of them, as they do even now. In a long, illuminating paragraph, MacIntyre contends that the solution to the dissolution of historically founded certitudes requires "imaginative conceptual innovation":

> The solution to a genuine epistemological crisis requires the invention or discovery of new concepts and the framing of some new type or types of theories which meet three highly exacting requirements. First, this in some ways radically new and conceptually enriched schema, if it is to put an end to epistemological crisis, must furnish a solution to the problems which had previously proved intractable in a systematic and coherent way. Second, it must also provide an explanation of just what it was which rendered the tradition, before it had acquired these new resources, sterile or incoherent, or both. And third, these first two tasks must be carried out in a way which exhibits some fundamental continuity of the new conceptual and theoretical structures with the shared beliefs in terms of which the tradition of enquiry has been defined up to this point.[41]

I have seen no better description than this of the task that Sayyid Ahmad Khan set himself in the wake of the events of 1857. He understood the Islamic tradition in precisely the manner that MacIntyre describes as his traditions of inquiry. His understanding of the rationality of his own tradition closely follows MacIntyre's account as well. And the solution that MacIntyre suggests was Khan's mission in life. What explains this strange symmetry? There are at least two reasons for this, one more obvious than the other. First, MacIntyre himself acknowledges that a broad Aristotelian schema was common to the various sciences of moral judgment in the theistic religions of the pre-modern age. The most relevant feature of this schema was a teleological understanding of human nature and a clear contrast between human-as-is and human-as-it-should-be. To be true to one's nature as a human being, one has to act in a manner that allows one to make a transition from the first state to the second. And the cultivation of the virtues attendant to being habituated to do this is to be properly human, in accord with one's true nature. This teleological understanding of human nature is complicated and added to, but not essentially altered, when it is placed within a framework of theistic beliefs, whether Christian as with Aquinas, or Jewish as with Maimonides, or Islamic with Ibn Roschd [*sic*]. The precepts of ethics now have to be understood not only as teleological injunctions but also as expressions of divinely ordained law. . . . But the threefold structure [of what-is -> Ethics -> what-should-be] . . . remains central to the theistic understanding of evaluative thought and judgment.[42]

Islam belongs within the larger set of traditions that presupposes a teleological conception of human nature. And that such nature is a function of one's actions in the world, not a condition of one's existence. The underlying unity of this schema rests on a rejection of the fact-value distinction, since "to say what someone ought to do is at one and the same time to say what course of action will in these circumstances lead toward a man's true end and to say what law, ordained by God and comprehended by reason, enjoins. Moral sentences are thus used within this framework to make claims which are true or false."[43] It is for this reason that Khan's particular conception of Islam and MacIntyre's general description of a tradition are so closely related.

There is, of course, another less obvious reason for this similarity. Both MacIntyre's tradition and Khan's Islam have been subjected to persistent attacks that threaten to destroy what MacIntyre calls "the unity of life" and what Khan calls *tauhid*. In either case, tradition has been identified with blind adherence to belief and submission to an arbitrary historical authority. To proclaim unity of one sort or another is to render human life static and staid and to wrest the freedom to change from the human individual. This is, after all, the common slur that liberals direct at all comers that do not prescribe to this or that version of modernity's dominant sociological and normative paradigms. It is in the regime of such constant insults that older traditions have often reacted badly to the dualistic choice put before them by their interrogators. As with Burkean conservatism, Muslims have produced their own version of so-called Islamists who identify a particular sedimentation of knowledge produced in their tradition as authoritative wisdom for all time. Burke's glorious revolution has its clear analog in the proclamation of seventh-century Arabia as the be-all and end-all of relevant knowledge about the good life. In modern times, this tradition-centered attack on the tradition itself has multiplied into a thousand different apostasies, each claiming for itself the mantle of authority. On the other hand, there are those who ostensibly seek to save the tradition but only by rejecting a "fundamental continuity of the new conceptual and theoretical structures with the shared beliefs in terms of which the tradition of enquiry has been defined up to this point." These are the liberal, enlightened saviors of Islam. They are both Muslim and non-Muslim, both liberal and neo-conservative, both young and old. As I have mentioned before, these "commensuralists" come in all shapes and sizes and some make for strange bedfellows. But they all reject the necessity of tradition to rational inquiry and notions of justice. To which MacIntyre exclaims: "Whose Justice? Which Rationality?" The teams appear to have taken their sides in a Cartesian field of mortal combat, across which they lob their verbal (or literal) grenades. But what of the field itself, the space in the middle? They fight over a fiction. But the real field of human action, of the nature and function of tradition in human life, they ignore entirely.

*   *   *

Tradition does ascribe unity to life, but these are not the staid, static unities of the liberal imagination. It is the unity of a story that is coherent and meaningful. It is the unity of history as a narrative that confers purpose and direction to those for which, and about which, it is written. It is the unity of harmony, not uniformity. It is unity in difference, not "like harmony passing into unison, or rhythm which has been reduced to a single foot."[44] Khan's entire intellectual oeuvre is one long and sustained proclamation of the primacy of *tauhid* in Muslim life. Yet so-called traditionalists and even some reform-minded Muslims barked in his face then.[45] Some even spit on his name now that he has been dead for over a century. It was the conservative reaction to Khan, and not any real engagement with his thought and work, that earned him the moniker of "liberal" among his British backers and his European interlocutors. For Khan on his own terms appears to have been wholly unintelligible to them, as he is now to much of their progeny.

MacIntyre describes the "unity of human life [as] the unity of a narrative quest." What are the ends of such a quest (and notice, of course, that at the end a *telos* is implied in the very name "quest")?

> It is in looking for a conception of *the* good which will enable us to order other goods, for a conception of *the* good which will enable us to extend our understanding of the purpose and content of the virtues, for a conception of *the* good which will enable us to understand the place of integrity and constancy in life, that we initially define the kind of life which is a quest for the good.[46]

Knowledge of the exact substance of such good need not be certain. It rarely is. Unity is a function of the telos, the quest, for finding harmony and meaning in a life composed of so many disparate elements and a multitude of desires and motivations. This unified good is what Khan identifies as *tauhid*, which in its active human form is the quest of *tatbi'a*, of seeking a language that can describe the world as a harmonious whole and our lives as meaningful unities within it.

For MacIntyre, the dialectical-historical character of traditional rationality means that such a quest always takes the form of a continuous, yet contested, conversation,

> for conversation understood widely enough is the form of human transactions in general. Conversational behavior is not a special sort or aspect of human behavior, even though forms of language-using and of human life are such that deeds of others speak for them as much as do their words. For that is possible only because they are deeds of those who have words.[47]

What is this conversation about? About the goods that constitute the good life. For Khan, this same conversation is identical to jihad, and the ends sought are the ethical imperatives that would allow human life to be lived in concordance with nature, the ends of our God-given humanity. One talks as one struggles only in the present, but it is a present securely tied to both a future and a past. It is time stitched together into a unity, and morality as the flow of time. Traditions necessarily proceed from what "the past has made available to the present." This, after all, is what the detractors of traditional modes of thinking are the first to point out. But tradition-constituted inquiry is bound by the demands of its teleological character, a rational voltage that pushes it inexorably and necessarily forward:

> There is no present which is not informed by some image of some future and an image of the future which always presents itself in the form of a *telos*—or of a variety of ends or goals—toward which we are either moving or failing to move in the present. Unpredictability and teleology therefore co-exist as part of our lives.[48]

This combination of unpredictability and teleology confounds the modern Western mind. For modern teleologies (e.g., Universal Spirits, Communist Utopias, Ends of History, Perpetual Peace) are by definition either predictable (in the sense of predictability being internal to the unfolding of history itself) or must be *made* predictable in order to be true teleologies (the only obstacles being the limitations in current knowledge or widespread ignorance or the absence of the proper institutions on a worldwide scale). Only life imagined as a narrative in which we humans "enter upon a stage which we did not design and we find ourselves part of an action that was not of our making," allows for both the possibility of contingency and the recognition that the story, as a story, has an *end*.[49] It is with this acknowledgment that we seek to know the parameters of this *end*, and our part in its elucidation, our personal role in the larger narrative of which we are, in the end, only a part. That this whole is prior to our part in it, and our part has no meaning without relation to this whole.

It is this acceptance of our part-ness that is often decried by modern liberals as a constraint on our freedom. But as Niebuhr put it, the freedom of the human is never freedom *from* constraints. It is the freedom *to* imagine the countless moral possibilities inherent within the specific constraints we necessarily find ourselves as human beings. For Khan, this condition of constraint, of *taklif*, is the very source of our rationality. Without it, we would be unable to even formulate viable moral questions and be incapable of having rational conversations to begin with. MacIntyre agrees: "To be outside all tradition is to be a stranger to enquiry: it is to be in a state of intellectual and moral destitution, a condition from which it is impossible to issue [any] challenge."[50] But it is one of the great intellectual feats of modern liberalism, an otherwise barren and impoverished moral system, that it has managed to effectively turn its own impoverishment into an advertisement! Most tellingly perhaps, MacIntyre notes that what Émile Durkheim described as a kind of social pathology, *anomie* or normless-ness, that attended the breakdown of traditional orders elsewhere, characterized by feelings of deprivation, loss, and suffering, "has been assigned the status of an achievement by and reward for the self [in the West] which had, by separating itself from the social relationships of traditions, succeeded, so it believed, in emancipating itself."[51] I am reminded once again of Niebuhr's wonderful definition of tragedy as the particular quest in which the hero's attempts to do the right thing land him in precisely the kind of trouble he seeks to avoid. The difference of course is that Greek tragedy finds its fulfillment, its meaning, in the eventual realization and acknowledgment that the hero's actions were always doomed to fail. MacIntyre contends that no such acknowledgment attends the heroes of modernity, to whom "what Durkheim saw as social pathology is now presented wearing the masks of philosophical pretensions."[52]

*   *   *

Delusions are a wonderful panacea for a sickness so far progressed that there is little hope of recovery. In this, at least, the modern West and modern Islam appear to be identical. The origins of their current dysfunction are also historically intertwined. When Sayyid Ahmad Khan discovered the true extent of the political and epistemological crisis after 1857, he wept for his community and his hair turned white. But eventually, Khan overcame such dejection and got back to the work of assessing the damage and offering prescriptions. MacIntyre's tone in *After Virtue* is obviously polemical, but there is a great deal of sadness too, and faith. This too shall pass. For the sickness, though advanced, is not incurable. Even as Rome fell, and Europe entered the Dark Ages, the virtues associated with civilized life were preserved in monasteries and churches everywhere. The rebirth of Europe in the middle ages was always already pregnant in the tradition of moral thought that preceded the dark ages. Ultimately, these past continuities were never as contingent as they may appear from our vantage point in the present. Just as our own continuities are never as certain as they appear to us in the present. Knowledge as such may not survive but the artifacts it leaves behind, the sedimentations that accrue, still remain. Fossilized perhaps, ossified but tangible. Wisdom persists.

The problems associated with the modern age are therefore neither intractable nor unique. The tussle between the freedom of knowledge and the gravity of wisdom has been a consistent feature of human life from the very beginning. Human societies are factories of knowledge production. As new knowledge accumulates, it is apt to declare for itself an independence from the past. This is the myopia of all presents. The present always has a veneer of uniqueness, of distinction: "It has never been so before." The particular form this tussle between knowledge and wisdom has taken in the present may appear to some of us as the most profound "moral calamity," the most remarkable "epistemological crisis" that history has ever produced. But after the fall of Rome, and the destruction of an older way of life, many in Europe may have felt the same way. And even before, some may have experienced a similar misery after the failure of the Roman republic. And so it has been throughout history. This is not to diminish the seriousness of the present crisis in both the Islamic world and the West. It is merely to put it in historical context.

That said, the particulars of the crisis may well be unique, even if the incidence of it is not. The scale of knowledge production in the present is so profound, and the varieties of its accumulations so multitudinous, that the capacity of human societies to manage this excess often appears compromised. The anxiety associated with this accumulation has produced the two paradigmatic responses that I have been talking about throughout this book. On the one hand, we have those that deny the need for any overarching organization, a single coherent story. It is in the regime of this understanding that knowledge becomes its own organizing principle, needing no wisdom to guide its path. The differentiation of modern spheres of a value is a symptom of such reasoning. So, economic knowledge (capital) becomes the sole standard of evaluation for itself. The same can be said of scientific knowledge, or political knowledge, or even religious knowledge. The list is long. But knowledge divorced from any outside standard of evaluation almost always confers on itself a single, simple standard: accumulation. So scientists contend that accumulation of scientific knowledge is its own end. And economists make a virtue out of greed; businesses are after all legitimately only interested in the bottom line. And nobody bats an eye at the contention that politicians are in it to win it. What else should they be expected to want to do? The problem of course is that accumulation is not directed growth. It is not like the tree in Sayyid Ahmad Khan's metaphor for a healthy society, but rather like a cancerous tumor. All it knows is to grow. Direction in modern society usually takes the form of regulation. But regulation lacks the moral seriousness of virtues and is often times only a function of this or that utilitarian calculation. And, as Hannah Arendt put it, moral meaning reduced to utility produces meaninglessness. It is against this propensity that MacIntyre counsels a return to the virtues of the past.

On the other hand, the anxiety associated with the pace of novelty in the modern age has begotten those that deny that all these new forms of knowledge are morally relevant at all. They proclaim the sedimented wisdom of one age or another, one place or another, as the standard of all evaluation for all time. I have already spent much time expounding on these characters and will spare the reader another long regurgitation of their sins. In short, these are the ones we sometimes call fundamentalists, or traditionalists, or extremists, and sometimes even radicals. Their worldview suffers from the peculiar myopia of the past. They have limited imagination, and the present interests them only as context for the recreation of their beatific visions of a mythical past. This is a conception of wisdom as a black hole from which the light of no knowledge can ever escape. It is against these disturbing, anachronistic visions that Sayyid Ahmad Khan counseled an engagement with the present.

So, MacIntyre and Khan are kindred spirits. But there is one important caveat. Khan was an eternal optimist and had aspirations of a conversation with the world itself as both subject and context. This was the gift of his particular tradition of Islam. For Sayyid Ahmad Khan's Islam is indeed universalist in its aspirations, not in the sense of world conquest but in its confidence that eventually the whole world can be rationally convinced of Islam's value. MacIntyre shares neither Khan's optimism nor his aspirations. Conversations across traditions are both possible and essential to their vitality and growth. But in the modern age, the task of preservation must take precedence. So he advocates local, limited communities of discourse within which the virtues of the past can be preserved for a future after the dark ages. It is in this sense that MacIntyre can sometimes appear needlessly alarmist. Perhaps this is by design. The modern institution of democracy, for example, has preserved many of the old virtues he so admires and added new ones to the mix.[53] As an aggregating mechanism, it is not ideal but adequate. And adequacy has been the way of human social life from the very beginning. Seeking perfection is, after all, the quintessential sin of pride.

* * *

Imagine a parallel universe, much like our own but sufficiently different to allow for the possibility of time travel. A medieval artist (henceforth, the Artist) is transported in time to the present to take part in an experiment devised by patrons of abstract expressionism. For many years now, debate has been raging about the value of abstract art. Some believe it the apotheosis of creative expression. Others call it self-referential gibberish. Abstract expressionists bristle at the notion that their art would be incomprehensible to anyone not already groomed and trained to admire it. This is art after all, timeless and beautiful, universal. So they are bringing in someone with no prior knowledge of abstract expressionism to confirm that anyone with an "artistic sensibility" from any time and any place would find value in their art.[54]

The Artist is given some indication of what he is doing so many hundreds of years in the future (in clear violation of the parameters of the experiment since he is supposed to come to conclusions about art on his own without prior signaling). He is then shown a painting by the famed American expressionist Jackson Pollock. Initially, the Artist is tempted to think of it as leftover paint from some *real* artistic rendering. When he is told that this is the art itself, he is dumbfounded, confused, even a little scared.[55] In what world would one call this art, he thinks to himself. These people are mad! But they are powerful; being in their time and in their place, they decide what is and is not such-and-such, not he, the one out of place and out of time. So he demurs, unwillingly but not showing his discomfort. This is indeed art, he says, and how beautiful, wonderful, timeless. Then they insist that it is not just art, but high art, *Abstract Expressionism*. He still goes along, not knowing what to say to these barbarians of the future. But of course, eventually, they want more than demurral and acceptance. They would like him to tell them why this art is timeless and beautiful in his own language and using his own terms. They do not want a lackey; they want a convert.

What the Artist does not know is that outside the little building in which he has been sequestered for some time now, there are many others who share his disdain for this art. In fact, there are many who have great facility and admiration for the kind of art that he made back in those days. And these folks, not out of time, knowing full well what abstract expressionism is, and appreciating its nuances, yet choose to think of it as an inferior kind of art. Even perhaps an unfortunate breakdown of "artistic sensibility," not the apotheosis of it. It is among those people that he would find the reception and the receptivity that could allow him to critically engage with such art and then begin to see where and how it fits in the larger conversation about art itself. Confusion will gradually give way to understanding, and a conversation can be had with those that he still disagrees with in a language that they can understand.

But he is not allowed to leave. He can blow up the building, kill his captors and escape, or he can accept the parameters of his captivity. If he does the former, he will be deemed a savage and a barbarian from the past, a superstitious traditionalist who cannot escape the binds of his own irrational beliefs. He is incapable of rational evaluation based on universal principles so his judgment is defective anyway. If he does the latter, they would declare victory, and pronounce the debate over. When exposed to reason, even those who are burdened by their own particular traditions can see the light of day. If they are honest. If they are willing to admit the inferiority of their systems of evaluation. Notice that there is no real debate here. There are two slots, two options, and neither does very much to account for the possibility that the Artist may know something that they do not. Confirmation or denial is dualistic logic. Either you are in or you are out.

So the Artist is faced with the choice of being a monster (a bomber, no longer an Artist) or an abstract expressionist (no longer an artist meaningful to himself). Is there no other way? Fortunately, there is. The Artist can ingratiate himself to his captors, so they let him carry on with his own work while he occasionally humors them by throwing paint on the wall and calling these his own contributions to abstract expressionism. Meanwhile, he bides his time. He figures that, eventually, they will let down their guard and he can escape unnoticed. And then he can go seeking for an ally out there in the world beyond the bounds of his captivity.

If the Artist is out of his time in the age of the abstract expressionists, then Muslims like Sayyid Ahmad Khan are similarly out of place in the modern West. They always have been to one extent or another. Often trimmed of their distinction to fit the molds that are already available, as friends or enemies but not critics. But as with the Artist, the situation is never as bad as it appears.

Because if Sayyid Ahmad Khan is the Muslim analog to the medieval artist, then MacIntyre is one among the many allies he would find in the present. Posthumously, of course, but not without benefit for both Islam and the West. For if MacIntyre is right, and the West is in an unacknowledged state of moral incoherence and senseless anomie, the pathologies attendant to such a situation would eventually need resolution. Like a housing bubble that just keeps growing and growing and growing, at some point it will pop. What will be needed when it does? Some may contend that it has been popping for quite some time already, in bits and pieces which are only getting bigger and harder to conceal. The monstrous chickens it has necessarily created as a consequence of its own incoherencies are already coming home to roost. Fundamentalisms abound, just as totalitarianisms did only a few generations ago. Imperialisms have given way to financial and economic exploitations on a grand scale. The world is on fire, from Tahrir Square to the Acropolis. Or as they say in America, from Wall Street to Main Street. MacIntyre now seems prophetic when in 1984 he counseled that all well-meaning actors should set themselves the task of building those kinds of communities "within which civility and the intellectual and moral life can be sustained through the new dark ages which are already upon us."[56] Khan's Islam is up this task, and more.

What will it mean to imagine Islam as an *immanent* critique of the West? It will mean to acknowledge that Islam is a tradition of rational inquiry and collective identity that has something to offer against what ails the world today. That its participation in the much-needed *resorgimento* of our broken social and moral order will be both necessary and critical. That Islam, far from being the religion of the barbarians may be a vital resource against the barbarians who "have already been governing us for quite some time."[57] But for this to happen, Islam itself will need to be reorganized and reimagined, and then re-presented to the world, in the way Sayyid Ahmad Khan imagined it. This book is written in the fervent hope that despite all the self-inflicted wounds and other calamities, such a reimagination and reorganization of Islam still remains well within the realm of possibility.

Epilogue: Can the Muslim Speak?

Back in 2011, *The New York Times Magazine* did a wide-ranging profile of Yasir Qadhi, a well-known Muslim-American cleric born in Houston to an immigrant family of Pakistani origins. Qadhi belongs to a small but growing movement of conservative Muslims called the Salafiyya, which literally means "the forebearers." As a fellow student in the Religious Studies Department at Yale University, he was also an acquaintance. The article was provocatively titled "Why Yasir Qadhi wants to talk about Jihad?"[1] The Salafiyya is a back-to-the-roots movement similar in theological orientation to modern neo-orthodox Christianity. It tries to look past the intervening innovations of the last thousand or so years and seeks moral guidance from the Qur'an and the earliest iterations of Prophetic Sunna. It has both theological and political manifestations. Radical Islamists and other militant fundamentalist groups like ISIS, al-Qaeda, or the Taliban are also broadly Salafi in their theological sensibilities. Many Salafi groups in the United States have come under increased scrutiny in the years since 9/11. As a sometimes spokesman for the movement, Qadhi has often found himself the subject of both scrutiny and suspicion. But for his willingness to engage with American authorities, he has also drawn the ire of his co-religionists. In the great but unenviable tradition of Muslim "mediums" of the last two centuries, Qadhi too finds himself in the middle of a mess.

Qadhi has an interesting background. His father is a doctor by trade and Qadhi himself has a degree in chemical engineering from the University of Houston. His mother is a microbiologist from Karachi, Pakistan, and together with her husband founded the first mosque in the Houston area in 1971. He grew up in a profoundly religious family that also had the peculiarly deep immigrant's love of America. In the years before attending college in Houston, Qadhi spent much of his childhood in Jeddah, Saudi Arabia, where his father had landed a job teaching medicine at the King Abdul-Aziz University. Shuttling back and forth between Jeddah and Houston, Qadhi was exposed to both the currents of modern Western life and a deeply conservative society in Saudi Arabia. He found the latter far more appealing and decided to pursue a graduate degree in Islamic theology at the University of Medina. The 9/11 attacks happened while he was in Medina and prompted much soul searching about where he properly belonged in the world, and what his life's work should be. He was troubled by the possibility that the theological movement to which he belonged had helped shape the militant ideologies of groups like al-Qaeda. "What type of Islam are we going to teach people?" he recalled thinking. "This isolationist Islam? This Islam of 'us' versus 'them'—is that healthy? Is that what my religion is?" When his father called him to say, "Come back to America, this is your land," Qadhi decided to switch from the University of Medina to the Yale program in Islamic Studies and returned home in 2004.

Qadhi was troubled by what he found in the United States upon his return. The leadership of the Salafi movement in the United States had been almost entirely wiped out by an increasingly unforgiving law enforcement atmosphere. Additionally, the leadership of the Muslim community as such was stuck between a rock and a hard place. Few wanted to speak too loudly for fear of being targeted by the authorities, and the community had become largely rudderless as a result. Mosques had become infested with informants and agents. Muslim charities and schools were under increased scrutiny. Many were closed down entirely, or worse, their leaders put in jail for tacit or explicit support of terrorism.[2] "No matter how strange this sounds, after having lived in Saudi Arabia for so long and also in America for so long, I could fully understand the fear, the anger, the frustration, the paranoia on both sides," Qadhi says. "I could understand 'they' and 'us.'" Fear was especially pervasive among young Muslim-Americans. Lacking any clear guidance, many were veering to one extreme or another, either abandoning Islam altogether to escape notice, or channeling their resentment into a militant and strident affirmation of their own difference. Qadhi had arrived home to find his community in some serious trouble.

It was in this kind of environment that Qadhi took on the important task of reaching out to his co-religionists and to other Americans and taking on a leadership role that had been left largely vacant since 2001. He became an instant hit in young Salafi circles that had been left without guidance for many years. In 2007, he made a pact of mutual respect and cooperation with American clerics of the Sufi disposition, trying to put to rest the longtime enmity between the Sufis and the Salafiyya. Earlier, he had created even more buzz during a conference in Copenhagen by shaking the hand of Mona Eltahawy, a female columnist on Arab and Muslim issues. For both these supposed transgressions, he was roundly criticized by his former colleagues in Medina and by the more conservative elements within the American Muslim community. Additionally, he also made efforts to reach out to Homeland Security officials, inviting them to Muslim conferences and even attending outreach seminars organized by the FBI. Many Muslims already resentful of being targeted indiscriminately by American law enforcement derided him as a sell-out and an opportunist.

Of course, Qadhi himself had been personally targeted many times by said law enforcement. On numerous occasions when reentering the country after foreign travel, he would spend hours with immigration authorities who would ask him probing questions about the nature of his travels, and about his Muslim colleagues among the Salafiyya. Even as he was co-operating with Homeland Security he was obviously on a terrorist watch list. When Qadhi ran into an acquaintance at Homeland Security conference in 2006, he pointedly asked him, "Don't you think it's ironic that on the one hand, you're reaching out for my expertise and wanting my help, and on the other hand, you're harassing and intimidating me as if I'm a potential terrorist?" He stopped traveling with his family because, as he said, "I'm not going to be humiliated in front of my kids." So Qadhi was not unaware of the humiliations that his fellow Muslims were undergoing on a regular basis at the hands of their own government. But resentment is wasted emotion. Qadhi was interested in constructive engagement.

*   *   *

In his own mind, Qadhi inhabits two ostensibly very different identities. He is a Salafi Muslim, a cleric who believes that many aspects of modern Western culture and life are detrimental toward true well-being. Yet, at the same time, though living somewhere in Saudi Arabia may be more comfortable for him, he says that "it's not my land at the end of the day. I am an American. What else can I say?" In fact, he sees life in America as an opportunity, not as an obstacle. Qadhi claims that there is no better place to be a Muslim than America, because as a minority, you "really feel your faith." But post-9/11 America presents Muslims with serious challenges. Qadhi believes that the only way to deal with the issue of militant Islam is to first engage in more sophisticated talk about Islam in the public mainstream here and elsewhere. This would entail having conversations about controversial issues, like the status of jihad in Islam, or the relationship between political citizenship and obligation to the *umma*, or the proper role of *shari'a* in modern Muslim life, or a critical Islamic take on the institution of secularism. These are all matters that need urgent engagement, if for no other reason than they are central to the development of a robust Muslim identity, no matter the place or time. In contemporary America, the urgency is even more profound because in the absence of frank conversation in the community, the young have a tendency to turn to the basement of communal life where darkness resides in all its most perverse manifestations. It is with this in mind that Qadhi advocates a greater emphasis on Islamic education, and on the development of a robust Muslim civil society in America, complete with Islamic centers, mosques, publications, schools and universities, charities, and other communal forums. Without such forums, Muslims life would tend to become even more ghettoized than it already is, and ghettos are not a safe space for any community.

It should be noted of course that there are no active pogroms against Muslims in the West. Nobody is throwing them out of their homes and putting them in actual, physical ghettos. Few are explicitly calling for their heads. Muslims are, for the most part, doing well financially in the United States and their children have better healthcare and education than their parents and grandparents ever did in their home countries. Many of them have been treated far better here in the West than they were in their ancestral lands. Many Muslim minorities find life here far more open and egalitarian than in those places they fled for religious, political, or economic reasons. But toleration too has its price. And the price has only become more exorbitant since 9/11. Islam as an active, engaged, and robust identity is gradually being squeezed out of Muslims by the vicelike grip of the "eithers" and "ors" of a depoliticized existence. Civic participation by practicing Muslim clerics has been reduced to taking part in largely vacuous interfaith dialogues and affirming their commitment to peace and toleration. In general, Muslim civil life in the public sphere has been largely muted in the last fifteen odd years. When it does appear on the scene, it is usually in the defensive mode of either pledging allegiance to American values or trying to explain themselves to a suspicious public. Conversation about Islam among Muslims and between Muslim-Americans and the larger public is so impoverished that even calling it a conversation is euphemism. And in this age of euphemisms, Islam itself is in danger of becoming a euphemism for itself; a tired and tamed version of a potent intellectual tradition reduced to bombs or clichés.

The case of Yasir Qadhi is most instructive in this regard. Qadhi serves as Academic Dean for the al-Maghrib Institute, a transnational center for Islamic learning that offers seminars and workshops in the United States, Canada, and Britain. In his role as both leader and teacher to an increasingly restive group of young Muslims, Qadhi finds himself caught in an unusual bind. In order to inform them on the aforementioned theological questions for which they need guidance (issues like secularism, jihad, sharia, etc.), he needs a public forum in which he can discuss these matters openly and frankly. When faced with the black-and-white simplicity concerning Islam, a feature of almost all media debates, he needs an intellectually safe space to prod them to think "in color" and to find a balance between loyalty to Islam and America. But no such safe space exists. "My hands are tied," he says, "and my tongue is silent." The reasons are not hard to understand. Though there is great demand for courses on the *fiqh* of jihad at the institute, for example, and young Muslims are craving guidance, no one is willing to touch the subject with a twelve-foot pole. Abu Easa Niamatullah, another al-Maghrib scholar puts it this way: "What stopped us [from offering courses on jihad]? Picture two bearded guys talking about the fiqh of jihad. We would be dead. We would be absolutely finished." Al-Maghrib is hardly the only place where such self-censorship is routine. It is well-established practice in the Muslim community at large at this point in time. Where Muslims venture out to stake out a place for conversation among themselves or with other Americans, they have found little or no appetite for nuance. "There is a way to stop extremism," Qadhi says, "but it is not palatable to Americans." While American critics of Islam often brand Qadhi "a wolf in sheep's clothing" and his al-Maghrib Institute, "Jihad U.," he is assailed by young members of his own community for not being more forthcoming with guidance on issues which are central to their Islamic identity. Jihad, *sharia, tauhid, khilafat,* and so on are not incidental to Islam, such that one can be Muslim without ever discussing these matters in public. Yet all these terms have become so toxic in the West that anyone who even mentions them draws immediate suspicion, and more often than not, also recrimination. So, laments Qadhi,

> it is an awkward position to be in. How can one simultaneously fight against a powerful government, a pervasive and sensationalist-prone media *and* a group of overzealous, rash youth who are already predisposed to reject your message, because they view you as being a part of the establishment (while, ironically, the "establishment" never ceases to view you as part of the radicals)?

But Qadhi will not lose hope. "We need to make sure that our children can live freely, and we're going to *fight* for that freedom. And every time I use that word, I need to make a disclaimer—I don't mean 'fight' in the Tea Party sense of overthrowing the government." Freedom in America is nebulous business, and this is how it has to be. Sometimes we are free to own guns but not free to marry who we love. Sometimes we are free to make money in whatever way we want but not free from pain and suffering. Sometimes it is just another form of nihilism, "just another word for nothing left to lose." Part of living in freedom is the ability to freely discuss the nature of that freedom. This is what Qadhi wants to reclaim in the aftermath of 9/11. He understands that in these traumatic times, the greatest danger is the loss of voice, the fear that can drive even the best of us dumb and mute. Dumb to the voices of others, and mute to their ears. Qadhi seeks neither acceptance nor rejection, but engagement, critically but without fear. In this age of drone strikes and bomb blasts, Qadhi seeks an audience. He wants to talk.

*   *   *

I began with Mahmoud Ahmadinejad and now end with Yasir Qadhi because neither of these men represents an easily tolerable case of Islam as critique. In their own distinct ways, their versions of Islam are largely not palatable to a Western audience (or even to me). Qadhi is deeply conservative and courts constant controversy in the media for his views, and also among America's Muslim population that is, on average, rather less conservative than him.[3] His positions on gender norms, homosexuality, and family life closely track other traditional religionists in America (including Christian and Jewish ones) and are similarly out of the liberal mainstream consensus.[4] And while he has repeatedly condemned extremist violence in the name of Islam, from an outside perspective his theological views are not that far removed from those of the radical outfits that encourage or commit such violence. For his part, Mahmoud Ahmadinejad built his political brand in Iran on virulent anti-Americanism and a deep, public distaste for what he calls "the Zionist entity" in historic Palestine. He was ridiculed in the American press for a 2007 speech at Columbia University where he claimed that homosexuality was a Western phenomenon and that there were no gay people in Iran.[5] His close alliance with the most conservative elements in the Iranian clerical establishment and his role in the American embassy hostage crisis (he was a student at that time) also made him a very unsympathetic figure for Western observers when he was president of Iran. Still, the test of viable critique can hardly be easy palatability or the character of the messenger if such critique is to have any credible relevance in public debates. As I mentioned before, the Western canon is replete with anti-Semites, racists, misogynists, and even outright Nazis, and there are few characters as distasteful as Winston Churchill who was nonetheless recently labeled "the greatest of all Anglo-Americans" by a famous British historian.[6] The point is not to ignore the various supposed shortcomings of this or that critic but rather to fairly assess their possible contributions to the broader debates about what it means to be a human being in the world today. And to assess and reassess the human condition from their particular vantage points, hemmed in by their peculiar limitations.

Consider, for example, that the anodyne perennialism of someone like the religion scholar Reza Aslan or the barely-there Islam of CNN anchor Fareed Zakaria might be easier to stomach for the mainstream American audiences but these kinds of figures provide no viable critiques from a Muslim perspective, rather only confirmations of already existing consensus in the West about what constitutes the good life. On the other hand, the theological and political musings of radical Islamic outfits and their intellectual antecedents are so clear in their rejections that their Islam often appears as pure negation of the West in the West. In either case, the commensurability thesis operates to siphon off the differences and familiarities into contrasting boxes of legibility for easy mass consumption. Folks like Qadhi and Ahmadinejad, who are both hated by the likes of al-Qaeda and ISIS and draw ridicule from the liberal mainstream in the West, resist being easily shoved into already existing registers of participation in public debates. Qadhi is unabashedly American, openly advocating his Islam as an aspect of his American identity and vice versa. And confounding the medievalist tropes about Muslims with long beards in thobes and turbans, Ahmadinejad is undeniably modern both in his appearance and in his aspirations for his native Iran on the world stage. They are not easy cases. And it is precisely on that account that they need to be properly accounted for.

What would such accounting entail? The first, simple task is to listen, "critically but without fear" as Ian Baruma said in a profile about Tariq Ramadan for the *New York Times Magazine* in 2007.[7] Baruma's credentials as a liberal critic are undisputable. The author of *Occidentalism*, Baruma has written extensively on the historical appeal of European fascism and other non-liberal ideologies for modern Islamist movements.[8] He was also horrified at the murder of the Dutch film maker Theo van Gogh by a homegrown Islamic fanatic in 2004. Van Gogh had collaborated with the well-known Somali-Dutch ex-Muslim Ayaan Hirsi Ali on the production of the documentary *Submission (2004),* a searing critique of the treatment of women in Muslim societies. Baruma wrote about this assassination in his book *Murder in Amsterdam* and clearly demonstrated an in-depth understanding of the danger of Islamism to European values.[9] His profile of Ramadan was therefore expected to be a blistering takedown. But Baruma refused to take the bait of these expectations. In listening to what Ramadan had to say with an open mind, he himself was surprised that they "agreed on most issues, and even when [they] didn't ([Ramadan] was more friendly toward the Pope than I was), our debate refused to catch fire."[10] After a long and only intermittently salutary discussion of Ramadan's ideas and concerns, Baruma notes that

Ramadan offers a different way, which insists that a reasoned but traditionalist approach to Islam offers values that are as universal as those of the European Enlightenment. From what I understand of Ramadan's enterprise, these values are neither secular, nor always liberal, but they are not part of a holy war against Western democracy either. His politics offer an alternative to violence, which, in the end, *is reason enough to engage with him, critically, but without fear.*[11]

It is this manner of engagement, of consistently listening critically but without fear, that opens up a middle space of contest over the meaning(s) of the modern world sans the summary judgments and rejections that often populate conversations about Islam in the West (and about the West in much of the Islamic world). It is this middle space that Hannah Arendt had in mind when she argued that "the world is not human just because it is made by human beings . . . [rather] we humanize what is going on in the world and in ourselves only by speaking of it, and in the course of speaking of it we learn to be human."[12] For it is only by speaking to each other, critically but without fear, into the middle space of appearance that we as human beings "become subjects as well as objects of modernization, to get a grip on the modern world and to make [ourselves] at home in it."[13] And it is toward the creation and maintenance of such open *agora* in the global public mainstream that this book is a small and humble effort.

* * *

Some years ago Yasir invited me to his place for *chai* and kebabs. We had somehow avoided being in a class together until we both found ourselves in a German for Reading Proficiency summer course. He was doing substantially better in the class than I was. Since he had learned the Qur'an by heart before he was fourteen, his facility with foreign languages came as no surprise to me. What was surprising was how gracious he was to someone like me, hardly the kind of practicing Muslim he would be expected to approve of. He invited me to come to the mosque to listen to him speak and meet other local Muslims. I said I would try. But even as I said it, I knew I would not go.

Some years earlier, a college friend of mine who was then working for Morgan Stanley in New York was picked up by the FBI and deported from the United States. His name had come up due to his involvement with a volunteer group run by a mosque in Jackson Heights, Queens. Apparently his name matched one on the terror watchlist. Without naming him, let me just say that his name is something like the equivalent of "Roger Smith" in English. The poor guy did not stand a chance. The FBI realized its mistake soon enough, but once the wheels of bureaucracy start turning, they take a while to stop. It was three years before he was allowed back into the country, and by then he had soured on America altogether. He accompanied his wife for the two years it took her to complete a graduate degree in International Economics from the Woodrow Wilson School of International Relations at Princeton University, and he used this time to get a master's degree in computer science from the University of Pennsylvania. Smart family! But he could not bring himself to live here, nor to have much sympathy for Americans anywhere. The trauma was not merely psychological, but existential. He had decided to shut up and continue on with his life without dealing with the issue of his Islam. This was unfortunate. At Bowdoin College, he had been a wonderful conversationalist and never shied away from discussing the ins and outs of Islam with anyone. In fact, after he was selected from among many other applicants to give the graduation day speech in 1999, he titled the speech "I am not a Terrorist." In the speech, he wanted the audience to appreciate the nuances of Islam, and the complexity of his own identity. Of course, no such complexity was on offer when some random mid-level operative at the FBI matched his name to one on a list, and that was that. And whatever my friend had to offer to the conversation about Islam in America, well, that is not on offer anymore.

I'd like to say I was righteously indignant or angry at this incident. But truth be told, the dominant feeling was fear. And fear drives all of us far more effectively than any other emotion. I too had decided to shut up. I would not join the Muslim Students Association at Yale, nor participate in any events for Muslims for fear of ending up on some list. Nor would I ever set foot in a mosque in the United States or attend conferences with largely Muslim audiences. I would have as little to do with the Muslim community here as I could. After all, my name too is something like the equivalent of "John Simon" in the Muslim world. What chance would I have? And so when Yasir asked me to come and listen to him speak with fellow Muslims in a local mosque, I knew I would not go. For fear, for self-preservation. And when petitions were sent around via e-mail regarding this or that case of discrimination against Muslim students, faculty, or others, I always deleted them immediately. Again, when the gaze of the other lacks any nuance or complexity, and demands conversion rather than conversation, one should keep things as simple as possible. And so it has been for some time now.

But there is great loss that attends such simplicity. Needless to say, I do not share Qadhi's politics or his particular account of Islam and its place in modernity. But the sounds that inhabit his silence are still whispering negations of our better natures as a human society. They parry us away from confidence against fear. This book is an attempt to begin filling these silences with fighting words, to ease out the fears, and demand engagement not mere toleration. To this end I have tried to show how the modern Muslim subject often experiences Western modernity as a curious assemblage of rat mazes that, short of blowing the maze up, offer only singular ways out. These mazes dot the discursive landscape, they are implicit in our conversations and deliberations about Islam, and often even explicit in political rhetoric about Muslims as a contagion, menace, or pest. And yet in spite of all this rhetoric, Muslims everywhere have tried to make sense of their situation in the world, and of this new emergent world itself, in ways that belie such binary restrictions. They have found ways out, so to say, by gnawing at the walls or refusing to play along. The hidden transcripts of their efforts are just as plentiful as the mazes they have vanquished, but these transcripts lack publicity.[14] In such circumstances, a contrapuntally mediated voice is better than no voice at all. In fact Sayyid Ahmad Khan himself would likely call the mediated voice the quintessentially Muslim voice, finding harmony in discord, and incorporating difference is an essential feature of a verdant, vigorous Islam. So in this sense, this project is both about Sayyid Ahmad Khan and undertaken in his stead. A voiceless, disengaged, fearful Islam is no Islam at all. The parameters of engagement may be less than ideal, but that is no reason to lose hope. It is an opportunity to find new avenues for improvement. As Ghalib puts it: "Alas, not all things in life are easy; Even man struggles to be human."

The legacy of Sayyid Ahmad Khan is something of a contested topic among South Asian Muslims. My particular take on his life and work is not within the mainstream of the study of Khan in Indian and Pakistani institutions of higher learning. The former tend to stress his educational works, and the latter his advancement of Muslim interests in pre-partition India. He is rarely studied as a systematic thinker, and his theological contributions have been largely ignored by the traditional *'ulama*. The desire to co-opt him for the nationalistic narratives of these states runs strong on both sides of the divide. More recently, the fundamentalist elements within the Islamic milieu have rediscovered him as a liberal stooge of the British, and a forerunner of the many contemporary elites that acquiesce to the West for their own petty interests. Khan, as I hope to have shown, is none of these caricatures of himself, and yet to some extent some combination of all of them. He was someone who collaborated with the British, and yet fought for the interests of his community. He believed that Hindus and Muslims could, and should, live together in peace in the subcontinent, and yet worried that Muslims were losing their distinction in the midst of all the different influences that India presented them with. He believed in the value of modern education, but at the same time was a firm traditionalist. All of these elements put together paint a picture of confusion, contradiction, and inconsistency only when viewed from the vantage point of ideological purity. But from Khan's own perspective, a good life was precisely the kind of life that balanced contradictions and mediated between the differences. It was the embodiment of *tatbi'a*, of harmonizing the different elements of one's experience into an effective plan for righteous action. It is in this sense that the example of Khan's life is so relevant to Muslim life today. For the Muslim can in fact speak, has spoken, and will keep on speaking. But do we have the good sense to let her in on our conversations? And the courage to *listen*?

Notes

Prologue

1 Christine Hauser, "Iranian Leader's Letter to Bush Emerges," *The New York Times*, May 9, 2006.

2 The Associated Press, "Rice Rejects Iranian Leader's Letter, Asserting Democracy Has Failed," *USA Today*, May 9, 2006.

3 Fred Kaplan, "Dear Mahmoud: How Bush Should Respond to the Iranian President's Letter," *Slate*, May 10, 2006.

4 Editorial Staff, "Iran Declares War," *The New York Sun*, May 11, 2006.

5 Kamal Zazir Yasin, "Unexpectedly, Iran's Leader Breaks a Few Old Taboos," *Dawn*, May 18, 2006.

6 Editorial Staff, "Ahmadinejad's Letter to Bush Inspires New Hope for Resolving Nuclear Issue," *The Daily Star*, May 9, 2006.

7 Alon Ben-Meir, "Engage Iran Directly," *Hurriyet Daily News*, May 17, 2006.

8 Editorial Staff, "Iranian President's Letter Opens Window into the Muslim World," *Daily News Egypt*, May 13, 2006.

9 Hauser, "Iranian Leader's Letter to Bush Emerges."

10 Appendix I, "Mahmoud Ahmadinejad's Letter to George W. Bush."

11 Editorial Staff, "Iranian President's Letter Opens Window into the Muslim World."

Introduction

1 Rudyard Kipling, "The Ballad of East and West," in T. S. Elliot, *A Choice of Kipling's Verse* (London: Faber & Faber, Main Edition, 1963).

2 The term "intersectionality" was first used by Kimberlé Crenshaw in "Demarginalizing the Intersection of Race and Sex: A Black Feminist Critique of Antidiscrimination Doctrine, Feminist Theory and Antiracist Politics" to describe the intersection of feminism with black identity politics (*University of Chicago Legal Forum*, 1989). But the idea that different aspects of one's identity can (and do) intersect in complex (and often contradictory) ways is of much older vintage. W. E. B. Du Bois was making a Marxist version of this argument (focusing on race, class, and nation) as far back as the early twentieth century. In the intervening

years, intellectuals as diverse as bell hooks, Anna Julia Cooper, and Sojourner Truth theorized some version of the theory of intersectionality now associated with Crenshaw.

3 Audre Lorde, *Sister Outsider: Essays and Speeches* (New York: Crossing Press, 1984), 116.

4 There is perhaps no better evidence of the fact the British authorities thought him a "liberal" (a euphemism for someone largely on board with their civilizational program in India) than the fact that he was knighted by the Queen, Sir Sayyid Ahmad Khan, in 1888.

5 Andrew March, "What Is Comparative Political Theory?" *The Review of Politics* 71 (2009): 547.

6 *Taklif* has the primary meaning of "obligation" in Arabic. But in Khan's native Urdu, the connotative domain of the word is centered around the feeling of "pain" or "burden." Khan was the first major Muslim thinker to do nearly all of his theological writing in Urdu rather than Arabic. This meant that theologically significant terms like *taklif* were often no longer bound strongly to their primary Arabic meaning for Khan (or his audience) but rather available for creative reinterpretation in the connotative domain of a new language. This manner of reinterpretation was of course controversial then as it is now, and it certainly made him no friends among the more traditionally minded Muslims of his day.

7 Irfan Ahmad, *Religion as Critique: Islamic Critical Thinking from Mecca to the Marketplace* (Chapel Hill: University of North Carolina Press, 2017).

8 From the Call for Papers, "Critical Muslim Studies: Decolonial Struggles and Liberation Theologies Granada, Spain - June 16–June 22, 2019," http://www.dialogoglobal.com/granada/

9 *ReOrient: The Journal of Critical Muslim Studies*, Pluto Journals, http://www.plutojournals.com/reorient/

10 "Our Mission," *Critical Muslim 01: The Arabs Are Alive*, Jan–March 2012, C. Hurst & Co (Publishers) Ltd., London, UK.

11 Sir William Muir, *The Life of Mahomet* (Whitefish: Kessinger Publishing LLC, 2003). The Muir text has made a rather remarkable comeback in the years since 9/11, being published and distributed widely by evangelical publishers. Cf.: a version of the book made available by Adamant Media Corporation, a well-known publisher of *Christian* books.

12 Syed Ahmad Khan and Francis Robinson (trans.), *The Causes of the Indian Revolt* (Oxford: Oxford University Press, 2000).

13 Thomas R. Metcalf, *The Aftermath of the Revolt in India: 1857–1870* (Westwood: Riverdale Company Inc., 1991), 298.

14 Sir Sayyid Ahmad Khan, "Lecture at the Education Conference in Delhi to Mark the Anniversary of the Foundation of the *Madrasat ul 'Ulūm*," December 28, 1889, quoted

in Altaf Husain Hali, K. H. Qadiri and David G. Matthews (trans.), *Hayat-i-Javed: A Biographical Account of Sir Sayyid* (Delhi: Idarah-i-Adabiyat-i-Delli, 1979), 56.

15 Khan and Robinson (trans.), *The Causes of the Indian Revolt*, 11–14.

16 Ibid., 12.

17 Edward W. Said, *Culture and Imperialism* (New York: Vintage Books, 1993), 33.

18 Andrea Eliot, "Why Yasir Qadhi Wants to Talk about Jihad?" *The New York Times Magazine,* March 17, 2011.

19 MacIntyre is, of course, still alive!

Chapter 1

1 For a wonderful, sympathetic account of these lives, please refer to William Dalrymple, *White Mughals: Love and Betrayal in late 18th Century India* (New York: Penguin Books, 2004).

2 Barbara D. Metcalfe (ed.), *Islam in South Asia in Practice* (Princeton: Princeton University Press, 2009), 95.

3 The years of Kabir's birth and death are unclear. Some historians like Linda Hess in *The Bijak of Kabir* (Oxford: Oxford University Press, 2006) favor 1398–1448, while others like David N. Lorenzen in *Who Invented Hinduism: Essays on Religion in History* (New Delhi: Yoda Press, 2002) argue for 1440–1518.

4 The term *tariqa* translates roughly to "way" or "method" and refers to mystical technique or esoteric knowledge of a particular order of Sufis. The term *silsila* is generally translated as "link" or "chain" and in this context refers to the continuous line of master-disciple relationships originating in the guidance of a particular Sufi master. Each *tariqa* can have many different *silsila*.

5 Sayyid Ahmad Khan, *Sīrat-i Farīdīyah* (this is Khan's portrait of his grandfather and grandmother written in August 1893) in M. Ismaʿīl Pānīpatī (ed.), *Maqālāt-i Sir Sayyid (PMaq),* 16 vols. (Lahore: Majlis-i Tariqqī-i adab, 1962–65), *PMaq XVI,* 687. Quoted in Christian W. Troll, *Sayyid Ahmad Khan: A Re-Interpretation of Muslim Theology* (New Delhi: Vikas Publishing House, Pvt Ltd., 1978), 29–30.

6 Hafeez Malik, *Sir Sayyid Ahmad Khan and Muslim Modernization in India and Pakistan* (New York: Columbia University Press, 1980), 256.

7 Ibid.

8 Ibid., 257.

9 Ibid., 258.

10 Troll, *Sayyid Ahmad Khan,* 33.

11 Ibid., 34.

12 Johannes Marinus Simon Baljon Jr., *The Reforms and Religious Ideas of Sir Sayyid Ahmad Khan* (Lahore: Ashraf Press, 1964), 72.

13 The idea of a *tariqa* of Muhammad is not entirely, conceptually distinct from the more common designation of the Sunna of Muhammad. The *tariqa* has a more devotional valence, having its roots in Sufi practice, whereas the Sunna has more legal connotations, as a primary source of guidance for *fiqh* of Muslim jurists.

14 Yohanan Friedman, *Shaykh Ahmad Sirhindī* (Montreal and London: McGill University Press, 1971), 40.

15 Troll, *Sayyid Ahmad Khan*, 44.

16 Annemarie Schimmel, *Mystical Dimensions of Islam* (Chapel Hill: University of North Carolina Press, 2011), 228.

17 Ibid., 226.

18 Sayyid Ahmad Khan, *Tusānīf-i Ahmadīyah (TFA)* in *PMaq XV*, 182–87. Quoted in Troll, *Sayyid Ahmad Khan*, 50.

19 *TFA* in *PMaq XV*, 272–73. Quoted in Troll, *Sayyid Ahmad Khan*, 45.

20 Cf.: *PMaq XIII*, 136, and Khan's paraphrase of Qur'an 28:49.

21 M. Ikram Chaghatai (ed.), *Herald of Nineteenth Century Muslim Thought: Sir Sayyid Ahmad Khan* (Lahore: Sang-e-Meel Publications, 2005), 298.

22 Cf.: Sayyid Ahmad Khan, "Lecture on Islam" to the *Anjuman-i himayat-I Islām*, section iv, "The Miracle of the Quran." Quoted in Troll, *Sayyid Ahmad Khan*, 325–27.

23 Troll, *Sayyid Ahmad Khan*, 56.

24 He produced a sociology, an anthropology, a philosophical theology of his anguish—this we now call the "Augustinian tradition," the closest thing to a theological orthodoxy in Christianity.

25 Wilfred Cantwell Smith, *Islam in Modern History* (Princeton: Princeton University Press, 1957), 41.

26 Altaf Hussain Hali, "Shikwa-e-Hind" (1888) in Iftikhar Ahmad Siddiqi (ed.), *Jawahar-e-Hali* (Lahore: Kereven-e-Adab, 1989), 314–30.

27 Ibid.

28 Ibid.

29 The use of the term "Middle East" to refer to the lands of South West Asia is so clearly problematic that its replacement here by the proper geographic descriptor should require no further explanation.

30 Hali, *Jawahar-e-Hali,* ibid.

31 By the time of the early Arab conquests North Africa and the South West Asia were already mostly Christian, and Persia was Zoroastrian with a large Christian minority.

32 A case in point is the famous *Quwwat-ul-Islam* mosque in Delhi, which was supposedly constructed out of the rubble of twenty-seven Jain temples torn down by the Mamluk king Qutb-ud-Din Aiback.

33 These practices and beliefs include (and this is NOT an exhaustive list) visiting and venerating tombs of saints and asking for intercession through prayer and

supplication, believing in magical and supernatural forces, ornate marriage ceremonies and the tradition of dowry, prohibition of a second marriage for women, the *Shi'i* practice of self-immolation and *tazia* (mourning), and even some Sufi notions like the *wahdat-al-wajud* (unity of being/creation) that were suggestive of pantheism and hence *shirk*.

34 The imam of Mecca, for example, declared that "this man (Sayyid Ahmad Khan) is erring and causes people to err. He is rather an agent of the devil and wants to mislead Muslims. It is a sin to support the college. May God damn the founder! And if this college (MAO College which in 1920 was converted into Aligarh Muslim University) has been founded, it must be demolished and its founder and his supporters thrown out of the fold of Islam." Quoted in Faizan Mustafa, "Misreading Syed Ahmad Khan," *The Indian Express,* November 17, 2017.

35 Sayyid Ahmad Khan's letter to Mahdī Ali Khan, June 20, 1870, in Shaikh Muhammad Isma'īl Panipati, *Maktūbat-i Sir Sayyid* (Lahore: Majlis Traqqi-I Adab, 1959), 124. Quoted in Malik, *Sir Sayyid Ahmad Khan and Muslim Modernization in India and Pakistan*, 98–99.

36 Sayyid Ahmad Khan, *Dāfi al-Buhtān* (Refuting False Accusations) in *Tahadhīb al Akhlaāq, I,* 15 Sha'bān, 1291 H., in *PMaq XIII,* 7–50. Quoted in Chaghatai (ed.), *Herald of Nineteenth Century Muslim Thought*, 353.

37 Sayyid Ahmad Khan, "Muslim Reformer," *Tahdhīb al-akhlāq (TA)* III: 194–203. Quoted in Troll, *Sayyid Ahmad Khan*, 305.

38 Sayyid Ahmad Khan, *TFA I* in *PMaq XV,* 182–87. Quoted in Troll, *Sayyid Ahmad Khan*, 306.

39 Sayyid Jamāl ad-Dīn al-Afghānī, "The Truth about the Neicheri Sect and an Explanation of the Neicheris," in Nikki R. Keddie and Hamid Algar (trans.), *An Islamic Response to Imperialism: Political and Religious Writings of Sayyid Jamāl ad-Dīn "al-Afghānī"* (Berkeley: University of California Press, 1983).

40 Sayyid Ahmad Khan, Introduction to *Khutubāt-i Ahmadīyah, TFA I & II,* 182–639, *PMaq XI,* 6–16. Quoted in Troll, *Sayyid Ahmad Khan*, 245–46.

41 Quran, 67:3-4.

42 Muhammad Iqbal in Khushwant Singh (trans.), *Shikwa and Jawab-i Shikwa: Iqbal's Dialogue with Allah* (New Delhi: Oxford University Press, 1991), 17.

43 Ibid., 19.

44 Ibid.

45 Ibid., 47.

46 Ibid., 52.

47 Malik, *Sir Sayyid Ahmad Khan and Muslim Modernization in India and Pakistan*, 99.

48 Ibid., 23.

49 Baljon, *The Reforms and Religious Ideas of Sir Sayyid Ahmad Khan*, 136.

Chapter 2

1   Jean-Luc Marion, *In Excess: Studies of Saturated Phenomena*, Robyn Horner and Vincent Berraud (trans.) (New York: Fordham University Press, 2002).

2   Parts of this paragraph have appeared before in Khurram Hussain, Review for Seema Alavi, *Muslim Cosmopolitanism in the Age of Empire* (Cambridge: Harvard University Press, 2015) in SCTIW Review Journal (March 14, 2017).

3   Marshall Berman, *All That Is Solid Melts into Air: The Experience of Modernity* (New York: Penguin Books, 1982), 5.

4   Hannah Arendt, *Men in Dark Times* (New York: Harvest Books, 1970), 24–25.

5   Alavi, *Muslim Cosmopolitanism in the Age of Empire.*

6   Cf.: David Motadel (ed.), *Islam and the European Empires* (Oxford: Oxford University Press, 2014).

7   Cf.: Thomas R. Metcalf, *Ideologies of the Raj* (Cambridge: Cambridge University Press, 1997).

8   Said, *Culture and Imperialism*, 33.

9   Hannah Arendt, *The Portable Hannah Arendt* (New York: Penguin Putnam Inc., 2000), 438.

10 Alasdair MacIntyre, *After Virtue* (Notre Dame: University of Notre Dame Press, 1984), 11.

11 Ibid., 263.

12 Alasdair MacIntyre, *Whose Justice? Which Rationality?* (Notre Dame: University of Notre Dame Press, 1988).

13 Cf.: Ibrahim A. Abu-Lughod, *The Arab Rediscovery of Europe: A Study in Cultural Encounters* (Princeton: Princeton University Press, 1963).

14 Dilyana Mancheva, "'Critical Islam' Debating/Negotiating Modernity," *Journal of Religion & Society* 14 (2002): 1.

15 Ibid., 13.

16 See also Tariq Ramadan, "Free Speech and Civic Responsibility," *The New York Times,* February 5, 2006. http://www.nytimes.com/2006/02/05/opinion/free-speech-and-civic-responsibility.html

17 Cf.: "Authority in Question: Secularity, Republicanism, and 'Communitarianism' in the Emerging Euro-Islamic Public Sphere," *Theory, Culture and Society* 24, no. 2 (2007): 135–60.

18 Mancheva, "'Critical Islam' Debating/Negotiating Modernity," 8.

19 Ziauddin Sardar, "Reformist Ideas and Muslim Intellectuals," in Abdullah Omar Naseef (ed.), *Today's Problems, Tomorrow's Solutions: Future Thoughts on the Structure of Muslim Society* (Mansell, London, 1988), 166.

20 Ziauddin Sardar, "Beyond Difference: Cultural Relations in a New Century," in Ehsan Masood (ed.), *How Do You Know: Reading Ziauddin Sardar on Islam, Science and Cultural Relations* (London: Pluto Press, 2006).

21 Cf.: Ziauddin Sardar, *The Future of Muslim Civilizations* (London: Croom Helkm Ltd., 1979), *Islamic Futures: The Shape of Ideas to Come* (London: Mansell Publishing, 1986).

22 "Pearl" here is with reference to Walter Benjamin's notion that the modern age represents such a catastrophic rupture from tradition and history that the only way to connect to our past is through diving for pearls in the ocean floor of history; to collect fragments of time, moments of thought and memory, shards of ideas and concepts, to craft out of these disparate elements so recovered some cohesive and coherent expedience in our experience of the present. I believe the efficacy of *re-membering* aspects of the work of Muslims thinkers cannot be overstated since the rupture from tradition and history in the Muslim world is of a whole different order than even the West.

23 Sayyid Ahmad Khan, *A Series of Essays on the Life of Muhammad and Subjects Subsidiary Thereto* (Lahore: Premier Bookhouse, 1968), 48–50.

24 Ibid., 36–48.

25 Ibid., 146.

26 Sayyid Ahmad Khan, *Mazhabi khayal zaman-e-qadim awr zaman-e-jadid ka* (Religious Thoughts about the Ancient Age and the Modern age), *PMaq III*, 23. Quoted in Faisal Devji, "Apologetic Modernity," *Modern Intellectual History* 4, no. 1 (2007): 61–76.

27 Carl Schmitt, *The Nomos of the Earth in the International Law of the Jus Publicum Europaeum* (New York: Telos Press Ltd., 2003).

28 Jose Casanova, *Public Religions in the Modern World* (Chicago: The University of Chicago Press, 1994), 234.

29 Ibid., 7. This way of phrasing the question is an obvious reference to the famous Kantian formulation in *The Critique of Pure Reason*, "What are the conditions of possibility for human consciousness?"

30 Ibid., 17.

31 Ibid., 8.

Chapter 3

1 Portions of this chapter have appeared before in slightly different form in Khurram Hussain, "Tragedy and History in Reinhold Niebuhr's Thought," *The American Journal of Theology and Philosophy* 31, no. 2 (May 2010): 147–59.

2 George Orwell, *Animal Farm* (New York: Brawtley Press, 2012), 12.

3 Jürgen Habermas, *The Postnational Constellation: Political Essays* (Cambridge: The MIT Press, 2001), 58.

4 Notice that the modern political project par excellence, nationalism, often entails both of these sensibilities, usually associated with opposing camps in the same

polity. To use the American case as an example, the *future-perfect* conforms to the version of nationalism assumed by Barack Obama's politics of hope, as well as to the notion of a civilizing manifest destiny in the nineteenth century (and beyond), the idea of an evolutionary advancement of the rights of man (per John Dewey, William James, and more recently Richard Rorty). To the *past-perfect* belong the nativist, and isolationist tendencies within the American sociopolitical milieu, constitutional originalism, fundamentalist accounts of the American founding as a Christian nation (and its slow decline into multi-culti confusion ever since). Of course, there are ways of imagining nationalism other than these two. In later sections of this chapter, we will encounter some of them. As a preview, let me suggest that Niebuhr's conception of a realistic nationalism, and Bella's notion of a civil religion both attempt to undo the Gordian knot that ties together these two opposing impulses while at the same time keeping them apart.

5 Habermas, *The Postnational Constellation*, 59.

6 Ibid., 58.

7 Imam Ruhullah Khomeini, "The Pillars of an Islamic State," in Mansoor Moaddel and Kamran Talattof (eds.), *Modernist and Fundamentalist Debates in Islam* (New York: Palgrave MacMillan, 2000), 247–48.

8 Ibid., 248.

9 Ibid., 258.

10 Ibid., 252.

11 Ibid., 253.

12 Cf.: Richard Dawkins, *The Magic of Reality* (New York: Free Press, 2012), *The God Delusion* (New York: Mariner Books, 2008), Christopher Hitchens, *And Yet... Essays* (New York: Simon & Schuster, 2015), *The Portable Atheist* (Boston: Da Capo Press, 2007), and Sam Harris, *The End of Faith* (New York: W.W. Norton & Company, 2006).

13 Sam Harris, *The Moral Landscape: How Science Can Determine Human Values* (New York: Free Press, 2010), 2.

14 Ibid., 11.

15 Ibid., 10.

16 Kant famously came up with an equation for moral knowledge! John Rawls' "veil of ignorance" and Thomas Nagel's "views from nowhere" are similarly formulas for the production of certain moral knowledge that implicitly, and sometimes explicitly, deny the relevance of "cultural invention." The later Rawls of *Political Liberalism* is of course much chastened and far more attendant to cultural concerns of particular social contexts. Hence his insistence on "overlapping consensus."

17 It is worth noting here that classical liberalism has in fact produced mutations (no pun intended) that seek to soften such utopianism. American pragmatism and, of course, Fabian socialism are critical interventions to the thoroughgoing optimism of liberal thinking.

18 Aldous Huxley, *Time Must Have a Stop* (New York: First Dalky Archive Edition, 1998).

19 For an excellent account of the state of Afghanistan in the early 1990s and the subsequent rise of the Taliban to power, cf.: Ahmad Rashid, *Taliban: Militant Islam, Oil and Fundamentalism in Central Asia* (New Haven: Yale University Press, 2000).

20 For more information on the political and intellectual biography of Maududi, cf.: Seyyed Vali Reza Nasr, *The Vanguard of the Islamic Revolution* (Berkeley: University of California Press, 1994), *Maududi and the Making of Islamic Revivalism* (New York: Oxford University Press, 1996).

21 Sayyid Abul A'la Maududi, "The Fallacy of Rationalism I & II," in S. Waqar Ahmad Gardezi and Abdul Waheed Khan (trans.), *West versus Islam* (New Delhi: International Islamic Publishers, 1992), 119.

22 Ibid., 114.

23 I am reminded here of the pre-Einstein/pre-Quantum Mechanics state of theoretical physics in the late nineteenth century when there was much discussion about the end of physics. Nearly all relevant laws had been discovered, nearly all relevant particles accounted for, and nearly all phenomena had become predictable and understandable. Science was on the verge of absolute triumph. But as it turned out, nearly was not nearly good enough. In the late twentieth century and up to the present, we are once again being told that physicists are on the verge of discovering the Grand Unified Theory, the so-called Theory of Everything. It is the nature of science to make such proclamations. As it is in the nature of the concept of *vilayat* to look forward to a time of moral perfection brought about by human experts.

24 How does one follow up, for example, "The Greatest Story Ever Told"?

25 Abul A'la Maududi, "The Political Theory of Islam," in John J. Donohue and John L. Esposito (eds.), *Islam in Transition: Muslim Perspectives* (New York: Oxford University Press, 1982), 254. He also used the term "Kingdom of God" but steadfastly refused to call an Islamic state a "theocracy," which he associated with the leadership of religious experts and theologically trained *ulama*.

26 For a detailed theological history of this important commandment, cf.: Michael Cook, *Commanding the Right and Forbidding the Wrong in Islamic Thought* (Cambridge: Cambridge University Press, 2000) and a shorter version of the same book, *Forbidding the Wrong in Islam* (Cambridge: Cambridge University Press, 2003).

27 Donohue and Esposito, *Islam in Transition*.

28 There is much resemblance between this model of governance and the grassroots, populist "Tea Party" movement in the United States. This movement also claims to represent American ideals or authentic American values that the political elites have abandoned and which the common people therefore must protect even from their own rulers. As with Maududi's emphasis on the time of the Prophet, and the example of his actions, the use of the term Tea Party also hearkens back to

the beginnings of the American Revolution, and the founding of the republic, the "golden age."

29 Cf.: Reinhold Niebuhr, *An Interpretation of Christian Ethics* (New York: Seabury Press, 1979).

30 Ibid.

31 And then quickly converted to Islam, making the blow more bearable in the long run.

32 Shan Muhammad, *Sayyid Ahmad Khan: A Political Biography* (Meerut: Meenakshi Prakashan, 1969), 38.

33 Reinhold Niebuhr, *The Children of Light and the Children of Darkness: A Vindication of Democracy and a Critique of Its Traditional Defense* (New York: Charles Scribner's Sons, 1944), X.

34 Tariq Ali, *The Clash of Fundamentalisms: Crusades, Jihads and Modernity* (London: Verso, 2002).

35 Reinhold Niebuhr, "Greek Tragedy and Modern Politics," *The Nation* 146 (January 1938): 740.

36 Ibid.

37 Ibid.

38 Cf.: Ben Quash, "Radical Orthodoxy's Critique of Niebuhr," in Richard Harries and Stephen Platten (eds.), *Reinhold Niebuhr and Contemporary Politics* (Oxford: Oxford University Press, 2010), and Justus D. Doenecke, "Reinhold Niebuhr and His Critics: The Interventionist Controversy in World War II," *Anglican and Episcopal History* 64, no. 4 (December 1995): 459–81.

39 Reinhold Niebuhr, *The Nature and Destiny of Man* (New York: Charles Scribner's Sons, 1964), 1:270.

40 Niebuhr's ultimate warrant for this understanding of human nature is his interpretation of Christian doctrine and myth. But as we shall see later in the essay, Niebuhr believes that he can provisionally defend such an understanding from purely historical or psychological experience as well. For Niebuhr it is the best, most coherent explanation of the human condition.

41 Robin W. Lovin, *Reinhold Niebuhr and Christian Realism* (Cambridge: Cambridge University Press, 1995), 123.

42 Niebuhr, *The Nature and Destiny of Man*, 1:75.

43 Lovin, *Reinhold Niebuhr and Christian Realism*, 126.

44 Ibid., 121.

45 It is important to distinguish between the kinds of reductive naturalisms that Niebuhr critiques and his own thinking which has also been understood as a kind of pragmatic "ethical naturalism," by Robin Lovin, among others.

46 Ibid., 75–76.

47 Niebuhr, *The Nature and Destiny of Man*, 1:167.

48 Lovin, *Reinhold Niebuhr and Christian Realism*, 132.

49 As evidenced by his affinity for the Greek notions of tragedy and irony, it is obvious that Niebuhr is much more sympathetic toward the Greek poet and dramatist than the Greek philosopher.

50 Niebuhr, *The Nature and Destiny of Man*, 2:3.

51 Lovin, *Reinhold Niebuhr and Christian Realism*, 123.

52 Colm McKeough, *The Political Realism of Reinhold Niebuhr* (New York: St. Martin's Press Inc., 1997), 60.

53 Lovin, *Reinhold Niebuhr and Christian Realism*, 125.

54 Niebuhr, *The Nature and Destiny of Man*, 1:182.

55 Ibid., 183.

56 Ibid., 182.

57 It is interesting that for Augustine *quaestio mihi factus sum* is a question raised in the presence of God "in whose eyes I have become a question for myself" (*Confessions*, x.33). It is also instructive in that, although Augustine does provide a tautological answer to the question "who am I?" (the answer: a man), the question "what am I?" remains *grande profundum*, a "profound mystery" (iv.14), for there is "something of man which the spirit of man which is in him itself knoweth not. But Thou, Lord, who has made him knowest everything of him" (x.5).

58 Lovin, *Reinhold Niebuhr and Christian Realism*, 130.

59 McKeough, *The Political Realism of Reinhold Niebuhr*, 39.

60 Niebuhr, *The Nature and Destiny of Man*, 2:80.

61 Reinhold Niebuhr, *Christian Realism and Political Problems* (New York: Charles Scribner's Sons, 1953), 119–20.

62 Lovin, *Reinhold Niebuhr and Christian Realism*, 5.

63 Walter Rauschenbusch, *Christianity and the Social Crisis* (Louisville: Westminster/John Knox, 1992). Quoted in Lovin, *Reinhold Niebuhr and Christian Realism*, 5.

64 Of course, the communists in Russia had a different system than the capitalists in the West, but the general idea was the same.

65 Cf.: Reinhold Niebuhr, *Moral Man and Immoral Society* (New York: Charles Scribner's Sons, 1960).

66 Lovin, *Reinhold Niebuhr and Christian Realism*, 6.

67 Both garden variety political realisms and Marxism, for example, would qualify as these kinds of reductive naturalisms.

68 Reinhold Niebuhr, *The Children of Light, and the Children of Darkness* (New York: Charles Scribner's Sons, 1972), viii.

69 Niebuhr, *An Interpretation of Christian Ethics*, 62.

70 Ibid., 5.

71 Niebuhr, *The Nature and Destiny of Man*, 1:16.

72 His oft-mentioned suspicion and criticism of classical thought notwithstanding.

73 Ibid.

74 Niebuhr, *The Nature and Destiny of Man*, 2:2.

75 Lovin, *Reinhold Niebuhr and Christian Realism*, 157.

76 Reinhold Niebuhr, *The Irony of American History* (Chicago: University of Chicago Press, 2008), 65.

77 Ibid., 66.

78 Ibid., 66–67.

79 Ibid., 67.

80 Ibid.

81 Ibid., 180.

82 Sir Sayyid Ahmad Khan, *A Series of Essays on the Life of Mohammad: And Subjects Subsidiary Thereto* (Memphis: General Books LLC, 2012).

83 Cf.: Greg Fisher (ed.), *Arabs and Empire before Islam* (Oxford: Oxford University Press, 2017), and Fred McGraw Donner, *The Early Islamic Conquests* (Princeton: Princeton University Press, 1981).

84 Khan, *A Series of Essays on the Life of Mohammad*, 50–61.

85 Muir makes three main accusations. As quoted in Khan, *A Series of Essays on the Life of Mohammad*, 50, "First: Polygamy, Divorce, and Slavery are maintained and perpetuated. . . . Second: Freedom of judgment in religion is crushed and annihilated. Toleration is unknown. Third, A barrier has been interposed against the reception of Christianity."

86 Khan, *A Series of Essays on the Life of Mohammad*, 103.

87 This is the Persian/Urdu pronunciation that Sayyid Ahmad Khan would have used. In Arabic, the term is pronounced *jahiliyya*.

88 Toshihiko Izatsu, *Ethico-Religious Concepts in the Quran* (Montreal and Kingston: McGill-Queens University Press, 2002), 29.

89 James A. Montgomery, "Dichotomy in Jahili Poetry," *Journal of Arabic Literature* 17 (1986): 15–16.

90 Durayd b. al-Simma in Suzanne Pinckney Stetkevych, *The Mute Immortals Speak* (Ithaca: Cornell University Press, 1993), 63.

91 Imru'u-l-Qays quoted in Carl Brockelmann, *A History of the Islamic Peoples* (New York: Capricon Books, 1972), 10.

92 Abid b. al-Abras quoted in Toshihiko Izutsu, *God and Man in the Quran* (Kuala Lumpur: Islamic Book Trust, 2002), 124.

93 Some examples from Khan, *A Series of Essays on the Life of Mohammad*, 36–47: "Adultery, fornication and incest were practiced unblushingly, and were shamelessly published and boasted of in all sorts of immoral poetry. . . . All of them were extremely addicted to wine and other strong liquors, and during a state of drunkenness, acts of the most shameless vice and profligacy were indulged in by the whole assembly. . . . Usury was also practiced generally and to a great

extent. . . . Robbery, pillage and murder were of common occurrence; human blood being almost daily shed without remorse or horror."

94 Ibid., 42–43. "Their belief was that the existence of man in this world is precisely the same as that of a plant or animal: he is born, and after arriving at maturity, gradually declines and dies, like any of the inferior animals and, like them, perishes utterly."

95 Quran, 14:4.

96 Philip K. Hitti, *History of the Arabs* (London: Palgrave MacMillan, 2002), 12.

97 Brockelmann, *A History of the Islamic Peoples*, 4.

98 Donner, *The Early Islamic Conquests*, 40.

99 Francesco Gabrieli, *The Arabs: A Compact History* (Westport: Greenwood Press), 11.

100 Donner, *The Early Islamic Conquests*, 39.

101 Hitti, *History of the Arabs*, 16.

102 *Jahiliyya* is replete with poets. As the old Arab adage goes, "The beauty of man lies in the eloquence of his tongue." So much so that Muhammad had to distinguish himself from these poets by saying explicitly that he was NOT a poet but a prophet. In fact, the Quran makes explicit mention of this confusion. It records the Meccans saying, "Shall we, then, give up our deities at the bidding of a mad poet?" (Quran, 37:36). To which God responds, "Nay, but he [whom you call a mad poet] has brought the truth; and he confirms the truth of [what the earlier of God's] message-bearers [have taught]" (Quran, 37:37).

103 Philip F. Kennedy, "*Khamr* and *Hikma* in Jāhilī Poetry," *Journal of Arabic Literature* 20, no. 2 (1989): 99.

104 Khan, *A Series of Essays on the Life of Mohammad*, 36–39.

105 Cf.: Sayyid Ahmad Khan, *Maslihah Jabr wa Ikhtiyar* (Treatise on Freedom and Determination) in *PMaq XI*, 245–54.

106 Sayyid Ahmad Khan, *Tafsīr al-Quran (TQ),* 6 Volumes (Aligarh: Institute Press, 1880–95), VI:141–42, quoted in Bashir Ahmad Dar, *The Religious Thought of Sayyid Ahmad Khan* (Lahore: Institute of Islamic Culture, 1957), 218.

107 Ibid.

108 Sayyid Ahmad Khan, *Insān ke Khayālāt* (The Ideas of Man) in *Tadhīb al-akhlāq (TA)* Vol. I, 15 Shawwāl, 1871, pp. 12–14/ *PMaq V*, 249–56. Quoted in Troll, *Sayyid Ahmad Khan*, 251–52.

109 Dar, *The Religious Thought of Sayyid Ahmad Khan.*

110 Ibid.

111 Ibid.

112 Sayyid Ahmad Khan, *TQ VI*, 164. Quoted in Troll, *Sayyid Ahmad Khan*, 209.

113 Sayyid Ahmad Khan, *Insān ke Khayalat, PMaq V*, 249–56. Quoted in Troll, *Sayyid Ahmad Khan*, 255–56.

114 Martin Heidegger, *Being and Time*, Joan Stambaugh (trans.) (Albany: State University of New York Press, 1996), 68.

115 Sayyid Ahmad Khan, *Insān kī Najāt kō Nabīyon kā ānā zurūr hai* (On the Necessity of the coming of prophets to save mankind), Chapter 1, *Tabyīn al-kalām (TK), Part 1* (Ghazipur: Author's Private Press, 1862), 2–6. Quoted in Troll, *Sayyid Ahmad Khan*, 237. Emphasis mine.

116 Sayyid Ahmad Khan, *Tahrīr fī usūl al-tafsīr (TUT)* (Agra: Mufid-i ām Press, 1892), 11/ *PMaq II*, 207. Quoted in Troll, *Sayyid Ahmad Khan*, 165.

117 Sayyid Ahmad Khan, *Insān ke Khayalat, PMaq V*, 256. Quoted in Troll, *Sayyid Ahmad Khan*, 214.

118 The most famous of these critics was of course Jamal al-Din al-Afghani who wrote the influential tract "Refutation of the Sect of the Neichiris" explicitly as a polemic against Sayyid Ahmad Khan (see pp. 58–60 of this volume). Scholars at *Dar-ul-Aloom*, a prominent madrasa in Deoband have also been perturbed by Sayyid Ahmad Khan's writings and statements on Islam, as were the Ahl al-Hadith and the Sufi-infused Barelwi sect. Interestingly, these different factions agreed on little else, and were in fact openly hostile to each other on most theological matters. Cf.: Barbara Metcalfe, *Islamic Contestations: Essays on Muslims in India and Pakistan* (Oxford: Oxford University Press, 2006).

119 Sayyid Ahmad Khan, *Azad-i Ra'y* in *Intikhabi Mazamin Sir Sayyid* (New Delhi: Muqataba Jamia Ltd., 2005), 43 (translated from Urdu).

120 Sayyid Ahmad Khan, *Insān kī Najāt kō Nabīyon kā ānā zurūr hai, TK I. Quoted* in Troll, *Sayyid Ahmad Khan*, 239. Notice, as before, Khan's juxtaposition of *tariqa* with *shari'a*.

121 Cf.: Sayyid Ahmad Khan, *TA III*, 124/ *PMaq XIII*, 43. Troll, *Sayyid Ahmad Khan*, 207.

122 Sayyid Ahmad Khan, *TA*, Vol. II (Aligarh: Institute Press, 1896), 220–21, quoted in Dar, *The Religious Thought of Sayyid Ahmad Khan*, 222.

123 Quran, 43:21.

124 Cf.: Sayyid Ahmad Khan, *Qaul-i matīn dar ibtal-i harakat-i zamīn* (Firm Assertion with Regard to Declaring False the Motion of the Earth, 1848), Delhi, Sayyid al-akhbār, 1848, *PMaq XVI*, 485–500.

125 Cf.: Sari Nusseibeh, *The Story of Reason in Islam* (Stanford: Stanford University Press, 2016).

126 Ibid., 190.

127 Sayyid Ahmad Khan, *PMaq II*, 27–28. Quoted in Troll, *Sayyid Ahmad Khan*, 160. Addressed here is Muhammad 'Ali of *Nūr al-āfāq* (Cawnpore).

128 Troll, *Sayyid Ahmad Khan*, 165. Cf: Sayyid Ahmad Khan, *PMaq II, 207*.

129 Cf.: Qur'an, 22:18; 21:79; 55:6; 57:1; 59:1; 61:1; 62:1; 64:1:59:24; 24:41; 38:18,19; 13:13. "There is nothing, but that which celebrates His praises." (17:44)

130 Qur'an, 2:164.

131 Sayyid Ahmad Khan, *TUT,* 3/ *PMaq II,* 199. Quoted in Troll, *Sayyid Ahmad Khan,* 145.

132 Quran, 4:108.

133 Classed as *sahih* by al-Albaani in *Sahih Sunan Ibn Mājah.*

134 Sayyid Ahmad Khan, *TUT,* 3/ *PMaq II,* 199. Quoted in Troll, *Sayyid Ahmad Khan,* 145.

135 Cf.: Immanuel Kant, Georg Wilhelm Friedrich Hegel, Friedrich Schleiermacher, for example, among many others.

136 Niebuhr, *The Irony of American History,* 180.

Chapter 4

1 Howard Fast, "The Trap," in Isaac Asimov et al. (eds.), *Isaac Asimov's Science Fiction Treasury* (New York: Gramercy Books 1980), 522–23.

2 This story is entirely fictional. It is a slightly modified version of one that appears in "The Trap" cited above. Its telling serves a heuristic purpose, not to be confused with historical reality! Of course, there exist many accounts from around the world, and of varying levels of veracity, about human beings raised by wolves.

3 Sayyid Ahmad Khan, *Wahshiyānah Nekī* (Goodness, Savage Style!), *PMaq IV,* 325 / John W. Wilder (trans.), *Selected Essays of Sir Sayyid Ahmad Khan* (Lahore: Sang-e-Meel Publications, 2006), 85–87.

4 Cf.: Michale Bonner, *Jihad in Islamic History* (Princeton: Princeton University press, 2008).

5 This particular understanding of jihad is especially important historically within Sufi circles as *al-jihad al-akbar* or the greater jihad as opposed to an external jihad (like warfare, for example) which is *al-jihad al-asghar* or the lesser jihad. In traditional circles, this particular formulation of a lesser and greater jihad among Sufis is often associated with *hadith* of dubious authenticity.

6 Cf.: Majid Khadduri, *War and Peace in the Law of Islam* (Baltimore: Johns Hopkins Press, 1955).

7 Ayesha Jalal, *Partisans of Allah: Jihad in South Asia* (Cambridge: Harvard University Press, 2008), 14. See also Fazlur Rahman, *Major Themes of the Quran* (Chicago: University of Chicago Press, 1980), and Mahmoud Ayoub, *Islam: Faith and History* (London: Oneworld Press, 2004).

8 Cf.: Bernard Lewis, *The Political Language of Islam* (Chicago: University of Chicago Press, 1991). Although Lewis was often skewered in some parts of the media as an Islamophobe, and his reputation was clearly dented by his close association with the neo-conservative right in the run up to the second Iraq War in 2003, much of his scholarship concerning the Arab Middle East is fairly sound.

9 It should be pointed out though that the Sufis were not entirely exempt from using jihad in its militant sense either in India and elsewhere. Many Sufi orders throughout history have had "militant wings," so to say and often participated in armed struggles against this or that foe.

10 Jalal, *Partisans of Allah*, 35.

11 I am reminded here of Germany's invasions of Poland and Czechoslovakia in 1939 based on the claim that German-speaking populations in those countries were being mistreated.

12 Jalal, *Partisans of Allah*, 33.

13 Ibid., 35.

14 Paraphrasing from Paul Simon's song "Diamonds on the Soles of Her Shoes," from the album *Graceland*.

15 Cf.: Sayyid Ahmad Khan, *Review on Dr. Hunter's Indian Musalmans: Are they bound in Conscience to Rebel against the Queen?* quoted in Hafeez Malik, *The Political Profile of Sayyid Ahmad Khan* (Islamabad: Institute of Islamic History, Culture and Civilization, 1982), 270–326.

16 Sayyid Ahmad Khan, *Mazhabi khayal zaman-e-qadim awr zaman-e-jadid ka, PMaq III*, 23. Quoted in Devji, "Apologetic Modernity," 61–76.

17 Sayyid Ahmad Khan did believe that a defensive armed struggle against the enemies of Islam or this or that Muslim polity qualified as jihad. But British rule in India met none of the conditions attendant to such use of jihad. This is the point he made repeatedly in his *Review on Dr. Hunter's Indian Musalmans: Are they bound in conscience to rebel against the Queen?*

18 Cf.: Wael Hallaq, *The Origins and Evolution of Islamic Law* (Cambridge: Cambridge University Press, 2005).

19 Cf.: Sayyid Ahmad Khan, *Azad-i Ra'y* (Freedom of Opinion), *PMaq IV*, 213. Quoted in Wilder, 49–68.

20 Ibid., 66.

21 For a discussion of the various iterations of the Deobandi movement in the South, cf: Barbara Metcalf, *Islamic Contestations*.

22 Barbara Metcalf, "'Traditionalist' Islamic Activism: Deoband, Tablighis, and Talibs," Social Science Research Council (SSRC), *Essays after 9/11*, http://essays. ssrc.org/sept11/essays/metcalf.htm

23 Cf.: Syed Ahmed Khan, *A Voyage to Modernism*, Mushirul Hasan and Nishat Zaidi (trans.) (New Delhi: Primus Books, 2011). This is collection of Khan's impressions of the journey (translated into English) during his long trip to Europe from 1869 to 1871. These letters were originally published in the newsletter of the Scientific Society of Aligarh as *Safarnama-i-Musafiran-I Landan*.

24 Cf.: "On the Advantages derived by Human Society in general from Islam," in Khan, *A Series of Essays on the Life of Muhammad and Subjects Subsidiary Thereto*, 48–50.

25 Cf.: Abdulaziz Sachedina, *The Islamic Roots of Democratic Pluralism* (New York: Oxford University Press, 2001).

26 Shafey Kidwai, *Cementing Ethics with Modernism: An Appraisal of Sir Sayyid Ahmed Khan's Writings* (Delhi: Gyan Publishing House, 2010), 263.

27 There is much debate (and no scholarly consensus) on the nature of the early Islamic state. Donner in *The Early Islamic Conquests* argues for a system of election by deliberation among prominent men in the community. More recently, C. G. Weeramantry, *Justice without Frontiers: Furthering Human Rights* (London: Kluwer Law International, 1997), and Len Evan Goodman, *Islamic Humanism* (Oxford: Oxford University Press, 2005)—suggest that the early Islamic polity was a kind proto-democratic state akin to Athenian and Roman democracy. There is no dearth of volumes about Islam and democracy in the popular and scholarly presses. But considering the paucity of primary sources from this period, any definitive claim about this polity is of course bound to be controversial. Still, inasmuch as Sayyid Ahmad Khan's understanding of this early state is concerned, he does appear fairly well wedded to the idea of this polity as having a deliberative core.

28 An interesting saying attributed to the Prophet in *Musnad Ahmad Ibn Hanbal*—a collection of *hadith* by the early Islamic scholar Ahmad Ibn Hanbal (780–855 CE) and founder of the Hanbali *madhab* (school of law)—appears to foresee this development: "Prophethood will remain among you as long as Allah wills. Then Caliphate (*Khilafah*) on the lines of Prophethood shall commence, and remain as long as Allah wills. Then corrupt/erosive monarchy would take place, and it will remain as long as Allah wills. After that, despotic kingship would emerge, and it will remain as long as Allah wills. Then, the Caliphate (*Khilafah*) shall come once again based on the precept of Prophethood."

29 Cf.: Sayyid Ahmad Khan, "India and English Government," in John J. Donohue and John L. Esposito (eds.), *Islam in Transition: Muslim Perspectives* (New York: Oxford University Press, 1982), 38–40.

30 Sayyid Ahmad Khan, in speech delivered on October 6, 1863, quoted in *The Proceedings of the Scientific Society of Ghazipur*, Sayyid Ahmad Khan's private press, 1864, 23–24.

31 Sayyid Ahmad Khan, in speech delivered on May 10, 1866, on the establishment of the British Indian Association, in *Majmua Lectures*, 26–27.

32 Ibid.

33 Sayyid Ahmad Khan, *TA II*, 33. Quoted in Muhammad, *Sir Syed Ahmad Khan*, 205. This is, as Sayyid Ahmad Khan himself admitted, an expansion of Mill's statement: "If all mankind minus one were of one opinion, and only one person were of the contrary opinion, mankind would be no more justified in silencing the one person, than he, if he had the power, would be justified in silencing mankind." See J. S. Mill, *Utilitarianism, Liberty and Representative Governance* (London: Everyman's Library, 1931), 79.

34 Sayyid Ahmad Khan, *TA II*, 36–39.

35 Ibid.

36 It should be noted that Sayyid Ahmad Khan never fully accounts for the extent to which a Muslim should have the liberty to question the teachings of the Qur'an and the rules of Muslim jurisprudence. The tension between these imperatives is usually dealt with only tangentially in Khan's work. When he does speak on the matter, it is usually to state that the many teachings of the Qur'an are open to free interpretation, and it is the duty of every Muslim to speak on these matters with others openly and without fear. The distinction between new *shari'a* for every age, yet the unity of *din*, allowed him to have it both ways, so to say, in his own mind at least. Of course, even this schema depends on an understanding of the Qur'an as a book meant for human engagement, and hence not divine in its essence. On this issue, as on many others, Khan was re-interpreting some settled debates within Islamic jurisprudence as being not so settled after all. *Ijtihad* was a persistent, constant obligation for Khan, not a once-and-done proposition. No debate could ever be settled entirely. The only certain settlement is on the Day of Judgment, not within human history.

37 Sayyid Ahmad Khan, speech quoted in Malik, *The Political Profile of Sayyid Ahmad Khan*, 383–84.

38 Mirza Lutfullah Khan Asadabadi, *Maqalat-i-Jamaliyah* (Tehran: Solar Press, 1312 A.H.), 113.

39 Afghani, *Al-'Urwat al-Wuthqa*, I (Beirut, 1328 A.H) in Anwar Moazzam, "Jamal al-Din al-Afghani: Views on Individual and Society," *Islamic Culture*, July 1982, 326.

40 Moazzam, "Jamal al-Din al-Afghani," 327.

41 Jamal al-Din al-Afghani, *Refutation of the Neichiris*, 1881, in Nikki R. Keddie, *An Islamic Response to Imperialism* (Berkeley: University of California Press, 1969), 140–41.

42 Tangentially, Sayyid Ahmad Khan was a staunch capitalist, believing the free markets to be far superior to any organized state economy. This obviously is consistent with his belief that the role of the state in the lives of its subjects should be minimal. Cf.: Deitrich Reetz, "Enlightenment and Islam: Sayyid Ahmad Khan's Plea to Indian Muslims for Reason," *The Indian Historical Review* XIV, no. 1–2 (1988): 206–18. In "The Religious Liberalism of Sir Sayyid Ahmad Khan," for example, Hafeez Malik also argues that during his trip to Europe, and "impressed with the comparatively high economic standard" particularly in England and France, Khan became an ardent fan of the theory of sentiments proposed in Adam Smith's *The Wealth of Nations* (1776), and "it is therefore not wrong to state that quite consciously Sir Sayyid became an apostle of *laissez faire* philosophy among the Muslims of India." Quoted in M. Ikram Chaghatai (ed.), *Heralds of Nineteenth*

Century Muslim Thought: Sir Sayyid Ahmad Khan (Lahore: Sang-e-Meel Publications, 2005), 303–04.

43 Sayyid Ahmad Khan, *Azad-i Ra'y* (Freedom of Opinion), *PMaq IV*, 213. Quoted in Moaddel and Talattof (eds.), *Modernist and Fundamentalist Debates in Islam*, 110–11.

44 Ibid., 110.

45 Ibid., 114.

46 Ibid., 115.

47 Ibid.

48 Ibid., 113.

49 Ibid., 115.

50 Cf.: Sayyid Amir 'Ali, one of Sayyid Ahmad Khan's sympathetic contemporaries, quoted in Rachel Fell McDermott, Leonard Gordon, Ainslie Embree, Frances Pritchett, and Dennis Dalton (eds.), *Sources of Indian Traditions: Modern India, Pakistan and Bangladesh* (New York: Columbia University Press, 2015), 154–55: "The present stagnation of Musulman communities is principally due to the notion which has foxed itself on the minds of the generality of Moslems, that the right exercise of private judgment *(ijtihad)* ceased with the early legists, that its exercise in modern times is sinful, and that a Moslem in order to be regarded an orthodox follower of Mohammed should belong to one or the other of the schools established by the schoolmen of Islām, and abandon his judgment absolutely to any interpretations of men who lived in the ninth century, and could have no conception of the necessities of the twentieth. . . . In the Western world, the Reformation was ushered in by the Renaissance and the progress of Europe commenced when it threw off the shackles of Ecclesiasticism. In Islām also, enlightenment must precede reform; and, before there can be a renovation of religious life, the mind must first escape from the bondage which centuries of literal interpretation and the doctrine of 'conformity' have imposed on it. The formalism that does not appeal to the heart of the worshipper must be abandoned; externals must be subordinated to the inner feelings; and the lessons of ethics must be impressed on the plastic mind; then alone can we hope for that enthusiasm in the principles of duty taught by the prophet of Islām."

51 Sayyid Ahmad Khan, *Azad-i Ra'y* (Freedom of Opinion), *PMaq IV*, 213. Quoted in Moaddel and Talattof (eds.), *Modernist and Fundamentalist Debates in Islam*, 117.

52 Ibid.

53 Ibid., 118.

54 Ibid., 120.

55 Cf.: Mohandas Gandhi, "Critique of Modern Civilization," in Rudrangshu Mukherjee (ed.), *The Penguin Gandhi Reader* (London: Pengin, 1956).

56 Hannah Arendt, *The Promise of Politics* (New York: Schocken Books, 2005), 201.

57 Ibid., 202.

58 Ibid., 203.

59 Ibid., 203–04.

60 Ibid., 202.

61 Hannah Arendt, *The Human Condition* (Chicago: The University of Chicago Press, 1998).

62 Ibid., 79–135.

63 Ibid., 136–74.

64 Ibid., 7.

65 Ibid. Italics in original.

66 Ibid., 8.

67 Ibid., 41.

68 Aristotle, *Politics*, in Richard McKeon (ed.), *The Basic Works of Aristotle* (New York: The Modern Library, 2001), 1252b12.

69 Ibid., 1252b28.

70 Ibid., 1280a31.

71 Dana R. Villa, *Arendt and Heidegger: The Fate of the Political* (Princeton: Princeton University Press, 1996), 18.

72 Aristotle, *Politics*, 1281a3.

73 Ibid., 1255b18.

74 Ibid., 1253b25–30.

75 Ibid.

76 Ibid., 1255b17.

77 Ibid.

78 Aristotle, *Nicomachean Ethics*, in Richard McKeon (ed.), *The Basic Works of Aristotle* (New York: The Modern Library, 2001), 1134a25–30. Political justice here means "unqualified" justice which is only possible between entities that are equal. The point becomes clearer later in the section quoted when Aristotle points out that "the justice of a master and that of a father are not the same as the justice of citizens . . . for there can be no injustice in the unqualified sense towards things that are one's own; but a man's chattel, and his child until he reaches a certain age and sets up for itself, are as it were part of himself, and no one chooses to hurt himself (for which reason there can be no injustice towards oneself)" (1134b7–11).

79 Ibid.

80 Aristotle, *Politics*, 1252b27–31.

81 Villa, *Arendt and Heidegger*, 19.

82 Aristotle, *Politics*, 1253a20.

83 Ibid., 1253a25.

84 Villa, *Arendt and Heidegger*, 19, also cf.: Aristotle, "Physics," 260a20–261b25.

85 Aristotle, *Politics*, 1253a2.

86 Ibid.

87 Ibid., 1253a10.

88 It, of course, goes without saying that Aristotle also includes the life of contemplation as a version of the good life.

89 Hannah Arendt, *The Human Condition* (Chicago: University of Chicago Press, 1958), 30.

90 Ibid., 31.

91 Ibid., 37.

92 Aristotle, *Politics*, 1252b35.

93 Villa, *Arendt and Heidegger*, 21.

94 Ibid.

95 Aristotle, *Ethics*, 1176b7.

96 Ibid., 1094a5.

97 "Artistic activities" is a loose translation. Aristotle gives more than thirty examples of activities which qualify as *technai* and these include crafts, medicine, sports, expressive and performing arts, and even military leadership, and medicine.

98 Aristotle, *Ethics*, 1140b6.

99 Ibid., 1140a5.

100 Villa, *Arendt and Heidegger*, 22.

101 Aristotle, *Ethics*, 1099a15.

102 Arendt, *The Human Condition*, 305.

103 Ibid., 154.

104 Ibid.

105 Villa, *Arendt and Heidegger*, 24.

106 Arendt, *The Human Condition*, 40.

107 Ibid.

108 Aristotle, *Politics*, 1263b31–36.

109 Villa, *Arendt and Heidegger*, 29.

110 Ibid.

111 Ibid. Examples of such revolutionary action which, at least briefly, resembled an Arendtian conception of politics are the American Revolution, the early *Soviets*, the Hungarian revolt, etc.

112 Hannah Arendt, *Between Past and Future* (New York: Penguin Books, 1968), 154.

113 Hannah Arendt in George Kateb, *Hannah Arendt: Politics, Conscience, Evil* (Totowa: Rowman & Allanheld, 1983), 32.

114 Aristotle, *Politics*, 1253a10.

115 Villa, *Arendt and Heidegger*, 31.

116 The "world" in Arendt's writings refers not to the natural world but more specifically the world of things, institutions, and communities created and produced by human beings, the world of human society and sociability. It is the

creation of what Arendt calls *Homo faber*, the fabricating and productive aspect of
the human condition.

117 Hannah Arendt quoted in Kateb, *Hannah Arendt*, 31.

118 Ibid., 33.

119 Villa, *Arendt and Heidegger*, 32.

120 Arendt, *The Human Condition*, 75.

121 Aristotle, *Ethics*, 1140a25.

122 Ibid., 1142b30.

123 Villa, *Arendt and Heidegger*, 33.

124 Ibid., 36.

125 Ibid., 37.

126 Patrick Riley, "Hannah Arendt on Kant, Truth and Politics," *Political Studies* 35, no.
3 (1987): 384.

127 Villa, *Arendt and Heidegger*, 39.

128 Seyla Benhabib, *The Reluctant Modernism of Hannah Arendt* (Rowan & Littlefield
Publishers Inc., 2003).

129 Khan, "India and English Government," 39.

130 Arendt, *Between Past and Future*, 220.

131 Ibid., 217.

132 Ibid.

133 Ibid., 218.

134 Jalal, *Partisans of Allah*, 4.

Chapter 5

1 I am thankful to Professor Helene Landemore of the Political Science Department,
Yale University, for this particular phrasing.

2 Emile Durkheim, *The Elementary Forms of Religious Life* (New York: The Free Press,
1995).

3 MacIntyre, *After Virtue*, ix.

4 Ibid., 204–25.

5 Edmund Burke and C. C. Obrien (eds.), *Reflections on the Revolution in France*
(London: Penguin Books, 2004), 129.

6 MacIntyre, *Whose Justice? Which Rationality?*, 217.

7 The famous document from the French Revolution.

8 MacIntyre, *After Virtue*, 221.

9 Interestingly, Burke made the same argument in his remarkable and persistent
attempts in Parliament against the dangers of corrupting India's social and political
order by the British colonial adventures there. He was unsuccessful, for the most
part, in changing many minds on that front.

10 MacIntyre, *Whose Justice? Which Rationality?*, 217.

11 Cf.: Jeffrey S. Stout, *Democracy and Tradition* (Princeton: Princeton University Press, 2004).

12 Cf.: Immanuel Kant, *Prolegomena to Any Future Metaphysics* (Cambridge: Cambridge University Press, 2004).

13 MacIntyre, *After Virtue*, 222.

14 Ibid.

15 Ibid., 32.

16 MacIntyre, *Whose Justice? Which Rationality?*, 353.

17 A good example of this is the notion of "false consciousness" that (primarily) Marxist sociologists use to describe the processes through which oppressed individuals participate in their own oppression. The term was first used by Karl Marx's associate Friedrich Engels in a letter to Franz Mehring in 1893, *Marx and Engels Correspondence* (New York: International Publishers, 1968).

18 Cf.: Adam Smith, *The Theory of Moral Sentiments* (Amherst: Prometheus Books, 2000). Most of Adam Smith's later works, including *A Treatise on Public Opulence* (1764) and *The Wealth of Nations* (1776), are predicated on using this theory as the normative and sociological basis of his claims. Smith's work was a self-conscious response to David Hume's theory of human passions, as was the case with Kant who makes the connection very explicit in his *Prolegomena*.

19 MacIntyre, *After Virtue*, 113.

20 Friedrich Wilhelm Nietzsche and Walter Kaufman (trans.), *The Gay Science* (New York: Vintage Books, 1974), 129.

21 MacIntyre, *Whose Justice? Which Rationality?*, 352.

22 Ibid., 353.

23 MacIntyre, *After Virtue*, 222.

24 Ibid.

25 Ibid.

26 Ibid., 219.

27 Michael Walzer, *Thick and Thin: Moral Argument at Home and Abroad* (Notre Dame: University of Notre Dame Press, 1994).

28 MacIntyre, *After Virtue*, 221. Emphasis mine.

29 Cf.: An excellent example of this mindset, MacIntyre, *Whose Justice? Which Rationality?*, 354.

30 Ibid., 220.

31 Ibid., 357.

32 Ibid., 356.

33 Ibid., 357.

34 Ibid., 359.

35 Ibid., 360.

36 MacIntyre, *After Virtue*, 223.

37 Ibid., 215–16. Emphasis mine.

38 MacIntyre, *Whose Justice? Which Rationality?*, 361.

39 Ibid., 362.

40 Smith, *Islam in Modern History*, 41.

41 MacIntyre, *Whose Justice? Which Rationality?*, 362.

42 MacIntyre, *After Virtue*, 53.

43 Ibid.

44 Aristotle, "Politics," 1263b31–36.

45 The critics of Sayyid Ahmad Khan are too numerous for me to provide an exhaustive list here. We already encountered Jamal al-Din al-Afghani in Chapter 1, and his critique of Khan as a *neichiri*. The famous Urdu poet Akbar Allahbadi was deeply suspicious of Khan's educational reforms and sarcastically mocked Khan's Europhilia in much of his poetry (although he did become more open to Khan's "liberal" disposition later in his life). Mohammad Qasim Nanatwi, the founder of Darul Uloom Madrassa in Deoband (1867) was also a frequent critic of Khan's West-facing reinterpretation of Islamic teaching and advocated a reorientation of the Muslim community to its "original" cultural and religious identity.

46 MacIntyre, *After Virtue*, 219.

47 Ibid., 211.

48 Ibid., 215.

49 Ibid., 213.

50 MacIntyre, *Whose Justice? Which Rationality?*, 357.

51 Ibid., 358.

52 Ibid., 369.

53 Cf.: Stout, *Democracy and Tradition*.

54 Of course, these are hypothetical abstract expressionists. In reality, I do not think abstract expressionists would make such a claim. But for the purposes of this story, let us imagine that in this universe, they do.

55 In all fairness, one does not need to be a medieval artist to be a little scared of modern abstract art. But that's another story.

56 MacIntyre, *After Virtue*, 263.

57 Ibid.

Epilogue: Can the Muslim Speak?

 1 Eliot, "Why Yasir Qadhi Wants to Talk about Jihad?". All quotations attributed to Yasir Qadhi in this chapter are from this article.

 2 Wikipedia has an actively updated list of charities accused of supporting terrorism (including Muslim charities in the United States) at https://en.wikipedia.org/wiki/

List_of_charities_accused_of_ties_to_terrorism. See also Kambiz GhaneaBassiri, "American Muslim Philanthropy after 9/11," *Journal on Muslim Philanthropy and Civil Society* 1, no. 1 (November 2017): 4–22.

3 The controversies are too numerous to list here. He has been accused of (and admitted to) calling the Holocaust a hoax (he later apologized). One of his students, Umar Farouk Abdulmutallab, was the infamous "underwear bomber" who (unsuccessfully) tried to blow up a transatlantic flight. His views on Jews and Christians are constantly under scrutiny for verging on the intolerant. His position on blasphemy in Islam has also drawn negative attention.

4 Qadhi has a popular YouTube channel which is an excellent resource for a general overview of his theological and political opinions (https://www.youtube.com/user/ YasirQadhi). He also has a blog on the website Muslim Matters where he opines on all manner of things, including "Do Muslim believe in Aliens?" (https://muslim matters.org/author/yasir-qadhi/).

5 "Full Transcript of Ahmadinejad Speech at Columbia University," September 24, 2007. https://www.globalresearch.ca/full-transcript-of-ahmadinejad-speech-at-columbia-university/6889

6 Niall Ferguson, *Civilization: The West and the Rest* (London: Penguin Books, 2011), 98. For a precis of Churchill's crimes, see for example, Shashi Tharoor, "In Winston Churchill, Hollywood Rewards a Mass Murderer," *Washington Post,* March 10, 2018. The racists, misogynists, and anti-Semites are too numerous to list here. The German philosopher Martin Heidegger and legal scholar Carl Schmidt were members of the Nazi party and are taught, usually without much explanation or explication, in most philosophy departments in the West.

7 Ian Baruma, "Tariq Ramadan has an Identity Issue," *The New York Times Magazine,* February 4, 2007.

8 Ian Baruma and Avishai Margalit, *Occidentalism: The West in the Eyes of Its Enemies* (New York: The Penguin Press, 2004).

9 Ian Baruma, *Murder in Amsterdam: Liberal Europe, Islam and the Limits of Tolerance* (London: Penguin Books, 2006).

10 Baruma, "Tariq Ramadan has an Identity Issue."

11 Ibid. Emphasis mine.

12 Arendt, *Men in Dark Times*, 24–25.

13 Berman, *All That Is Solid Melts into Air*, 5.

14 Cf.: James C. Scott, *Domination and the Art of Resistance: Hidden Transcripts* (New Haven: Yale University Press, 1990).

Bibliography

Abdelkader, Deina Ali, *Islamic Activists: The Anti-Enlightenment Democrats* (New York: Pluto Press, 2011).

Abu-Lughod, Ibrahim A., *The Arab Rediscovery of Europe: A Study in Cultural Encounters* (Princeton: Princeton University Press, 1963).

Ahmad, Irfan, *Religion as Critique: Islamic Critical Thinking from Mecca to the Marketplace* (Chapel Hill: University of North Carolina Press, 2017).

Ahmad, N., *Muslim Separatism in British India: A Retrospective Study* (Lahore: Ferozsons Pvt. Ltd., 1991).

Ahmad, Syed Nisar, *Origins of Muslim Consciousness in India: A World-System Perspective* (New York: Greenwood Press, 2004).

Ahmed, Safdar, *Reform and Modernity in Islam: The Philosophical, Cultural and Political Discourses among Muslim Reformers* (New York: I.B. Tauris, 2013).

al-Afghānī, Sayyid Jamāl ad-Dīn, Nikki R. Keddie, and Hamid Algar (trans.), *An Islamic Response to Imperialism: Political and Religious Writings of Sayyid Jamāl ad-Dīn al-Afghānī* (Berkeley: University of California Press, 1983).

Alavi, Seema, *Muslim Cosmopolitanism in the Age of Empire* (Cambridge: Harvard University Press, 2015).

Ali, Tariq, *The Clash of Fundamentalisms: Crusades, Jihads and Modernity* (London: Verso Books, 2002).

Allana, G., *Muslim Political Thought through the Ages: 1562–1947* (Karachi: Royal Book Company, 2006).

Ansari, Asloob A., *Sir Syed Ahmad Khan: A Centenary Tribute* (Delhi: Adam Publishers and Distributors, 2001).

Ansary, Tamim, *Destiny Disrupted: A History of the World through Islamic Eyes* (New York: Public Affairs, 2009).

Arendt, Hannah, *Between Past and Future* (New York: Penguin Books, 1968).

Arendt, Hannah, *The Human Condition* (Chicago: The University of Chicago Press, 1998).

Arendt, Hannah, *The Life of the Mind* (New York: Mariner Books, 1981).

Arendt, Hannah, *Men in Dark Times* (New York: Harvest Books, 1970).

Arendt, Hannah, *The Portable Hannah Arendt* (New York: Penguin Putnam Inc., 2000).

Arendt, Hannah, *The Promise of Politics* (New York: Schocken Books, 2005).

Aristotle, "Politics," in Richard McKeon (ed.), *The Basic Works of Aristotle* (New York: The Modern Library, 2001).

Arjana, Sophia Rose, *Muslims in the Western Imagination* (Oxford: Oxford University Press, 2015).

Asad, Talal, Wendy Brown, Judith Butler, and Saba Mahmood, *Is Critique Secular: Blasphemy, Injury, and Free Speech* (New York: Fordham University Press, 2013).

Asadabadi, Mirza Lutfullah Khan, *Maqalat-i-Jamaliyah* (Tehran: Solar Press, 1312 A.H.).

Aydin, Cemil, *The Idea of the Muslim World: A Global Intellectual History* (Cambridge: Harvard University Press, 2017).

Ayoub, Mahmoud (ed.), *Contemporary Approaches to the Qur'an and Sunnah* (London: The International Institute of Islamic Thought, 2012).

Ayoub, Mahmoud, *Islam: Faith and History* (London: Oneworld Press, 2004).

Baljon, Johannes Marinus Simon Jr., *The Reforms and Religious Ideas of Sir Sayyid Ahmad Khan* (Lahore: Ashraf Press, 1964).

Baruma, Ian, *Murder in Amsterdam: The Death of Theo van Gogh and the Limits of Tolerance* (New York: The Penguin Press, 2006).

Baruma, Ian, and Avishai Margalit, *Occidentalism: The West in the Eyes of Its Enemies* (New York: The Penguin Press, 2004).

Baum, Gregory, *The Theology of Tariq Ramadan: A Catholic Perspective* (Toronto: Novalis Publishing Inc., 2009).

Begum, Rehmani, *Sir Syed Ahmad Khan: The Politics of Educational Reform* (Lahore: Vanguard Books, 1985).

Behloul, Samuel M., Susanne Leuenberger, and Andreas Tunger-Zanetti (eds.), *Debating Islam: Negotiating Europe, Religion and the Self* (Bielefeld: Transcript, 2013).

Benhabib, Seyla, *The Claims of Culture: Equality and Diversity in the Global Era* (Princeton: Princeton University Press, 2002).

Benhabib, Seyla, *The Reluctant Modernism of Hannah Arendt* (New York: Rowan & Littlefield Publishers Inc., 2003).

Bennett, Clinton, *Muslims and Modernity: An Introduction to the Issues and Debates* (New York: Continuum, 2005).

Berman, Marshall, *All That Is Solid Melts into Air: The Experience of Modernity* (New York: Penguin Books, 1982).

Berman, Paul, *The Flight of the Intellectuals* (New York: Melville House, 2010).

Black, Antony, *The History of Islamic Political Thought: From the Prophet (PBUH) to the Present* (Karachi: Oxford University Press, 2001).

Bonner, Michale, *Jihad in Islamic History* (Princeton: Princeton University Press, 2008).

Brockelmann, Carl, *A History of the Islamic Peoples* (New York: Capricorn Books, 1972).

Burke, Edmund, and C. C. Obrien (eds.), *Reflections on the Revolution in France* (London: Penguin Books, 2004).

Carey, W. H., *The Mahomedan Rebellion: Its Premonitory Symptoms and the Outbreak and Suppression* (Lahore: Sang-e-Meel Publications, 2007).

Casanova, Jose, *Public Religions in the Modern World* (Chicago: The University of Chicago Press, 1994).

Chaghatai, M. Ikram (ed.), *1857 in the Muslim Historiography* (Lahore: Sang-e-Meel Publications, 2007).

Chaghatai, M. Ikram (ed.), *Herald of Nineteenth Century Muslim Thought: Sir Sayyid Ahmad Khan* (Lahore: Sang-e-Meel Publications, 2005).

Chaghatai, M. Ikram (ed.), *Jamal al-din al-Afghani: An Apostle of Islamic Resurgence* (Lahore: Sang-e-Meel Publications, 2005).

Chaghatai, M. Ikram (ed.), *Sir Sayyid Ahmad Khan: A Prominent Muslim Politician and Educationist* (Lahore: Sang-e-Meel Publications, 2005).

Cook, Michael, *Commanding the Right and Forbidding the Wrong in Islamic Thought* (Cambridge: Cambridge University Press, 2000).

Curtis, Edward E. IV (ed.), *The Bloomsbury Reader on Islam in the West* (London: Bloomsbury Press, 2015).

Dabashi, Hamid, *Can Non-Europeans Think?* (London: Zed Books, 2015).

Dalrymple, William, *The Last Mughal: The Fall of a Dynasty, 1857* (New York: Vintage Books, 2006).

Dalrymple, William, *White Mughals: Love and Betrayal in Late 18th Century India* (New York: Penguin Books, 2004).

Dar, Bashir Ahmad, *The Religious Thought of Sayyid Ahmad Khan* (Lahore: Institute of Islamic Culture, 1957).

Dawkins, Richard, *The Magic of Reality* (New York: Free Press, 2012).

de Bellaigue, Christopher, *The Islamic Enlightenment: The Struggle between Faith and Reason, 1798 to Modern Times* (New York: Liveright Publishing Corp., 2017).

Devji, Faisal, *Muslim Zion: Pakistan as a Political Idea* (Cambridge: Harvard University Press, 2013).

Diagne, Souleymane Bachir, *Open to Reason: Muslim Philosophers in Conversation with the Western Tradition* (New York: Columbia University Press, 2018).

Donner, Fred McGraw, *The Early Islamic Conquests* (Princeton: Princeton University Press, 1981).

Donohue, John J., and John L. Esposito (eds.), *Islam in Transition: Muslim Perspectives* (New York: Oxford University Press, 1982).

Durkheim, Emile, *The Elementary Forms of Religious Life* (New York: The Free Press, 1995).

el Fadl, Khaled Abou, *The Great Theft: Wresting Islam from the Extremists* (New York: HarperCollins, 2007).

el Fadl, Khaled Abou, "Islam and the Challenge of Democracy," *The Boston Review* April/May 2003.

Eliade, Mircea, *Myth and Reality* (New York: Harper & Rowland Press, 1963).

Elliot, Andrea, "Why Yasir Qadhi Wants to Talk about Jihad?" *The New York Times Magazine*, March 17, 2011.

Elliot, T. S., *A Choice of Kipling's Verse* (London: Faber & Faber, Main Edition, 1963).

Esposito, John L., *Who Speaks for Islam* (New York: Oxford University Press, 2009).

Esposito, John L., and John Obert Voll, *Islam and Democracy* (Oxford: Oxford University Press, 1996).

Euben, Roxanne L., *Enemy in the Mirror: Islamic Fundamentalism and the Limits of Modern Rationalism* (Princeton: Princeton University Press, 1999).

Euben, Roxanne L., and Muhammad Qasim Zaman (eds.), *Princeton Readings in Islamist Thought: Texts and Contexts from al-Banna to Bin Laden* (Princeton: Princeton University Press, 2009).

Fast, Howard, *The Hunter and the Trap* (New York: Dial Press, 1968).

Fisher, Greg (ed.), *Arabs and Empire before Islam* (Oxford: Oxford University Press, 2017).

Friedman, Yohanan, *Shaykh Ahmad Sirhindī* (Montreal and London: McGill University Press, 1971).

Fuerst, Ilyse R. Morgenstein, *Indian Muslim Minorities and the 1857 Rebellion: Religion, Rebels and Jihad* (New York: I.B. Tauris, 2017).

Gabrieli, Francesco, *The Arabs: A Compact History* (Westport: Greenwood Press, 1981).

Gardezi, S. Waqar Ahmad, and Abdul Waheed Khan (trans.), *West versus Islam* (New Delhi: International Islamic Publishers, 1992).

Garret, H. L. O., *The Trial of Bahadur Shah Zafar* (New Delhi: Roli Books, 2007).

Gill, Mohammad Akram, *Modernity and the Muslim World* (Bloomington: Authorhouse, 2006).

Graham, G. F. I., *The Life and Work of Syed Ahmad Khan* (Delhi: Idarah-i-Adabiyat-i-Delli, 1985).

Grewal, Zareena, *Islam Is a Foreign Country: American Muslims and the Global Crisis of Authority* (New York: New York University Press, 2014).

Habermas, Jürgen, *The Inclusion of the Other* (Cambridge: The MIT Press, 1998).

Habermas, Jürgen, *The Post-National Constellation* (Cambridge: The MIT Press, 2001).

Hajj, Samira, *Reconfiguring Islamic Tradition: Reform, Rationality and Modernity* (Stanford: Stanford University Press, 2009).

Hali, Altaf Hussain, *Jawahar-e-Hali*, Iftikhar Ahmad Siddiqi (ed.) (Lahore: Kereven-e-Adab, 1989).

Hali, Altaf Hussain, K. H. Qadiri, and David G. Matthews (trans.), *Hayat-i-Javed* (Delhi: Jagowal Printing Press, 1979).

Hallaq, Wael, *The Origins and Evolution of Islamic Law* (Cambridge: Cambridge University Press, 2005).

Hamid, Mohsin, *The Reluctant Fundamentalist* (New Delhi: Penguin Books India, 2007).

Harries, Richard, and Stephen Platten (eds.), *Reinhold Niebuhr and Contemporary Politics* (Oxford: Oxford University Press, 2010).

Harris, Sam, *The End of Faith* (New York: W.W. Norton & Company, 2006).

Harris, Sam, *The Moral Landscape: How Science Can Determine Human Values* (New York: Free Press, 2010).

Hasan, Mona, *Longing for the Lost Caliphate: A Transregional History* (Princeton: Princeton University Press, 2016).

Hasan, Tariq, *The Aligarh Movement and the Making of the Indian Muslim Mind, 1857–1902* (New Delhi: Rupa & Co., 2006).

Hashmi, Sohail H., *Islamic Political Ethics: Civil Society, Pluralism, and Conflict* (Princeton: Princeton University Press, 2002).

Heidegger, Martin, *Being and Time*, Joan Stambaugh (trans.) (Albany: State University of New York Press, 1996).

Hitchens, Christopher, *And Yet... Essays* (New York: Simon & Schuster, 2015).

Hitti, Philip K., *History of the Arabs* (London: Palgrave MacMillan, 2002).

Hobsbawm, Eric, *The Age of Extremes: The Short Twentieth Century, 1914–1991* (New York: Time Warner Books, 2002).

Hodgson, Marshall, *The Venture of Islam,* Vols. 1–3 (Chicago: University of Chicago Press, 1974).

Hourani, Albert, *Islam in European Thought* (Cambridge: Cambridge University Press, 1991).

Huntington, Samuel P., *Who Are We: The Challenges to American National Identity* (New York: Simon and Shuster, 2005).

Hunter, Shireen T., *Reformist Voices of Islam: Mediating Islam and Modernity* (New York: M.E. Sharpe, 2009).

Hunter, William W., *The Indian Musalmans* (New Delhi: Rupa & Co., 2002).

Huxley, Aldous, *Time Must Have a Stop* (New York: First Dalky Archive Edition, 1998).

Iqbal, Muhammad, and Khushwant Singh (trans.), *Shikwa and Jawab-I Shikwa: Iqbal's Dialogue with Allah* (New Delhi: Oxford University Press, 1991).

Izutsu, Toshihiko, *Ethico-Religious Concepts in the Quran* (Montreal & Kingston: McGill-Queens University Press, 2002).

Izutsu, Toshihiko, *God and Man in the Quran* (Kuala Lumpur: Islamic Book Trust, 2002).

Jalal, Ayesha, *Partisans of Allah: Jihad in South Asia* (Cambridge: Harvard University Press, 2010).

Kant, Immanuel, *Prolegomena to Any Future Metaphysics* (Cambridge: Cambridge University Press, 2004).

Kateb, George, *Hannah Arendt: Politics, Conscience, Evil* (Totowa: Rowman & Allanheld, 1983).

Keddie, Nikki R., and Hamid Algar (trans.), *An Islamic Response to Imperialism: Political and Religious Writings of Sayyid Jamāl ad-Dīn "al-Afghānī"* (Berkeley: University of California Press, 1983).

Kedwai, Shafey, *Cementing Ethics with Modernism: An Appraisal of Sir Sayyed Ahmed Khan's Writings* (New Delhi: Gyan Publishing House, 2010).

Kennedy, Philip F., "*Khamr* and *Hikma* in Jāhilī Poetry," *Journal of Arabic Literature* 20:2, pp. 97–114 (1989).

Kepel, Gilles, *The War for Muslim Minds: Islam and the West* (Cambridge: Belknap Press, 2004).

Khadduri, Majid, *War and Peace in the Law of Islam* (Baltimore: Johns Hopkins Press, 1955).

Khair, Tabish, and Renu Kaul Verma (eds.), *Muslim Modernities: Essays on Moderation and Mayhem* (New Delhi: Vitasta Publishing Pvt. Ltd., 2008).

Khan, Naveeda, *Muslim Becoming: Aspiration and Skepticism in Pakistan* (Durham: Duke University Press, 2012).

Khan, Sayyid Ahmad, *Intikhabi Mazamin Sir Sayyid* (New Delhi: Muqataba Jamia Ltd., 2005).

Khan, Sayyid Ahmad, *A Series of Essays on the Life of Muhammad and Subjects Subsidiary Thereto* (Lahore: Premier Bookhouse, 1968).

Khan, Sayyid Ahmad, *Tabyīn al-kalām (TK)*, 3 Volumes (Ghazipur: Author's Private Press, 1862).

Khan, Sayyid Ahmad, *Tadhīb al-akhlāq (TA)*, 2 Volumes (Aligarh: Institute Press, 1896).

Khan, Sayyid Ahmad, *Tafsīr al-Quran (TQ)*, 6 Volumes (Aligarh: Institute Press, 1880–95).

Khan, Sayyid Ahmad, *Tahrīr fī usūl al-tafsīr (TUT)* (Agra: Mufid-i ām Press, 1892).

Khan, Sayyid Ahmad, *Tusānīf-i Ahmadīyah (TFA)*, 2 Volumes (Aligarh: Institute Press, 1883–87).

Khan, Sayyid Ahmad, *Selected Essays Sir Sayyid* (Aligarh: Education Book House, 2007).

Khan, Sir Sayyid Ahmad, *Maqalat-e-Sir Sayyid (PMaq)*, 16 Volumes (Lahore: Majlis-eTariqi-e-Adab, 1996).

Khan, Sayyid Ahmad, and Dr. Nasrin Mumtaz Baseer (eds.), *The Letters of Sir Sayyid* [in Urdu] (Aligarh: Education Book House, 1995).

Khan, Sayyid Ahmad, and Shan Mohammad (eds. and trans.), *Writings and Speeches of Sir Syed Ahmad Khan* (Bombay: Nachiketa Publications Ltd., 1972).

Khan, Sayyid Ahmad, and Aiza Qureishi (eds.), *The Views of Sir Sayyid* [in Urdu] (New Delhi: Akif Book Depot, 2005).

Khan, Syed Ahmad, and Francis Robinson (trans.), *The Causes of the Indian Revolt* (Oxford: Oxford University Press, 2000).

Khan, Sayyid Ahmad, and John W. Wilder (trans.), *Selected Essays by Sir Sayyid Ahmad Khan* (New Delhi: Sang-e-Meel Publications, 2006).

Khan, Syed Ahmed, Mushirul Hasan, and Nishat Zaidi (trans.), *A Voyage to Modernism* (New Delhi: Primus Books, 2011).

Kidwai, Shafey, *Cementing Ethics with Modernism: An Appraisal of Sir Sayyed Ahmed Khan's Writings* (Delhi: Gyan Publishing House, 2010).

Kurzman, Charles (ed.), *Modernist Islam 1840-1940: A Sourcebook* (New York: Oxford University Press, 2002).

Lamptey, Jerusha Tanner, *Never Wholly Other: A Muslima Theology of Religious Pluralism* (New York: Oxford University Press, 2014).

Lapidus, Ira M., *A History of Islamic Societies* (Cambridge: Cambridge University Press, 2002).

Lewis, Bernard, *Islam and the West* (Oxford: Oxford University Press, 1993).

Lewis, Bernard, *The Muslim Discovery of Europe* (New York: W.W. Norton & Company Inc., 2001).

Lewis, Bernard, *The Political Language of Islam* (Chicago: University of Chicago Press, 1991).

Lilla, Mark, *The Stillborn God: Religion, Politics and the Modern West* (New York: Vintage Books, 2008).

Lorde, Audre, *Sister Outsider: Essays and Speeches* (New York: Crossing Press, 1984).

Lovin, Robin W., *Reinhold Niebuhr and Christian Realism* (Cambridge: Cambridge University Press, 1995).

Lynch, Timothy J., "Virtuous Muslims? Neo-Conservatives and the Middle East," presented at *The MidWest Political Science Association 63rd Annual Conference in Chicago*, April 7–11, 2005.

MacIntyre, Alasdair, *After Virtue* (Notre Dame: University of Notre Dame Press, 1984).

MacIntyre, Alasdair, *Against the Self-Images of the Age: Essays on Ideology and Philosophy* (Notre Dame: University of Notre Dame Press, 1989).

MacIntyre, Alasdair, *Whose Justice? Which Rationality?* (Notre Dame: University of Notre Dame Press, 1988).

Malik, Hafeez, *The Political Profile of Sayyid Ahmad Khan* (Islamabad: Institute of Islamic History, Culture and Civilization, 1982).

Malik, Hafeez, *Sir Sayyid Ahmad Khan and Muslim Modernization in India and Pakistan* (New York: Columbia University Press, 1980).

Mamdani, Mahmood, *Good Muslim, Bad Muslim: America, the Cold War and the Roots of Terror* (New York: Three Leaves Press, 2004).

Manji, Irshad, *The Trouble with Islam Today: A Muslim's Call for Reform of Her Faith* (New York: MacMillan, 2003).

March, Andrew, *Islam and Liberal Citizenship: The Search for an Overlapping Consensus* (New York: Oxford University Press USA, 2009).

Marion, Jean-Luc, *In Excess: Studies of Saturated Phenomena*, Robyn Horner and Vincent Berraud (trans.) (New York: Fordham University Press, 2002).

Marzouki, Nadia, *Islam: An American Religion* (New York: Columbia University Press, 2017).

Mayer, Ann Elizabeth, *Islam and Human Rights: Tradition and Politics* (Boulder: Westview Press, 2013).

McDermott, Rachel Fell, Leonard Gordon, Ainslie Embree, Frances Pritchett, and Dennis Dalton (eds.), *Sources of Indian Traditions*, 2 Volumes (New York: Columbia University Press, 2015).

McDonough, Sheila, *Muslim Ethics and Modernity: A Comparative Study of the Ethical Thought of Sayyid Ahmad Khan and Mawlana Mawdudi* (Waterloo: Wilfred Laurier University Press, 1984).

McKeough, Colm, *The Political Realism of Reinhold Niebuhr* (New York: St. Martin's Press Inc., 1997).

Metcalf, Thomas R., *The Aftermath of the Revolt in India: 1857–1870* (Westwood: Riverdale Company Inc., 1991).

Metcalf, Thomas R., *Ideologies of the Raj* (Cambridge: Cambridge University Press, 1997).

Metcalf, Barbara D. (ed.), *Islam in South Asia in Practice* (Princeton: Princeton University Press, 2009).

Metcalf, Barbara D., *Islamic Contestations: Essays on Muslims in India and Pakistan* (Oxford: Oxford University Press, 2006).

Metcalf, Barbara D., *Islamic Revival in British India: Deoband, 1860–1900* (Royal Book Company, 1989).

Mill, J. S., *Utilitarianism, Liberty and Representative Governance* (London: Everyman's Library, 1931).

Mishra, Pankaj, *From the Ruins of Empire: The Revolt against the West and the Remaking of Asia* (New York: Picador, 2012).

Moaddel, Mansoor, and Kamran Talattof (eds.), *Modernist and Fundamentalist Debates in Islam: A Reader* (New York: Palgrave Macmillan, 2002).

Moazzam, Anwar, *Jamal al-Din al-Afghani: A Muslim Intellectual* (New Delhi: Concept Publishing Company, 1984).

Motadel, David (ed.), *Islam and the European Empires* (Oxford: Oxford University Press, 2014).

Muhammad, Shan, *Sayyid Ahmad Khan: A Political Biography* (Meerut: Meenakshi Prakashan, 1969).

Muhammad, Shan, *Successors of Sir Syed Ahmad Khan* (Lahore: Islamic Book Center, 1986).

Muir, Sir William, *The Life of Mahomet* (Whitefish: Kessinger Publishing LLC, 2003).

Nasr, Sayyed Hossein, *Islamic Philosophy from Its Origin to the Present* (Albany: State University of New York Press, 2006).

Nasr, Seyyed Vali Reza, *Maududi and the Making of Islamic Revivalism* (New York: Oxford University Press, 1996).

Nasr, Seyyed Vali Reza, *The Vanguard of the Islamic Revolution* (Berkeley: University of California Press, 1994).

Nayar, Pramod K., *The Trial of Bahadur Shah Zafar* (New York: Orient Blackswan, 2007).

Niebuhr, Reinhold, *The Children of Light, and the Children of Darkness* (New York: Charles Scribner's Sons, 1972).

Niebuhr, Reinhold, *The Children of Light and the Children of Darkness: A Vindication of Democracy and a Critique of Its Traditional Defense* (New York: Charles Scribner's Sons, 1944).

Niebuhr, Reinhold, *Christian Realism and Political Problems* (New York: Charles Scribner's Sons, 1953).

Niebuhr, Reinhold, "Greek Tragedy and Modern Politics," *The Nation*, 146 (January 1938).

Niebuhr, Reinhold, *An Interpretation of Christian Ethics* (New York: Seabury Press, 1979).

Niebuhr, Reinhold, *The Irony of American History* (Chicago: University of Chicago Press, 2008).

Niebuhr, Reinhold, *Moral Man and Immoral Society* (New York: Charles Scribner's Sons, 1960).

Niebuhr, Reinhold, *The Nature and Destiny of Man* (New York: Charles Scribner's Sons, 1964).

Nietzsche, Frederick Wilhelm, *The Gay Science*, Walter Kaufman (trans.) (New York: Vintage Books, 1974).

Novak, Michael, *The Universal Hunger for Liberty: Why a Clash of Civilizations Is Not Inevitable* (New York: Basic Books, 2004).

Nusseibeh, Sari, *The Story of Reason in Islam* (Stanford: Stanford University Press, 2016).

O'Brien, Peter, *The Muslim Question in Europe: Political Controversies and Public Philosophies* (Philadelphia: Temple University Press, 2016).

Orwell, George, *Animal Farm* (New York: Brawtley Press, 2012).

Pati, Muhammad Ismail Pani (ed.), *Letters to and from Sir Syed Ahmad Khan* (Lahore: Sadat Art Press, 1993).

Quddus, Syed Abdul, *Islamic Polity in Modern Times* (Lahore: Ferozsons Pvt. Ltd., 1987).

Qutb, Sayyid, *Milestones* (Chicago: Kazi Publications, 2007).

Rahman, Fazlur, *Major Themes of the Quran* (Chicago: University of Chicago Press, 1980).

Ramadan, Tariq, *Islam, the West, and Modernity* (Markfield: The Islamic Foundation, 2009).

Ramadan, Tariq, *To be a European Muslim* (Markfield: The Islamic Foundation, 2003).

Ramadan, Tariq, *Western Muslims and the Future of Islam* (Oxford: Oxford University Press, 2003).

Rashid, Ahmad, *Taliban: Militant Islam, Oil and Fundamentalism in Central Asia* (New Haven: Yale University Press, 2000).

Rauschenbusch, Walter, *Christianity and the Social Crisis* (Louisville: Westminster/John Knox, 1992).

Rawls, John, *Political Liberalism* (New York: Columbia University Press, 1995).

Rodinson, Maxime, *Europe and the Mystique of Islam* (New York: I.B. Tauris, 2009).

Sachedina, Abdulaziz, *The Islamic Roots of Democratic Pluralism* (New York: Oxford University Press, 2001).

Safi, Omid (ed.), *Progressive Muslims: On Justice, Gender and Pluralism* (Oxford: Oneworld Publications, 2003).

Said, Edward W., *Culture and Imperialism* (New York: Vintage Books, 1993).

Said, Edward W., *Orientalism* (New York: Vintage Books, 1979).

Sardar, Ziauddin, *The Future of Muslim Civilizations* (London: Croom Helkm Ltd., 1979).

Sardar, Ziauddin, *Islamic Futures: The Shape of Ideas to Come* (London: Mansell Publishing, 1986).

Sardar, Ziauddin, *What Do Muslims Believe? The Roots and Realities of Modern Islam* (New York: Walker & Company, 2007).

Schaebler, Brigit, and Leif Stenberg (eds.), *Globalization and the Muslim World: Culture, Religion and Modernity* (Syracuse: Syracuse University Press, 2004).

Schimmel, Annemarie, *Mystical Dimensions of Islam* (Chapel Hill: University of North Carolina Press, 2011).

Schmitt, Carl, *The Nomos of the Earth in the International Law of the Jus Publicum Europaeum* (New York: Telos Press, Ltd., 2003).

Scott, James C., *Domination and the Arts of Resistance: Hidden Transcripts* (New Haven: Yale University Press, 1992).

Shapiro, Ian, *The Moral Foundations of Politics* (New Haven: Yale University Press, 2004).

Shryock, Andrew, *Islamophobia Islamophilia: Beyond the Politics of Friend and Enemy* (Bloomington: Indiana University Press, 2010).

Smith, Adam, *The Theory of Moral Sentiments* (Amherst: Prometheus Books, 2000).

Smith, Wilfred Cantwell, *Islam in Modern History* (Princeton: Princeton University Press, 1957).

Stetkevych, Suzanne Pinckney (trans.), *The Mute Immortals Speak* (Ithaca: Cornell University Press, 1993).

Stout, Jeffrey, *Democracy and Tradition* (Princeton: Princeton University Press, 2004).

Thompson, Michael J., *Islam and the West: Critical Perspectives on Modernity* (New York: Rowan & Littlefield Publishers Inc., 2003).

Troll, Christian W., *Sayyid Ahmad Khan: A Re-Interpretation of Muslim Theology* (New Delhi: Vikas Publishing House, Pvt Ltd., 1978).

Van Norden, Bryan W., *Taking Back Philosophy* (New York: Columbia University Press, 2017).

Villa, Dana R., *Arendt and Heidegger: The Fate of the Political* (Princeton: Princeton University Press, 1996).

Walzer, Michael, *Thick and Thin* (Notre Dame: University of Notre Dame Press, 1994).

Watt, William Montgomery, *The Formative Period of Islamic Thought* (Oxford: Oneworld Publications, 2006).

Yazdi, Mehdi Ha'iri, *The Principles of Epistemology in Islamic Philosophy: Knowledge by Presence* (Albany: State University of New York Press, 1992).

Zaman, Muhammad Qasim, *Modern Islamic Thought in a Radical Age: Religious Authority and Internal Criticism* (Cambridge: Cambridge University Press, 2012).

Zaman, Muhammad Qasim, *The Ulama in Contemporary Islam* (Princeton: Princeton University Press, 2002).

Index

Abduh, Muhammad   109
Abdulmutallab, Umar Farouk   193 n.3
abstract expressionism   153–5
action, Arendt's theory of   7, 15, 123–4,
     132–5
adultery   180 n.93
Afghani(s)   116–17
Afghanistan   66, 110
After Virtue (MacIntyre)   137, 138, 151
age of ignorance   55, 56, 57, 84–6, 99
aggression   85, 86
ahadith (traditions of Prophet)   28
Ahmad, Irfan   8
Ahmadinejad, Mahmoud   162–3
ajlaf (native Muslims)   24
al-Afghani, Jamal al-Din   8, 36, 40–1, 57,
     109, 115–16, 182 n.118, 192 n.45
A'la Maududi, Abul   177 n.25
Alavi, Seema   50
al-fitrah (nature)   26, 94
al-Hallaj, Mansur   24
al-haram (sacred truce in around
     Ka'ba)   87
Ali, Ayaan Hirsi   163
Ali, Sayyid Amir   187 n.50
Ali, Shaykh Ghulam   24
Ali, Tariq   70
Aligarh movement   67
Aligarh Scientific Gazette   10, 114
al-Ikhlas (*surah* of Sincerity)   20
alim (religious scholar)   28
al-jihad al-akbar   183 n.5
al-jihad al-asghar   183 n.5
al-jihad fi sabil Allah (striving in path of
     God)   105
Allah. See God
Allah, Shah Wali   6, 48
Allahbadi, Akbar   192 n.45
Al-lat   19–20
al-Maghrib Institute   160
al-masalih (salutary purposes)   26, 94
al-Muhit (God)   99

al-Qaeda   67, 157, 158
al-Qays, Imru'   85
al-Simma, Durayd b.   85
Al-Uzza   19–20
American Muslim community   16,
     158–62
American society   62
ana al-Haqq (I am truth/real)   24
ancient period   56, 109
animal laborans   123
anomie (normless-ness)   150
anti-modern   62, 124, 134
anxiety   74–8, 85–6, 92–4, 100, 151–2
'aql (capacity to reason)   93, 95, 140
Arab society   19, 55, 56, 83–4, 86
     jahili   86–7, 95, 98, 105, 111, 122
     life   87
     poetry   87
Arendt, Hannah   7, 14, 15, 16, 17, 49, 51,
     52, 122, 133–4, 165, 189–90 n.116
     action, theory of   7, 15, 123–4, 132–5
     critiques   124
     freedom, views on   129
     human affairs, public and private
          in   128–30
     modern depoliticization, critique
          of   125–6
     neo-Aristotelianism   15, 138
     pessimism   124, 136
     representative democracy, views
          on   131–2
     work   124
     worldlessness   122–3
Aristotelianism   15, 138
Aristotle   124–32, 188 n.78, 189 n.97
     critiques   124
     "good life"   129
     oikia vs. polis   125–8, 129
     politics, views on   131–4
     praxis *vs.* poesis   129–30
     Western modernity, views on   124–5
     writings   131–2

artistic activities   189 n.97
artistic sensibility   153–4
asabiyyat (human sociality, ideal of)   6
Asbab-i-bhagavat-i-Hind (Khan)   11,
    36–7
ashraf classes   24, 33, 36
Aslan, Reza   163
associationism   28, 37, 41
ateleis   129–30, 132
Augustinian tradition   172 n.24
Austen, Jane   14, 50
Ayoub, Mahmoud   106

Baruma, Ian   163–4
battle at Plassey, 1757   21–2
Bedouins   30, 84–5, 87–8
beliefs   14, 27, 34–5, 37, 38, 40, 43, 56,
    60, 65, 69, 81, 113, 117, 120, 124,
    144–8, 154
Benhabib, Seyla   134
Benjamin, Walter   175 n.22
Benslama, Fethi   54
Bentham's theory of Utilitarianism   140
Berman, Marshall   48
biblical faith   73
bida'at (innovations)   25–6, 31, 35–6,
    39, 68
bihisht (hole paradise)   61
black   2
blind following   26, 36, 120
Bourke, Richard Southwell   10
British   10–11, 21–3, 26–7, 31, 36
    colonial India   1, 47, 103
    East India Company   21, 47
    imperial rule in India   50, 110
Brockelmann, Carl   87
burden   7, 14–15, 92–6, 105, 150, 170 n.5
Burke, Edmund   138–9, 147

Cairo   50
Calcutta   103, 112
caliphate   116–17, 185 n.28
capacity to reason   93, 95, 140
Carlyle, Thomas   55–6, 83
Casanova, Jose   59–60
Catholicism   72
Chabel, Malek   8, 54
Changa (Assam)   103
*The Children of Light and the Children of
    Darkness* (Niebuhr)   69

Christianity
    emergence   32, 57
    faith   76
    liberal   77, 78, 80
    realism   51–2, 77–81, 78–81
    Zionism   63
Christian nation   175–6 n.4
Churchill, Winston   162
communism   59, 65, 81
community, important men of   112, 114
Company Raj   83
complaints   33, 42–3
conflicts   145–8
consciousness   29, 72, 99–100, 176 n.16
Constantinianism   111
Cooper, Anna Julia   169–70 n.2
Copernican worldview   96–7
Crenshaw, Kimberlé   169–70 n.2
Critical Islam   8, 17, 55, 60
The Critique of Judgment (Kant)   134
Critique of Practical Reason (CPR)   134
The Critique of Taste   135
customary law   87

dahr (fate)   85, 86
Dalton, Dennis   187 n.50
dar al-harb (abode of war)   42, 108
dar al-Islam (abode of Islam/peace)   42
Dar-ul-Ulum, Deoband   110, 182 n.118
Day of Judgment   30–1, 86, 100
deed/action   143
Delhi   22–4, 48, 56
Demiurge   61–2
democracies   12, 50, 59, 69, 112, 124,
    131, 153, 164
Deobandis   110–11
depoliticization   4–5, 125, 130
despotikon   125, 127
devotional practices   24, 28, 29, 31, 35, 110
Dewey, John   175–6 n.4
din. See religion
disclosure   29
duality   94, 105
Du Bois, W. E. B.   169–70 n.2
dunyawi communities   109
Durkheim, Émile   150
dystopia   66

Eden   61–2
ego   29, 57

Egypt   53, 116
eloquent clarity   30
Eltahawy, Mona   158
Embree, Ainslie   187 n.50
emotivist culture   52–3
enemy, raid on   87, 95–6
English   112
enlarged mentality   134
Enlightenment(s)   4, 6
    critique   60, 140
    European   13, 164
    ideals   78
    liberal   7
    moral perspectivism   141
    moral relativism   141
    progressivism   45
    project   52, 140–1, 144
    religion   60
    scientism   65
epistemological crisis   145–6, 151
escapism   122
European imperialism   41, 142–3
European languages   112
European society   1
    civilization   3
    vs. Islam   1–5, 9, 51
    and Muslim neighbors   38
events of 1857   9, 12–13, 21–3, 47, 50,
        109–10, 146
experiential knowledge/gnosis   28

Fabian socialism   176 n.17
factum (deed/action)   143
faculty of godliness   90–1
faculty of iniquity   90–1
faculty of moral discernment   91
faculty of reason   91–4
faith   93–4, 106
false consciousness   191 n.17
fana al-rusul (annihilation in
        Prophet)   29
fana al-shaykh (own ego in person)   29
Fanon, Frantz   14, 50
fasāhat o balāghat (eloquent clarity)   30
fate   85, 86
fatwas   36
feminism   2, 60
fiqh (legal tradition)   16, 27–8, 54
fitna (chaotic series of events)   58

foreign languages   112–13
fornication   180 n.93
freedom   14, 72, 133–4
    active principle   15
    American   161–2
    human   72–7, 129, 150
    knowledge   151
    natural capacity   72–5
    vs. necessity, realm of   128–9
    of opinion   111, 113, 117–18
    self-transcendence   82–3
free press   114
free will   89, 91, 93–4
French revolution   50, 131, 138
Friedman, Yohanan   27
fujur (iniquity)   91
fundamentalisms   67–8
The Future of Muslim Civilization and
        *Islamic Futures: The Shape of Ideas
        to Come* (Sardar)   54
future-perfect sensibility   14, 62, 63, 64,
        66, 68–9, 101, 175–6 n.4

Gandhi, Mahatma   133
Germany   135–6
Ghalib, Mirza Asadullah   136
gharaniq (beautiful cranes)   19–20, 38
ghaziya (raid on enemy)   87, 95–6
God   19–21, 41–5, 67, 99
    annihilation in   29
    consciousness   29
    creation   24, 41–2
    divinity   31
    law   29, 62
    presence   32–3
    reality, perception of   24–5
    reliance on   25
    and Self   24
    striving in path of   105
    transcendent   25
goddesses   19–20, 23
good conduct   106
"good life"   4, 49, 119, 125–30, 132, 142,
        147, 149, 163
Goodman, Len Evan   185 n.27
goodness   104–5
Gordon, Leonard   187 n.50
government of Law   64
Grand Unified Theory   177 n.23

Greek
  astronomy 39, 97
  philosophy 39, 97, 99
  sciences 39, 98–9
  tragedy 70–1, 76, 81, 150
Grenada 56
guardianship 67
  of jurists 64
  of scientists 65

Habermas, Jürgen 63–4
Hadith 31, 183 n.5, 185 n.28
hakimiyya (sovereignty) 57
Hali, Altaf Hussain 33–4, 36
Hanbal, Ahmad Ibn 185 n.28
Hanbali *madhab* (school of law) 185
  n.28
harb (killing/violence) 107
harmonization 26–7, 41–2, 48, 95, 149
Harris, Sam 65
Hegel, G. W. F. 50
heliocentrism 65
Hess, Linda 171 n.3
Hijaz 19
Hindus 10, 22
  cultural patterns 25
  culture, polytheistic influences of 26
  idolatry 26
  Muslims relationship 31, 166
  Vedantism 24
history 71–2, 75–6
  flow 62
  meaning 6
History of the Arabs (Hitti) 87
Hitti, Philip K. 87
hole paradise 61
holy war 106–11
Homeland Security 158–9
Homo faber 123, 189–90 n.116
households 125–30
  and city-state 125–7
  Muslim 9, 113
  national 130
  nature 126
  necessities 128–9
  oikia and 125–7
  political association and 126–7
  private 111
  slave and 127
Houston 157

human beings 30, 42, 62, 68–9, 72–3,
  103–4
  affairs, public and private in 128–30
  animality 104–6
  as communal creature 90
  condition 13–15, 50–1, 58, 62–3, 65,
    68–72, 75–82, 86, 88, 101, 105, 120,
    123, 134, 162, 178 n.40
  dignity 72
  freedom 72–7, 129, 150
  godliness, faculty of 90–1
  goodness to 104–5
  iniquity, faculty of 90–1
  intelligence, nature of 119–21
  nature 72–5, 94, 178 n.40
  rationality 140–1
  reason, demands of 119–21
  savagery 105
  self 6, 57, 72–3, 141
  sociality 6, 119–21
  as socio-historical creature 90
  space for 133–4
  will 91–6
The Human Condition (Arendt) 123
human existence 13, 31, 35, 52, 76
  be-all and end-all of 88
  freedom for 129
  instrumental activity and 130
  internal feature of 91
  laws of 65
  limitations of 71
  natural states of 66
  oasis fit for 122–3
  possibilities 71
  productive activity and 130
  unnaturalness 123
  worldlessness and 123
humanism 14, 48–60
humanity 52, 124
humility 90
Huxley, Aldous 66

Ibn ʿArabi, Muhyiddin 24
idealism *vs.* realism 77–81
ihsan (good conduct) 106
ijmaʿ (Islamic polity) 33, 114, 117, 184
  n.17, 185 n.27
ijtihad (reasoned interpretation) 26, 36,
  94, 109–11, 116–17, 186 n.36, 187
  n.50

ikhtiyar (ability/capacity to control/
    power) 89
ilm. See knowledge
'ilm al-kalam (theology for Muslims) 11,
    23–31, 36, 48
imago dei (image of God) 72
iman (faith) 93–4, 106
inability 76
incest 180 n.93
India 1, 6, 9–11, 21–7, 31–42, 112
Indian
    Muslims 5–6, 10, 11, 14, 26–7, 31, 35,
        38, 48, 69
    rebellion 12–13
Indic Muslims 25, 26
individualism 59, 135
    liberal 139–40
    pre-Islamic Arab 87
    Western 57, 86
iniquity 91
innovation 34–5
    imaginative conceptual 146
    theological 36
    traditional moral orders and 34–6
insaniyyat (human self) 6, 72
Insan ke Khayalat 91, 93
internationalism 52, 62–3, 78
interpretive reasoning 98
intersectionality 169–70 n.2
Iqbal, Muhammad 6, 8, 42–3
Iran 63, 67–8, 162
The Irony of American History
    (Niebuhr) 81
Islam 1, 37–9, 106
    abode of 42
    antithesis of 13
    attacks on 10
    authentic 5
    constitutive of 106
    as critique 2–3, 13, 155, 162–3
    decline 64
    definition 44
    distinction 7, 51
    vs. European society 1–5, 9, 51
    harmonization and 26–7
    historical religion 55
    identity 159–60
    individualism 57
    jihad and 105–11
    language 9, 33, 34, 44, 58

Laws 64–6, 120
    modern 6–7, 44
    as political ideology 66–8
    polity 33, 114, 117, 184 n.17, 185
        n.27
    re-emergence in human history 40–1
    revivalism 25
    socialist conception 110
    spiritual crisis 32–3
    Sufis in 28
    tauhid 13–14, 23, 30, 35, 37–8
    theology 6, 11, 23, 25–7, 29, 36, 48
    traditions 15
    voice 13
    Wali Allah's contribution to 26
    in West 164
Islamic Obscurantism 44
Islamic outfits 163
Islamic revolution of 1979 64
Islamic State of Iraq and Syria (ISIS) 67,
    157
Islam in Modern History 145
Islamophobia 4, 10
Istanbul 50

Jabal an-Nur 19
jabr wa ikhtiyar (predestination and free
    will) 89, 91, 93–4
jadidiyyat (novelty) 6, 55, 56, 57
jahili Arab society 86–7, 95, 98, 99, 105,
    111, 122
jahiliyyah 25, 181 n.102
jahiliyyat (age of ignorance) 55, 56, 57,
    84–6, 99
jahilli 85–6, 87–8
    anxieties 88–9
    poets 87–8
Jalal, Ayesha 106, 107
James, William 175–6 n.4
Jawab-e-Shikwa 42–3
Jeddah 157
jihad 106–11, 116–17, 119, 149, 157,
    159, 183 n.5, 184 n.17
    against British 109–10
    fiqh of 161
    of hand 106
    of heart 106
    Islamic imperative 7, 15, 16, 105
    Islam without 106
    Khan's conception of 15, 111, 135

legal conception of 107
in mind 106
private moralistic conception of
110–11
qur'anic concept 106
spiritual aspects 107
"statist" conception 107
of sword 106
of tongue 106
jihad bi-l lisan (jihad of tongue) 106
jihad bi-l qalb/nafs (jihad of heart) 106
jihad bi-l saif (jihad of sword) 106
jihad bi-l yad (jihad of hand) 106
Jila al-qulub bi dhikr al-Mahbub. See
Polishing of the Hearts by
Remembering the Beloved
juridical traditions 36, 120
jurists, guardianship of 64
Just War Theory 107

Ka'ba 19, 87
Kabir 24, 171 n.3
Kalamat al-haqq 29–30, 31
Kant, Immanuel
The Critique of Judgment 134
*Critique of Practical Reason
(CPR)* 134
The Critique of Taste 135
political philosophy 134–5
kashf (disclosure) 29
Kateb, George 132
Khalifa-i-Rashidun 108
Khan, Sayyid Ahmad 5–17, 62, 166–7,
170 n.4, 172 n.24, 180 n.93
Afghani, views on 116–17
background 10, 24
as educationalist 11–12
eternal optimist 152
family 24
feedback loops 101
foreign languages, views on 112–13
human intelligence nature, views
on 119–21
humanism 14, 48–60
human reason demands, views
on 119–21
innovation influence on local
environment, views on 34–6
institutes and associations 114–19
Islam for 13–14, 23–31, 38–41, 152

Islamic distinction 51
on *jihad* 15, 105–11, 135
legacy of 166–7
loyalty 10
as modernist 14, 48–60
modernity 48–60
as *na'ib munsif* 31
project 10, 49
realism 105
as reformer 11–12, 48
reformulated Islam 15
scientific progress and education,
emphasis on 43–4
Sufi life and 25
taklif, reinterpretation of 14–15
theology of Islam and 11, 23–31
tradition, Islam in relation to 15
universe, Ptolemaic view of 96–100
writings 10, 11–12, 25, 27–31
Khomeini, Imam Ruhullah 64–6
khudi (ego/self) 57
killing 107, 162
Kingdom of God 177 n.25
King Jr., Martin Luther 133
Kipling, Rudyard 1
knowledge 6, 7, 15, 84, 93–4, 101,
137–55
economic 152
freedom of 151
moral 176 n.16
political 152
religious 152
scientific 152
self-reflexive 137
traditions for 138
wisdom and 137–55

labor 123
language of Islam 9, 23, 33, 34, 44, 58
Law of God 62, 93
laws
of Islam 64–6, 120
of love 68–70, 80–1
of man 65
of nature 72, 97
of Qur'an 67
of Science 65–6
legal tradition 16, 27–8, 54
Legislative Council of India 12–13
lex talionis (customary law) 87

liberal   170 n.4
liberalism   63, 66–7, 82, 140, 141, 150,
        176 n.16
liberal utopianism   78
liberty   114, 134 (*see also* freedom)
life-enhancing traditions   54
The Life of Mahomet (Muir)   10
lineage   24, 28, 171 n.4
Lorde, Audre   3
Lorenzen, David   N.   171 n.3
Lovin, Robin   78, 81, 178 n.45

McDermott, Rachel Fell   187 n.50
MacIntyre, Alasdair   7, 14, 15, 16, 17,
        51, 137
    emotivist culture   52–3
    on morality   52–3, 141–4
    on tradition   7, 15, 138–42, 145–52
    unity of human life   148–50
    Western modernity, views on   138
madhahib (juridical traditions/schools of
        law)   36, 120
madrassas   66, 111
majlis (important men of
        community)   112, 114
Manat   19–20
mard-i-momin (man of perfect faith)   43
ma'rifa (experiential knowledge/
        gnosis)   28
Marion, Jean-Luc   47
Marx, Karl   191 n.17
Marxism   62–3
mass society   123–4
Maududi, Sayyid Abul A'la   66–8
maulud risalah (biography of
        Prophet)   27
Mecca   19, 36, 38, 50, 87, 111
Meccans   19–20
medieval artist   153–5
Medina   36, 111
Meerut   115
men   72–3
    as communal creature   90
    godliness, faculty of   90–1
    inability   76
    iniquity, faculty of   90–1
    material and non-material aspects
        of   89–90
    nature   92
    of perfect faith   43

as political animal   127, 131
political life *vs.* good life   127–8
reason   92
self-sufficiency   126–7
as socio-historical creature   90
Mernissi, Fatima   8
Middle East   172 n.29
Mill, John Stuart   112, 113
mind   144
Mir Dard, Khwajāh   28
modern age   175 n.22
modern culture   50
modernism   48–60
modernity   3, 6, 44, 138
    archive   14, 50
    cartography   7
    contrapuntal approach to   14, 50
    European   56
    future-perfect sensibility of   63
    Indian Muslims   14
    nature of   6
    normative tenses of   62
    past-perfect sensibility of   62–3
    self-images   141–4
    sociological tense of   63–4
    traditions and   15
    Western   52, 56–60, 82
modern nationalism   15
modern times   56, 109
monotheism   86
moral
    calamity   138, 145
    certainty   76
    imagination   70
    knowledge   176 n.16
    optimism   69–70, 81
    perspectivism   141–2
    pessimism   69–70, 79–80
    realism   70, 79–80
    relativism   141–2
morality   52–3, 62, 94, 104, 140–4
    and Law   62
    for power   140
The Moral Landscape   65
mourning   172–3 n.33
Mughal Empire   22
Muhammad   19–22, 25, 42, 55
    biography of   83, 86
    devotion to   29
    messages   86

Muhammad, Shan 69
Muhammad al rusul Allah 19
Muhammadan Anglo-Oriental (MAO)
    College 10–11, 102, 115
Muhammadan Literary Society,
    Calcutta 112
Muhammadan revolution 83, 84
Muir, William 10, 55, 83, 84, 86
mujahidin movement 108, 109–10
Murder in Amsterdam (Baruma) 163
murid 29
muruwah 84–5, 95–6
Muslims 2–4, 8, 39–40, 136
    American 16, 158–62
    civilization 3
    civil life 160
    community 20, 27–8, 30–1, 37–8, 40,
        48, 66, 69, 108–9, 111–12, 116–17,
        158–9, 161, 165
    conventional 40–1
    depoliticization 4–5, 125, 130
    detachment from Islam 37–8
    disloyalty, conspiracy theories
        about 11–13
    exploitation 4
    guidance 111–12
    Hindus to relationship 31, 166
    household 9, 113
    humanist 48–60
    identity 58, 159–60
    ignominy of 34
    Indian 5–6, 10, 11, 14, 26–7, 31, 35,
        38, 48, 69
    innovation in 25
    jihad and 105–11
    law 54
    loyalty 13
    modernity, experience of 4–5, 10,
        48–60
    on native customs 35
    political power 34
    polity 33, 114, 115–17, 184 n.17, 185
        n.27
    rebellion 10, 12–13
    Salafi 159
    sovereignty 22
    vs. Sufis 27–8
    totalitarianism in 122–3
    tradition, theological anthropology
        within 91–6

universe, Ptolemaic view of 96–100
value systems 39–40
voices and concerns of 113–14, 166
in Western societies 58
women 2, 163
The Muslim Social Reformer 10
Musnad Ahmad Ibn Hanbal 185 n.28
Mutiny of 1857 110

Nagel, Thomas 176 n.16
Nanatwi, Mohammad Qasim 192 n.45
naql (transmitted knowledge) 93, 95
Naqshbandiyya Mujaddidiyya 24, 28
nation 115
The Nation 70
national household 130
nationalism 115, 116–18, 135, 175–6 n.4
naturalism 41, 57, 178 n.45
nature 40, 41, 72–4
necessities 128–9
neicheris (pejorative bastardization of
    "naturalist") 41
neichiriat (naturalism) 41, 57
neo-Aristotelianism 15, 138
neo-conservatism 52, 63, 66, 148
Newton, Isaac 118, 143
New World 59
Niamatullah, Abu Easa 161
Nicomachean Ethics 125–6, 129
Niebuhr, Reinhold 7, 14, 16, 17, 51, 62,
    70–1, 175–6 n.4, 178 n.40
    Christian realism 51–2, 78–81
    essay 70–1
    ethical naturalism 79
    feedback loops 101
    on freedom 72–6
    Greek tragedy and 71
    on history 71–2
    on law of love 68–70
    liberal utopianisms, views on 15, 48,
        52, 62–3, 78
    as modernist 52
    moral action, views on 81–2
    moral praxis for 52
    moral realism, views on 79–80, 105
    natural law, theories of 72–3
    political realism, views on 78–81
    politics, views on 82–6
    realism *vs.* idealism, views on 77–81
    as relentless pessimist 71

self for　73
worldview　76–7
niechiri　117
Nietzsche, Friedrich　140–1
no-man rule　124
normless-ness　150
novelty　6, 55, 56, 57

Obama, Barack　175–6 n.4
obligations　7, 14–15, 92–6, 105, 150,
　　170 n.5
Occidentalism (Baruma)　163
oikia　125–8
one-man rule　124
oneness　21
optimism　52, 65, 69–70, 78
　　of future-perfect sensibility　14
　　of liberal thinking　176 n.17
　　moral　69, 81
　　oozing　78
　　positivism and　65
　　Western liberal　7, 136
Ottoman Caliphate　116–17

Pakistan　66
Palestine　162
past-perfect sensibility　62, 68, 101,
　　175–6 n.4
past-perfect worldview　14
peace　19
peril　7, 51, 69
Persian poetry　33
pessimisms　15, 100
Pfander, Reverend　86
Pitkin, Hannah　132
Plassey battle (1757)　21–2
pleasures　88
polis
　　existence　128–9
　　nature of　128
　　vs. oikia　125–8
　　self-sufficiency and　128–9
Polishing of the Hearts by Remembering
　　the Beloved　27
political
　　animal　127, 131
　　justice　188 n.78
　　realism　78–81
politics　82–6, 131–4
Pollock, Jackson　153

positive law　63
positivism　15, 63, 65
post-Hegelian sociology　63–4
powers　77, 81
　　Axis　71
　　divine　89, 90
　　European　10, 17, 57
　　Muslim　13, 22, 26, 34, 40–3, 69,
　　　107–8
　　non-Muslim　108
　　political　107–8
　　Prophet　30
　　social　87
　　state　108
praxis *vs.* poesis　129–30
predestination　89, 91, 93–4
pride　76
Pritchett, Frances　187 n.50
progress　14
promise　7
The Promise of Politics (Arendt)　122
Prophet　10, 19, 21, 25, 67, 69
　　annihilation in　29
　　biography of　27
　　devotional link to　28–30
　　Muslim's relationship to　27–30
　　as *pir*　28–30
　　tariqa Muhammadiyya　27
　　traditions　28–9
Punjab　108
purification　19, 37

Qadhi, Yasir　16, 157–65, 193 n.4
　　as Academic Dean for the al-Maghrib
　　　Institute　160
　　American Muslim community
　　　and　158–62
　　background　157–8
　　freedom, views on　161–2
　　Homeland Security and　158–9
　　Islamic education, emphasis on　160
　　Salafiyya　157–9
　　views　162–3
qānūn-i qudrat (law of nature)　97
qaum (nation)　115
qital (killing/violence)　107
qudrat (nature)　40, 41, 72–4
queer　2
Quran　26, 28–31, 35, 41, 57, 67, 69, 86,
　　94, 98, 105, 107, 109, 157, 186 n.36

Qutb, Sayyid 57
quwat-i fujur (faculty of iniquity) 90–1
quwat-i taqwa (faculty of godliness) 90–1
Quwwat-ul-Islam mosque, Delhi 172
    n.32

Rahman, Fazlur 106
Ramadan, Tariq 8, 9, 54, 163–4
rationality 93–4, 140–8
rational law 63
Rauschenbusch, Walter 77
Rawls, John 176 n.16
Razi, Fakhr al-Din 97
realism *vs.* idealism 77–81
reality 13–14, 25–6, 95
reasoned interpretation 26, 36, 94,
    109–11, 116–17, 186 n.36, 187
    n.50
Reflections on the Revolution in France
    (Burke) 138
Reinhold Niebuhr and Christian Realism
    (Lovin) 78
religion 40, 96
    naturalism in 41
    unitary 94
Religion as Critique: Islamic Critical
    Thinking from Mecca to the
    Marketplace? (Ahmad) 8
religious scholar 28
representative democracy 131
rights of man 175–6 n.4
Rorty, Richard 175–6 n.4
rouhani haqiqat (spiritual reality) 97

Said, Edward 14, 50, 51
St. Augustine 31–2
Salafi Muslims 159
Salafiyya 157–9
salam (peace) 19
salutary purposes 26
Sans 49
Sardar, Ziauddin 8, 54
Saudi Arabia 157, 158, 159
savage 104–6
Sayyid 24
Schmitt, Carl 58–9
schools of law 26, 120
science 9, 116–19, 177 n.23
Scientific Revolution in Europe 99
Scientific Society of Ghazipur 112

scientists, guardianship of 65
Second World War 71
self 57, 72–3, 141
self-assertion 85–7, 117
self-consciousness 72
self-deception 37
self-determination 118–19
self-images 141–4
self-interest 77, 140
self-realization 31–2
self-reflection 92
self-reliance 86
self-sufficiency 126–8, 132
Shahid, Sayyid Ahmad 108
Shari'a 16, 28, 29, 30, 35, 54, 69, 94, 95,
    186 n.36
Shariati, Ali 8
sharif 24
Shi'i millenarianism 14
shikwa (complaints) 33, 42–3
Shikwa-i-Hind 33
shirk (associationism) 28, 37, 41
shukr (thankfulness) 90–1
shura 112
Sikhs 108
silsila (lineage) 24, 28, 171 n.4
Simon, John 165
sin, Christian conception 7, 14, 75
Sirhindi, Shaykh Ahmad 24–5
Smith, Adam 140, 191 n.18
Smith, Roger 164
Smith, Wilfred Cantwell 32, 145
Social Gospel movement 77, 78
sociality 117–18
social (re)-engineering 63
Soroush, Abdul Karim 8
sovereignty 57
space of appearance 133–4
spirit 74
spiritual reality 97
statism 117–18
statist, jihad 107, 108
stipend 24
struggle 7, 15, 16, 105–11, 116
submission 106
Submission (documentary) 163
Sufis 24–6
    devotionalism of 29–30
    in Islam 28
    vs. Muslims 27–8

Sunna of Prophet   25–9, 35, 41, 94, 98,
      109, 157
Sunni Islam   36
surah of Sincerity   20

Tablighi Jamaat (Missionary Party)   110
Tafsir al-kabir   97
tahdhīb al-akhlāq   28–9
taklif. See burden; obligations
Talib, ʻAli ibn Abi   90
Taliban   66, 67, 110, 157
taqlid (blind following)   26, 36, 120
taqwa (humility)   90
tarikh. See history
tariqa Muhammadiyya   27, 28, 172 n.13
tariqa (way/method)   171 n.4, 172 n.13
Tasawwur   29
tasawwur-i-shaykh   28
tatbiʻa (harmonization)   26, 48, 149
tatbiq (harmony)   42
tauhid (harmonization)   13–14, 23, 30,
      35, 37–8, 55, 148–9
tawakkul (reliance on God)   25
taʼwil (interpretive reasoning)   98
tazia (mourning)   172–3 n.33
tazkiya (purification)   19, 37
Tea Party movement, United States
      177–8 n.28
technologies, emerging   100
teleologies   149
thankfulness   90–1
theo-democratic   68
theology for Muslims   11, 23–31, 36, 48
Theory of Everything   177 n.23
Theory of Gravity   118
The Theory of Moral Sentiments
      (Smith)   191 n.18
time   52, 61–2, 85
toleration   118–19
totalitarian movements   122–3
traditions   7, 15, 53
      authority   139
      Burke's brand   139–40
      challenges   145
      conflict and   145–8
      constitutive of   145–8
      of enquiry   147–8
      for knowledge   138
      of moral thinking   138
      notion of   138–9

rationality of   144–8
self-images of modernity   141–4
social constraints, set of   140
in traditional sense   142
unity to life and   148–50
for wisdom   138
transmitted knowledge   93, 95
transmodernity   54
A Treatise on Public Opulence
      (Smith)   191 n.18
tribalism   84
The True Discourse   29–30, 31
Trump, Donald   60
Truth, Sojourner   169–70 n.2
Turkey   116

ʻulama-i-akhirat (scholars)   107
ʻulama-i-duniya (worldly scholars)
      107
ʻulama-i-rabbani (godly scholars)
      107
ulama (scholars)   24, 28, 29, 31, 35, 110
umma   16, 109, 112, 159
underwear bomber   193 n.3
unities   41
      of being   24, 26, 172–3 n.33
      of harmony   148
      of history   148
      of human life   148–50
      liberal imagination   148–50
      of perception   24, 26, 172–3 n.33
universe, Ptolemaic view of   96–100
unreasonable reality   63
Urdu   33, 112
Usuli   66
usury   180 n.93
utilitarianism   140
utopianisms   15, 48, 52, 62–3, 78

van Gogh, Theo   163
veil of ignorance   176 n.16
velayat (guardianship)   67
Velayat-i-daneshmandan (guardianship of
      scientists)   65
Velayat-i-Faqih (guardianship of
      jurists)   64
views from nowhere   176 n.16
vilayat   177 n.23
violence   107, 162
voice of people   12–13

wahdat al-shuhud (unity of
    perception) 24, 26, 172–3 n.33
wahdat al-wujud (unity of being) 24, 26,
    172–3 n.33
Wali Allah, Shah 25–7, 94
Walzer, Michael 142
war, abode of 42
way/method 171 n.4, 172 n.13
wazifa. See stipend
The Wealth of Nations (Smith) 191 n.18
Weeramantry, C. G. 185 n.27
West 1–5, 155
Western modernity 59–60, 82, 138
    danger of 121–4
    dehumanizing aspects of 121–4
    Muslim commensurability with 10–11
    pessimisms 15, 100
    utopian optimisms 15, 48, 52, 62–3,
    78, 100
Western society 58
Whose Justice? Which Rationality?
    (MacIntyre) 138
Wilder, John W. 104
will, human 91–6
wisdom 15, 118–19, 137
    for Afghani 116
    of ages 30

human 82
knowledge and 137–55
moral 70
Newton's 118
practical 132
traditions for 138–9
without reflection 138–9
wolf 103–4
women 2, 88
    modernization 48
    Muslims 2, 163
    second marriage for 25, 172–3 n.33
world 189–90 n.116
worldlessness 122–3

Yangon 47
yaum-i qiyamat (Day of Judgment)
    30–1, 86, 100

Zafar, Bahadur Shah 22, 47
Zakaria, Fareed 163
zaman-e-qadim (ancient period)
    56, 109
zaman-i-jadid (modern times) 56, 109
Zionism, Christian 63
Zionist entity 162
zōon politikon (political animal) 127, 131